CAMBRIDGE WORLD ARCHAEOLOGY

AFRICAN ARCHAEOLOGY

AFRICAN ARCHAEOLOGY

DAVID W. PHILLIPSON

Curator,
Museum of Archaeology and Anthropology,
University of Cambridge

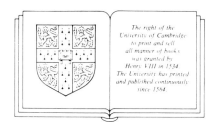

CAMBRIDGE UNIVERSITY PRESS

CAMBRIDGE

NEW YORK NEW ROCHELLE

MELBOURNE   SYDNEY

Published by the Press Syndicate of the University of Cambridge
The Pitt Building, Trumpington Street, Cambridge CB2 1RP
32 East 57th Street, New York, N.Y. 10022, U.S.A.
10 Stamford Road, Oakleigh, Melbourne 3166, Australia

First published 1985
Reprinted with revisions 1988

Printed in Great Britain at The Bath Press, Avon

Library of Congress catalogue card number: 83–25235

British Library Cataloguing in Publication Data
Phillipson, David W.
African archaeology.—(Cambridge World Archaeology)
1. Africa—Antiquities
I. Title
960   DT13

ISBN 0 521 25234 2 hard covers
ISBN 0 521 27236 x paperback

P.P.

CONTENTS

Acknowledgements   *page* xi

1 Introduction   1
The discovery of the African past   1
Archaeology in Africa   3
Linguistics   5
Oral tradition   8
Africa in world prehistory   8

2 The emergence of man in Africa   11
Man's precursors   11
The earliest hominids   13
The oldest East African discoveries   16
Olduvai and Koobi Fora   22
South Africa   28
Conclusions: the earliest tool-makers   30

3 The consolidation of basic human skills   32
The Acheulian techno-complex in Africa   32
Koobi Fora, Olduvai and the earliest Acheulian   37
Olorgesailie   42
Kalambo Falls   45
Broken Hill mine, Kabwe   47
Southern Africa   48
West Africa and the Sahara   49
North Africa   51
The makers of Acheulian industries   54

4 Regional diversification   58
The 'Middle Stone Age' and the 'Late Stone Age'   58
Southern Africa   60
Central Africa   78
Eastern Africa   80
West Africa   85
North Africa and the Sahara   87
The Nile Valley   94
Changing life-styles and technology   97

5 The beginnings of permanent settlement   **99**
    The Nile Valley   99
    East Africa   103
    The southern and central Sahara   105
    Overview   108
    Africa 10,000 years ago   109

6 Early farmers   **113**
    Food-production   113
    The Sudanese Nile Valley   116
    The Egyptian Nile Valley   122
    North Africa   130
    The Sahara   131
    West and Central Africa   135
    Ethiopia and the Horn   139
    East Africa   141

7 Iron-using peoples before A.D. 1000   **148**
    Iron   148
    North Africa   150
    Egypt and the Arab invasion   154
    The Sudan   156
    Ethiopia and adjacent regions   158
    West Africa   163
    Bantu-speaking Africa   171
    Stone-tool-using pastoralists of south-western Africa   183

8 The second millennium A.D. in sub-Saharan Africa   **187**
    The last 1,000 years   187
    West Africa   188
    Ethiopia, the southern Sudan, and adjacent regions   194
    The east coast of Africa   197
    Bantu-speakers north of the Zambezi   199
    Zimbabwe   203
    South of the Limpopo   207

    References   212
    Index   229

ILLUSTRATIONS

		page
1.1	Physical map of Africa	2
1.2	Classification of African languages	6
1.3	Distribution of African language families	6
2.1	Geological periods and hominoid types	11
2.2	Hominids within the order Primates	12
2.3	Skeletons of gorilla, *Australopithecus africanus* and *Homo sapiens*	14
2.4	Family tree of African hominids	16
2.5	Skulls of *Australopithecus africanus*, *A. boisei* and *Homo habilis*	17
2.6	*Australopithecus* and *Homo habilis* sites	18
2.7	Hominid footprints at Laetoli	20
2.8	Stone artefacts from Hadar and the Omo Valley	21
2.9	Koobi Fora stratigraphy	22
2.10	Olduvai Gorge	24
2.11	Butchery site at Koobi Fora	25
2.12	Plan of stone circle at Olduvai Gorge	26
2.13	Artefacts from Bed I, Olduvai	27
2.14	Ages of South African australopithecine sites	29
3.1	Acheulian stone implement types	33
3.2	The Levallois technique	35
3.3	Victoria Falls from the air	36
3.4	Artefacts of the Karari industry	38
3.5	Artefacts from Bed II, Olduvai	39
3.6	The archaeological sequence at Olduvai Gorge	40
3.7	*Homo erectus* skull from Koobi Fora	41
3.8	Principal Acheulian and related sites in Africa	43
3.9	Implements at Olorgesailie	44
3.10	Kalambo Falls	46
3.11	Skull from Broken Hill mine, Kabwe	48
3.12	West African Acheulian implements	50
3.13	Artefacts from Ain Hanech and Sidi Zin	52
3.14	Sidi Abderrahman quarry section	53
3.15	Jaw of *Homo erectus* from Ternifine	55
4.1	How backed microliths were hafted	59
4.2	Artefacts from Klasies River Mouth and other southern African sites	61

4.3	Sequence of deposits at Klasies River Mouth	62
4.4	Stone settings at Orangia	66
4.5	Kalemba rockshelter	69
4.6	Artefacts from Kalemba and Gwisho	71
4.7	Human burial at Gwisho	72
4.8	Rock paintings showing people in trance	73
4.9	Rock engravings from the Transvaal	74
4.10	Sites described in chapter 4	76–7
4.11	Sangoan and Lupemban implements	79
4.12	Artefacts from Hargeisa, Gobedra and Gamble's Cave	83
4.13	Sangoan and mode 3 artefacts from Nigeria	85
4.14	Artefacts from Tiemassas and Rop	86
4.15	Aterian implements	89
4.16	Artefacts from Haua Fteah	91
4.17	Iberomaurusian artefacts	93
4.18	Khormusan and Halfan artefacts	95
5.1	Location of settlement sites	100
5.2	Khartoum-related and Shamarkian artefacts from Nubia	101
5.3	Artefacts from Early Khartoum	102
5.4	The Lowasera site	104
5.5	Artefacts from Lowasera	105
5.6	Pottery from Amekni	107
5.7	Distribution of African populations	109
5.8	Human skull from Iwo Eleru	111
6.1	Initial domestication areas of indigenous African crops	114
6.2	Artefacts from Esh Shaheinab	117
6.3	Sites with evidence for early food-production	118
6.4	A-Group artefacts from near Wadi Halfa	120
6.5	Brick substructure of royal burial mound at Kerma	121
6.6	Temples at Abu Simbel	122
6.7	Pre-dynastic Egyptian artefacts	123
6.8	The chronology of ancient Egypt	125
6.9	Ancient Egyptian hieroglyphic writing	126
6.10	Egyptian royal graves	127
6.11	Relief carving at Kalabsha	128
6.12	Tuthmosis III	129
6.13	Rock engravings at Jebel Uweinat	132
6.14	Artefacts from Adrar Bous	133
6.15	Kintampo artefacts	137
6.16	Excavation at Daima	138
6.17	Paintings of cattle at Genda Biftu	141
6.18	The Land of Punt	142
6.19	Stone bowl from North Horr	143

6.20   Artefacts from Hyrax Hill   145
7.1   Traditional African iron-smelting   149
7.2   Rock painting of horse-drawn chariot, Acacus   150
7.3   Greek and Phoenician colonies in North Africa   151
7.4   Roman city at Timgad   152
7.5   Septimius Severus   153
7.6   Mosque of Sidi Okba at Kairouan   155
7.7   Meroitic temple at Naqa   157
7.8   Saint Anna on Faras wall painting   158
7.9   North-eastern Africa   159
7.10   Pre-Axumite altar   160
7.11   Axumite coins   161
7.12   Stela at Axum   162
7.13   Nok terracotta heads   164
7.14   Iron-smelting furnace at Taruga   165
7.15   Megalithic stone circle at Sine Saloum   167
7.16   Bronzes from Igbo Ukwu   168
7.17   West African sites with early metal   169
7.18   Urewe ware   172
7.19   The Chifumbaze complex in eastern and southern Africa   174
7.20   Chifumbaze complex pottery from Malawi   176
7.21   Terracotta head from Lydenburg   177
7.22   Rock painting at Silozwane   182
7.23   Rock painting at Sakwe   183
7.24   Sheep before A.D. 1000 in south-western Africa   184
7.25   Cape coastal pottery   185
8.1   Ruins at Kumbi Saleh   189
8.2   West African sites and kingdoms   190
8.3   Pottery discs from Begho   191
8.4   Terracotta heads from Ife   192
8.5   Early-style Benin bronze head   193
8.6   Second-millennium sites in eastern and southern Africa   195
8.7   Church of Abba Libanos, Lalibela   196
8.8   Ruins at Gedi   198
8.9   Luangwa-tradition pottery   201
8.10   Kisalian grave at Sanga   202
8.11   Inside the great enclosure, Great Zimbabwe   204
8.12   Reconstruction of Nhunguza Ruin   206
8.13   Copper cross-ingot from Ingombe Ilede   207
8.14   Stone walling at Naletale   207
8.15   Stone-walled enclosure at Makgwareṅg   209
8.16   Rock painting at Mpongweni   211

ACKNOWLEDGEMENTS

This book owes much to the comments and advice of Drs J. Alexander, P. L. Carter, G. Connah, G. Ll. Isaac, F. van Noten, L. Phillipson and P. L. Shinnie who have read parts or all of the manuscript. They do not, of course, share my responsibility for any errors which remain.

I am most grateful to all who have assisted with selecting and providing illustrations. The line drawings have been prepared by Dr L. Phillipson, apart from nos. 4.1, 4.9, 6.17, 6.19, 6.20, 7.10, 7.11, 7.18, 7.25, 8.9 and 8.12 which are the work of the late J. Ochieng'.

I would also like to thank the staff of Cambridge University Press for their help, patience and advice.

Acknowledgement is due to the following for their permission to reproduce the photographs indicated: **2.7** John Reader. **2.10** Cambridge University Press 1971: M. D. Leakey, *Olduvai Gorge*, III. **2.11** Survival Anglia Ltd and J. Matternes. **3.3** Zambia Survey Department. **3.7** National Museums of Kenya. **3.11** By courtesy of the Trustees, British Museum (Natural History). **3.15** Musée de l'Homme, Paris, *Archives de l'Institut de Paléontologie Humaine*, XXXII. **4.8** Cambridge University Press 1983: J. D. Lewis-Williams, *Rock Art of Southern Africa*. **5.8** University Museum of Archaeology and Anthropology, Cambridge. **6.5** Courtesy, Museum of Fine Arts, Boston. **6.12** By courtesy of the Trustees of the British Museum. **6.13** Dr F. van Noten, *Rock Art of the Jebel Uweinat*, 1978 (Akademische Druck-u. Verlagsanstalt, Graz). **6.16** Professor G. Connah, 'The Daima sequence', *Journal of African History*, XVII, 1976 (Cambridge University Press). **7.1** L. M. Pole. **7.4** Thomas Nelson & Sons Ltd 1959: A. A. M. van der Heyelen and H. H. Scullard (eds.), *Atlas of the Classical World*. **7.5** Fitzwilliam Museum, Cambridge. **7.7** Dr P. L. Carter. **7.8** The John Hillelson Agency Ltd. **7.13** Professor F. Willett. **7.15** Professor M. Posnansky. **7.16** Professor Thurstan Shaw, *Igbo Ukwu*, 1970 (Faber & Faber). **7.21** R. R. Inskeep and T. Maggs, 'Unique art objects in the Iron Age of the Transvaal, South Africa', *South African Archaeological Bulletin*, XXX, 1975. **8.1** Weidenfeld & Nicolson Archives 1966: B. Davidson, *Africa – history of a continent*. **8.4** and **8.5** Professor F. Willett, *Ife in the History of West African Sculpture*, 1967 (Thames & Hudson). **8.10** Dr F. van Noten, *The Archaeology of Central Africa*, 1982 (Akademische Druck- u. Verlagsanstalt, Graz). **8.15** Dr T. Maggs, *Iron Age Communities of the Southern Highveld*, 1976 (Natal Museum). **8.16** A. R. Willcox, *The Rock Art of South Africa*, 1963 (Nelson). All other photographs are my own.

CHAPTER 1

INTRODUCTION

The discovery of the African past

This book attempts to provide an up-to-date summary and interpretation of the archaeological evidence for the past of human beings in Africa from their first appearance up to the time when written history becomes the primary source of information. In chronological terms, this period covers all but a tiny fraction of the time that the earth has had human inhabitants. It now seems very probable that it was in Africa that mankind first evolved, at a date well before 3.0 million years ago. At the other end of the time-scale, the earliest written records relating to Africa, those of the ancient Egyptians, began about 5,000 years ago; for other parts of the continent, notably the interior regions south of the equator, no such relevant records exist which are more than one or two centuries old.

The period of time before written history is conventionally known as prehistory. The term is not entirely appropriate for Africa, for a number of reasons. First, there were long periods, especially in the northern part of the continent, about which written records, although available, are not generally informative on many aspects of contemporary life. There are also numerous instances where the only available written records were produced by outsiders and frequently give an incomplete account of matters which the writers did not properly understand. These are situations which confront prehistorians in many parts of the world, but they give rise to particular problems in some parts of Africa because of the generally shallow time-depth of indigenous literacy. A different approach is required to those aspects of African culture which, to a very large extent, take the place of written literature in other regions. These include the developed oral traditions which, in many societies, preserve the accumulated wisdom of the people, including details of their past history. Again, language itself plays a large part in determining a people's or an individual's sense of identity. Where written examples of ancient languages do not exist, much can be learned through the study of present-day linguistic forms and distributions concerning the nature and interactions of past populations. The methods of interpreting these sources of information about the African past will be discussed below, and an attempt made to link their evidence with that derived from archaeology.

In view of the enormous time-span of African prehistory and the great variety of the human societies that have inhabited the continent, it is clear that very varied methods have to be employed in elucidating the past. Studies of linguistics and oral traditions are, of course, only applicable to relatively recent periods. For the vast majority of the period of time with which this book is concerned archaeology is our main and often our only source of primary information about human activities.

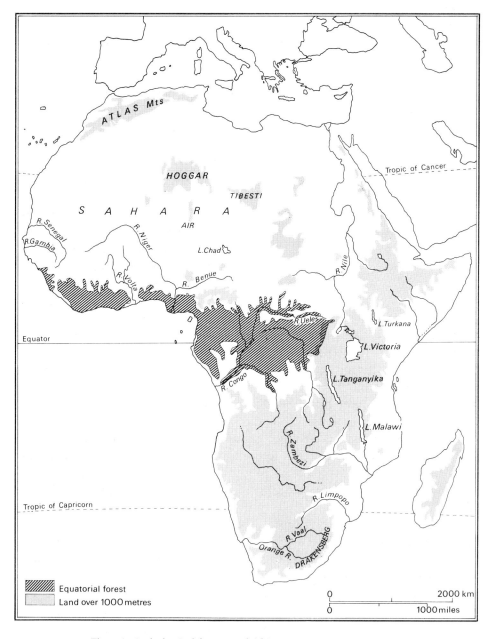

1.1 The principal physical features of Africa.

Archaeology in Africa

Archaeological data provide a picture of the past which is essentially different from, and in many ways complementary to, that which may be reconstructed from written or oral sources. The archaeologist studying the remains of a pre-literate people will hardly ever be able to learn the names or characters of individuals. He will often find it difficult to make more than very general inferences about social systems or political situations. On the other hand, his interpretation of technological skills or economic practices, particularly hunting, agriculture or the herding of domestic animals, will generally be far more complete and reliable than those that can be obtained by other types of study. For this reason it is not just to the study of prehistory that archaeology can make an important contribution; it is also an approach that greatly aids our understanding of more recent societies, even those for which abundant written records are available.

To the student of Africa, the findings of archaeological research represent a major source of information about the continent's past; it is the principal source for most of prehistory, and it makes a significant contribution to our understanding of more recent periods. In Africa, the shallow time-depths to which archaeological investigations may often be usefully applied greatly increase our historical perspective of recent trends and events; and it may justly be claimed that our understanding of such pressing and disparate problems as desertification and tribalism is enhanced through the results of archaeological research, with obvious implications for economic and political development. But African archaeology is relevant far beyond its own continent. The archaeologists and prehistorians of other regions have much to learn from the African record, not only from its unparalleled evidence for the earliest periods of human development, but also methodologically. Because most of Africa has undergone environmental change on a scale which is relatively minor when compared with the glaciated regions of Eurasia and North America, abundant data are fairly readily available to aid the interpretation of prehistoric subsistence practices. Africa also provides excellent opportunities for contrasting the testimony of archaeology with that of linguistic and oral historical studies, and for interpreting the meaning of rock art in the light of the belief systems of recent peoples, as will be discussed below.

The study of African archaeology has developed in two principal directions. The literate civilisations of ancient Egypt and North Africa have been investigated through two hundred years of changing approaches, while the prehistory of more southerly regions first received serious attention in South Africa at the end of the nineteenth century. The two studies have long remained separate, and their methodologies are only now beginning to converge. In the Saharan and sub-Saharan latitudes the emphasis and geographical coverage of research has always been irregular, and the archaeology of large areas remains virtually unexplored. Of necessity, much effort has gone into demonstrating basic sequences and setting up a terminological framework for prehistory. Only fairly recently has it been practicable to present a comprehensive overview of the type here attempted.

The classification of archaeological material into successive phases, industries and complexes is now seen as to some extent an artificial compartmentalisation of what is in fact a continuous variation, both in time and space. It must, however, be recognised that closely defined boundaries between culture areas could and did exist in certain circumstances, and that stylistic and technological change proceeded more rapidly at some times than at others.

Contrary to the assumptions frequently made in the past, it is now recognised that the parameters of material culture distributions do not necessarily coincide with those of human societies as recognised on socio-political, linguistic or other bases. Uncertainty about the significance of material culture groupings is greatest in the case of the earlier prehistoric industries, because we do not yet understand the purposes to which artefacts were put. It is frequently difficult to distinguish between variation due to different function, to stylistic tradition and preference, or to other factors such as availability of raw materials. Furthermore, a single society may engage in distinct life-styles, sometimes on a seasonal basis, perhaps in separate areas and environments: contrasting archaeological assemblages may thus represent different activities of a single community. On the other hand, it has also been shown that certain items or styles of material culture may fulfil a symbolic function through their association with a particular society.

For reasons such as these, African prehistory is here presented with emphasis on economic development and general life-style, correspondingly less attention being paid to the definition, succession and inter-relationship of named industries. However, in the present state of African archaeological studies, we need a partial retention of the old framework. In many parts of the continent, as will be made apparent in the following chapters, concerted programmes of archaeological research have never been undertaken. There are several regions, even whole countries, where chance discoveries or isolated excavations, often poorly documented, provide the only data on which a synthesis may be based. Here, the archaeologist may consider himself fortunate where he can propose an outline succession of industrial stages, such being an essential prerequisite for the detailed study of ancient life-styles and resource-exploitation patterns.

In the building up of an overview of African prehistory, we must pay particular attention to erecting a sound chronological framework. Age estimates based on radiocarbon analyses are particularly problematic, since it is only for the more recent periods that the relationship between radiocarbon and true ages is known. In this book ages are cited in the following manners in order to minimise confusion and to aid comparison between dates derived from different sources and methods.

(a) In chapters 2–5 ages are given in the form 'about . . . years ago'. These ages apply to periods beyond the last 7,000 years and should all be regarded as approximations. They are derived from a variety of sources, mostly – for the last 50,000 years or so – radiocarbon, and no attempt has been made to calibrate or correct them unless otherwise stated.

(b) In chapters 6–8 dates since *c.* 5,000 B.C. are given in years B.C. or A.D. Here, radiocarbon dates have been calibrated and are expressed in calendar years according to the calculations presented by Ralph *et al.* (1973). This calibration must be regarded as provisional since we are not yet sure that it applies in tropical latitudes. Precise dates, e.g. 146 B.C., are derived from historical sources. All ages noted in these three chapters are thus intended to be comparable with one another, but they are not necessarily compatible with those cited in chapters 2–5.

Since more plentiful data relating to absolute chronology are now available than could be employed by the writers of previous syntheses, and in view of the evidence, cited above, for disparate rates of development in different areas, we are not going to use the conventional terminology based upon broad techno-logical/chronological subdivisions such as 'Late Stone Age', 'Neolithic' or 'Iron Age'. It has long been recognised that such terms cannot be precisely defined, but their informal use has continued, often at the expense of clarity; they are avoided in this book.

Linguistics

Language provides an important means of classification for African peoples. It is a criterion which has a major bearing on an individual's sense of identity and membership of a group. It also has historical validity since an individual obtains his knowledge of his first language from the other members of that group to which he belongs by birth and/or upbringing.

There is good general agreement between linguists concerning the major language families of Africa (Greenberg, 1963; fig. 1.2). Their present distribution is shown in outline form in fig. 1.3. In the northern and north-eastern regions of the continent, the languages which are spoken today belong to the super-family generally known as Afroasiatic or Erythraic. This includes the Berber languages of North Africa, the Cushitic tongues centred on Ethiopia and Somalia as well as the widespread Semitic family, the modern members of which include Arabic, Amharic and Hebrew.

To the south is a very irregularly shaped area covering much of the central and southern Sahara, the southern Sudan and parts of the adjacent savanna with an extension into parts of East Africa, where most of the modern languages are classed as Nilo-Saharan, with Nilotic and Sudanic as the principal subdivisions. Some linguists believe that Songhai, spoken around the Niger bend, is also of Nilo-Saharan affinity. It may be that the present fragmented distribution of the

Family	Main divisions	Examples
Afroasiatic	Semitic	Arabic, Amharic, Gurage, Tigrinya
	Berber	Berber, Tuareg
	Cushitic	Somali, Galla, Afar, Sidamo, Beja
	Chadic	Fali, Hausa
Nilo-Saharan	Sudanic	Acholi, Shilluk, Mangbetu, Jie
	Saharan	Kanuri, Teda, Zaghawa
	Songhai	Songhai
Congo-Kordofanian	West Atlantic	Dyola, Fulani, Temne
	Mande	Mwa, Mende
	Voltaic	Dogon, Mossi, Talensi
	Kwa	Akan, Bini, Ibo, Igala, Yoruba
	Bantu	Gikuyu, Bemba, Shona, Xhosa, Kongo
	Adamawa-Eastern	Mbaka, Zande
Khoisan	South African Khoisan	!Kung, ‡Khomani, Nama
	Sandawe	Sandawe
	Hadza	Hadza

1.2 The classification of recent African languages (after Greenberg, 1963).

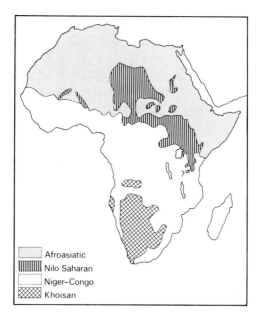

Afroasiatic
Nilo Saharán
Niger–Congo
Khoisan

1.3 The distribution of Africa's major language families in recent times (simplified from Greenberg, 1963).

Nilo-Saharan languages indicates that they were formerly spoken over a more extensive area.

Most of the modern languages of West Africa belong to the Niger–Congo family, which may also be extended to include Kordofanian, spoken in the western Sudan.* Within West Africa these languages have developed considerable diversity. On the other hand, the distribution of one sub-group of Niger–Congo extends over the greater part of central and southern Africa, excluding the extreme south-west. These are the Bantu languages which, despite the enormous area of their distribution, show a relatively strong degree of similarity with one another. The northern limit of the Bantu languages approximates to the northern edge of the equatorial forest. In the savanna woodland to the north, the Adamawa and Ubangian languages also belong to the Niger–Congo family.

As will be shown in chapter 7, there is good evidence that the Bantu-speaking peoples have expanded from a north-western area into the sub-equatorial latitudes during the course of the last few thousand years. In much of this region these populations replaced or absorbed people who spoke languages of the Khoisan family, such as still survive in the south-westernmost parts of the continent. These are the languages of the Khoi and San peoples (still sometimes called by the derogatory terms Hottentots and Bushmen), who have retained into recent times their traditional herding or hunting life-styles beyond the country of the Bantu-speakers. There are indications that in earlier times the Khoisan languages were spoken as far to the north as the modern Kenya/Tanzania border area, but in regions further to the west their northerly extent is less certain.

These modern languages provide the data on which the historical linguist bases his conclusions (Ehret, 1976). Through studying the distribution of recent linguistic forms he is able to reconstruct certain features of the past languages from which the modern ones are derived, and to suggest the areas in which these ancestral languages may have been spoken. The vocabulary that is attested for these ancestral languages can tell us something about the life-styles of the people who spoke them, and about the things with which they were familiar. As different peoples came into contact with one another words were borrowed from one language into neighbouring ones; these 'loanwords' too can often be traced. It is through studies such as these that the linguistic prehistory of Africa may tentatively be reconstructed.

We have of course no precise information about the varying speeds at which linguistic change proceeds. It is only in the case of languages which have a long written history that such speeds can be calculated at all precisely. Linguistics

---

* In this book 'Sudan' with a capital 'S' refers to the modern Republic of the Sudan. Spelled with a small 's', 'sudan' refers to the open savanna country which extends across Africa south of the Sahara and north of the equatorial forest. The word is derived from the Arabic, meaning black people.

alone can provide only a relative ordering of processes and events, together with a rough estimate of the lengths of time that have been involved. Glottochronological formulae (a method of calculating the ages at which linguistic developments took place) should be regarded with great suspicion, particularly when applied in non-literate contexts, since these formulae assume that language change takes place at an even rate. However, when there are links between independent sequences, based respectively on archaeology and on linguistics, the chronology of the latter is placed on firmer ground. Historical reconstructions based on linguistic studies may be of particular value in adding to testimony of archaeology in areas where little excavation can be undertaken; and because many aspects of inter-group relationships illustrated by linguistic studies are difficult to demonstrate on the basis of archaeological evidence. Such linguistic reconstructions mostly relate to the past five thousand or six thousand years, although attempts have been made tentatively to apply these methods to still earlier periods.

Oral tradition

In order properly to interpret the oral historical traditions which are preserved in many African societies, we must understand the role that they play in that society and the reasons for their recollection (Vansina, 1965; Henige, 1974). It is generally found that oral traditions are most carefully preserved and re-told among peoples who have a strong centralised state system. In such cases the function of the historical traditions is often to support the established political authority, for example by explaining the origin of the ruling clan or family and the manner by which its members claim their right to rule. Several societies recognise this aspect of oral tradition and have official historians, whose task it is to preserve and transmit orthodox versions of state history.

It is generally agreed that traditions which purport to relate to events of more than four or five centuries ago must be interpreted with particular caution. Absolute chronology (in the western sense) is not often a major interest of the custodians of oral tradition, and events may sometimes have taken place at a significantly earlier period than a literal interpretation of the traditions suggests (e.g. J. C. Miller, 1972; 1976). As with written history, oral historical traditions tend to concentrate their attentions on political events and on the activities of important individuals. They are not therefore a substitute for archaeology as a source of historical information; and a comprehensive picture of the African past can only be built up through the use of all available sources.

Africa in world prehistory

The archaeological picture now discernible of the African past is one of paramount importance for the study of human prehistory. As will be shown below, evidence for the life-style and physical characteristics of the earliest hominids comes at present only from African sites. While it cannot be conclusively demonstrated that mankind first evolved in Africa alone, there is a strong possibility that this was indeed the case. Virtually every major subsequent stage in mankind's development may be illustrated from the African record.

The succession of African hunter-gatherer societies is the longest and one of the most varied known. It extends from the origins of humanity to the present day and, potentially, provides an evolutionary link between the studies of the primate behaviour specialist and the social anthropologist. It illustrates adaptation to environments of great diversity, ranging from deserts and high-altitude glacial margins on the one hand to rain-forests and coastal swamps on the other. Major environmental changes have, of course, taken place during the period of some two to three million years with which we are here concerned, but these have not generally been so drastic as those in more northerly latitudes and, although their distribution has undergone great shifts, the range of situations exploited by prehistoric hunter-gatherers has been preserved in Africa to an extent not paralleled in other continents that were settled in Middle Pleistocene or earlier times. This continuity, both in environment and in the hunter-gatherer life-style itself, offers in Africa an unrivalled series of opportunities for interpreting the major trends and processes in human development.

It has been noted by J. G. D. Clark (1969) that developments in stone-tool technology were broadly similar throughout much of the world. Backed-blade industries of the type represented in the European and West Asian 'Upper Palaeolithic' were thought prerequisite for the development of food-production and, ultimately, of literate civilisation. This premise, at least so far as Africa is concerned, has been seriously questioned (Shaw, 1971), and the point made that, although industries of this type are uncommon in Africa south of the Sahara, microlithic industries such as were made by the earliest European and Near Eastern food-producers were produced in Africa at a remarkably early date. More recent research, summarised below, has confirmed this observation, and microlithic technology is now attested in southern Africa at a date far earlier than in any other part of the world; not only is it significantly older than the European or Asian blade industries, but it is apparently associated with the oldest fossils so far known which may confidently be attributed to fully modern man, *Homo sapiens sapiens*. Far from being a backwater therefore, as has sometimes been suggested, Upper Pleistocene Africa may have been a world leader both in the evolution of our species and in its technological development.

Current research has also involved a major re-evaluation of the evidence for early African settled life and food-production. At least south of the Sahara, these developments are now seen to have taken place very gradually and essentially independently of comparable processes in other parts of the world. Settled life appears to have come about in what is now the southern Sahara and sahel in response to the rich and well-watered environments which prevailed there at the start of the Holocene. This same general area is now recognised as the homeland of many plant species which were subsequently brought under cultivation and dispersed to become important food crops here and in most other parts of sub-Saharan Africa. Although the domestic animals of the latter region appear all to have been introduced from elsewhere, it is now clear that Africa was a major area for the initial cultivation of vegetable foods as diverse as yams, rice, ensete and dry-grown cereals.

With the exception of the Egyptian Nile Valley, no part of Africa saw the rise of an indigenous literate civilisation, for strong external influences made a major contribution to civilisation at Axum, Meroe and on the East African coast. What were the main factors contributing to the rise of literate civilisation in Egypt and elsewhere which were absent in other parts of Africa? The Egyptian Nile Valley is given great fertility by the annual inundations of the Nile. The surrounding desert stopped the physical expansion of the dense population which the fertile valley could support. Comparable situations prevailed in other centres of early civilisation: the Indus Valley, Mesopotamia, the Hwang Ho Valley and Mexico (cf. Shaw, 1971). The resultant stress required for its control the development of an elaborate socio-political system, an established sanctioned order of a complexity which would have been out of keeping with the smaller, less constrained societies of most other parts of the continent. It may be argued, at least in part, that it was the richness of the African environment and its lack of physical barriers which permitted African society to develop its own form and order without the constraints imposed by literate civilisation.

But it is far more relevant to consider what Africa did achieve, rather than what it did not. It is pertinent to view the development of African societies, as revealed by archaeology and other disciplines, from an essentially internal viewpoint before comparison is made with their counterparts in other parts of the world. Thus we are able to evaluate African achievements in terms of their African context and to appreciate the range of economic practices, technologies, socio-political systems and beliefs which was developed in response to varied population densities, physical boundaries, communications and available resources. Then we can see the comprehensive manner in which varied environments were exploited. We can begin to understand why indigenous technology reached the high level of expertise evidenced, for example, in West African bronze casting, while other aspects – such as transport – saw little change over prolonged periods. We can appreciate oral tradition as a counterpart of written literature, and wonder at the possible antiquity of art forms in wood and other perishable materials which are at present only known from the most recent periods. African archaeology provides a unique view of local cultural development leading to recent societies that are now appreciated, not as failures that have fallen by the wayside in the rise of industrial civilisation, but as examples of different – perhaps in the long term more viable – expressions of human culture fully adapted to their practitioners' circumstances.

CHAPTER 2

THE EMERGENCE OF MAN IN AFRICA

Man's precursors

The story of the emergence of man extends far back into geological time (fig. 2.1). The modern species of Old World and New World monkeys, apes and humans are all classed as members of the Anthropoidea sub-order of the order Primates (fig. 2.2). Other members of this order, with which we are not here concerned, include such animals as tarsiers and tree-shrews. Fossil remains of early primates have been recovered at many sites in the Americas, Europe and

Million years ago	Geological period	African hominoids
0	Pleistocene/Recent	Homo
2	Pliocene	Australo-pithecus
4		
6		
8	Miocene	
10		Ramapith-ecus
12		
14		
16		Dryo-pithecus
18		
20		
22		
24	Oligocene	
26		Oligopithecus
28		Aegyptopithecus
30		

2.1 The geological periods of the last thirty million years, showing the ages of the principal hominoid types attested in the fossil record.

Asia as well as in Africa, extending back in time as far as the end of the Cretaceous period about 70 million years ago.

The modern Old World Anthropoidea are believed to be descended from small but ape-like primates, notably that named *Aegyptopithecus*, whose remains are best known from deposits in the Fayum Depression of Egypt, dating from the Oligocene period of between 36 and 23 million years ago (Simons, 1972; Szalay and Delson, 1978).

By the beginning of the subsequent Miocene, it appears that primate evolution had proceeded sufficiently far to permit the differentiation of lines of descent that have led, on the one hand, to the modern monkeys, and on the other to the great apes and man. On the latter (hominoid) line, some of the most important fossils are those from western Kenya attributed to the genus *Dryopithecus*, which show important developments in skull, teeth and wrist. *Dryopithecus* probably lived in the forests that were widespread in East Africa in Miocene times, before the completion of the great earth movements which resulted in the formation of the Rift Valley. Fossils attributed to the same genus are also recorded from Europe and south-eastern Asia. *Dryopithecus* limb bones show that these creatures could use their fore-limbs as arms and also walk on all four limbs, while the teeth suggest that fruit may have been an important part of the diet.

In later Miocene times, between about 14 and 10 million years ago, further evolutionary development took place which eventually led to the emergence of the hominid family to which all types of man, past and present, belong. With greater geographical spread, resulting in the colonisation of new environments and subsequent isolation, several distinct early hominoid species now developed; of greatest relevance to the study of human origins are those attributed to the

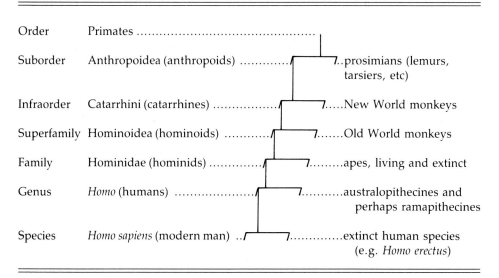

Order	Primates ....
Suborder	Anthropoidea (anthropoids) ....⌐ ⌐..prosimians (lemurs, tarsiers, etc)
Infraorder	Catarrhini (catarrhines) ....⌐ ⌐.....New World monkeys
Superfamily	Hominoidea (hominoids) ....⌐ ⌐.......Old World monkeys
Family	Hominidae (hominids) ....⌐ ⌐.........apes, living and extinct
Genus	*Homo* (humans) ....⌐ ⌐..........australopithecines and perhaps ramapithecines
Species	*Homo sapiens* (modern man) ..⌐ ⌐.............extinct human species (e.g. *Homo erectus*)

2.2 The classification of the hominids within the order Primates.

genus *Ramapithecus*. The faces of these creatures were less snout-like than those of their ancestors, the jaws were more massive and the teeth were further adapted to use as grinders. One type of ramapithecine has been found at Fort Ternan in Kenya, but most of the other significant discoveries come from south-east Europe and from southern Asia. Other fossils from the same sites indicate that these creatures favoured open savanna woodland environments in contrast with the forest habitat of *Dryopithecus*. This adaptation to a less circumscribed habitat, doubtless linked (as the teeth indicate) with the adoption of a more omnivorous diet, may have been a major step in the evolutionary processes which led to the emergence of man (Simons, 1977). It has even been suggested that *Ramapithecus* should be classified as the earliest known hominid, but the evidence is inconclusive.

Between about 10 million years ago and some time between 4.0 and 3.0 million years ago there is a major gap in the available fossil evidence for human ancestry. This covers the end of the Miocene and much of the Pliocene periods. Fossil-bearing deposits of this time are relatively rare in Africa, for reasons that are not fully understood; and in those that have been investigated primate remains are extremely uncommon. When the fossil record resumes, late in the Pliocene, it is exclusively in eastern and southern Africa that fossils of true hominids are found; and they occur with an abundance that contrasts markedly with the earlier periods. Despite the wide Old World distribution of the ramapithecines, the evidence currently available suggests that it was probably in Africa that man first evolved.

The earliest hominids

It is now clear from the results of recent research that it was in the period between about 6.0 and 4.0 million years ago that the first creatures generally acknowledged as hominids developed. Virtually all the important fossils which illustrate this development have been recovered from sites in eastern and southern Africa. Before discussing these sites it is first necessary to describe the different types of hominid that have been recognised in this crucial time-span, and the theories that have been put forward concerning their inter-relationships.

There can now be little reasonable doubt that, by about 2.0 million years ago if not before, several distinct types of hominid were co-existing in broadly similar environments. The exact number of parallel hominid lineages and their relationship to each other are subjects of controversy. This is partly because many of the fossils are fragmentary, and also because it is not known how much variation could exist between the sexes and individuals of a single species or genus at any one time.

The most widely accepted classification of the early hominids places them in two distinct genera (Tobias, 1978a; 1980). Of these, the earliest to evolve was *Australopithecus*. The first australopithecines were of a lightly built, or gracile type, which first appeared at least 4.5 million years ago. The earlier East African fossils of this type – before about 3.4 million years ago – are generally classed as *Australopithecus afarensis*, the later ones as *A. africanus* (Johanson and White, 1979; Day *et al.*, 1980). The gracile australopithecines were probably extinct by about 2.0 million years ago in South Africa, perhaps surviving rather later further to the north. In both areas more heavily built, or robust, forms – *A. robustus* in South Africa and *A. boisei* in East Africa – are attested between 2.0 and 1.0 million years ago.

It is instructive briefly to compare *Australopithecus africanus* both with modern man and with a modern great ape, such as a gorilla (fig. 2.3). The first point that one notices is the small size of the australopithecine: an adult specimen stood less than 1.5 m high and weighed only 25 to 45 kg (Suzman, 1980). Comparison

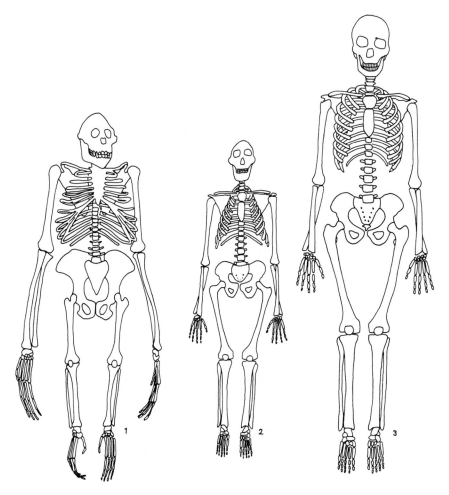

2.3 Skeletons, to the same scale, of 1 – gorilla, 2 – *Australopithecus africanus*, 3 – *Homo sapiens*.

of the skulls shows that the jaws and teeth of *Australopithecus*, despite the creature's small overall size, were actually larger than those of modern man. The brain, on the other hand, was only about one-third as large, at about 450 cubic centimetres. This is approximately the same size as the modern gorilla's brain. In the gorilla the brain is placed behind the face, and the neck-muscle attachment is at the back of the skull. In man, the brain extends over the face, with the development of a true forehead, and the muscle is attached to the base of the skull. In both respects, the australopithecine occupies a position intermediate between the gorilla and modern man. In two important ways, *Australopithecus* was, however, clearly much closer to man than to the gorilla: his posture was completely upright, and his canine teeth were much reduced in size. A gorilla's molar teeth serve essentially a crushing function: in man and the australopithecines they are primarily grinders.

Although these characteristics are true of both types of australopithecine, there were nevertheless significant differences between them (Tobias, 1967; Bilsborough, 1972). The front teeth (incisors and canines) of *A. africanus* were appreciably larger than those of his robust counterparts; this is in contrast to the generally more substantial build of the latter species. While *A. africanus* was essentially omnivorous, *A. robustus* may have evolved a specialised predominantly vegetarian diet to which large grinding teeth – molars – were well suited. To this feature may be linked also his massive musculature, especially that of the jaw, which in turn gave rise to the large ridges of bone to which the muscles were attached. This was the sole function of the 'sagittal crest' of bone running along the top of the skull from front to back, a feature which both *A. robustus* and *A. boisei* shared with the modern male gorilla. There were also significant postcranial differences, as yet imperfectly understood, between skeletons of the two australopithecine species.

The earliest representatives of the genus *Homo*, to a single species of which all types of modern man belong, may be dated somewhat earlier than 2.0 million years ago. *Homo* probably evolved from a gracile australopithecine (Tobias, 1978a). The earliest known specimens are of the type designated *Homo habilis*; the more advanced *H. erectus* first appeared around 1.5 million years ago. One way in which the early hominid types may have been related to one another is shown in figure 2.4. However, there is much controversy concerning the relationship between *Australopithecus africanus* and the earliest members of the genus *Homo* (J. T. Robinson, 1967; Wood, 1978; Tobias, 1978a; R. E. Leakey and Walker, 1976; Walker and Leakey, 1978). Some authorities deny that two genera are represented, regarding *H. habilis* as a gracile australopithecine. The dispute serves to show how difficult it is to describe evolutionary processes in 'Linnaean' terms, which were originally designed to classify modern genera and species (Campbell, 1978).

Specimens attributed to *Homo habilis* differ from those accepted as australopithecine most importantly in their larger brain size – averaging about 640 cubic

Million years ago

2.4 A tentative 'family tree' of African hominids during the last four million years. *Australopithecus robustus* and *A. boisei* are regarded as regional races, found in South and East Africa respectively. Likewise, *A. afarensis* appears to be the East African equivalent of the earliest South African examples of *A. africanus*.

centimetres, which is 45 per cent greater than the equivalent figure for *A. africanus* (fig. 2.5). The teeth also more closely resemble those of modern man, as do the bones of the hand. The posture of *H. habilis* seems to have been completely upright and there is no evidence for such massive muscles, with bony ridges for their attachment, as were characteristic of the contemporary *A. boisei* (L. S. B. Leakey *et al.*, 1964). At one site, Koobi Fora in northern Kenya, there is evidence for a contemporary or variant of *H. habilis* with an even larger brain, and this creature may have been the direct ancestor of the *Homo erectus* types that are attested in East Africa from about 1.5 million years ago, and which are described in more detail in chapter 3.

The oldest East African discoveries

It must be emphasised that the distribution of fossil discoveries is controlled not only by the former geographical extent of the relevant species, but also by the presence or absence of conditions suitable for their preservation, survival and eventual recovery. These conditions have occurred in both East and South Africa, but in very different situations (fig. 2.6). In East Africa the lake basins of the Rift Valley provided favoured habitats for the early hominids and their associated faunas. Rapid sedimentation rates ensured their preservation and the volcanic activity of the area provided materials that can be dated, notably by potassium/argon analysis. Lastly, more recent developments have often led to the erosion of the fossil-bearing deposits, thus exposing their contents for collection or excavation and subsequent study. In South Africa, on the other hand, bones accumulated in limestone caves, in deposits that were consolidated by minerals carried down by water seepage. They have subsequently been exposed, for the most part, in the course of mining operations. Direct dating of these cave deposits has not yet proved possible (Howell, 1982).

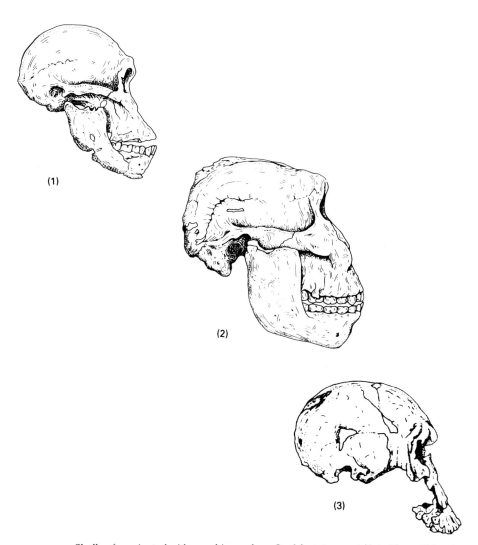

2.5 Skulls of 1 – *Australopithecus africanus* from Sterkfontein, 2 – *A. boisei* from Olduvai, 3 – *Homo habilis* (1470) from Koobi Fora.

In both regions where remains of *Australopithecus* have been found, open
savanna conditions with patches of woodland are indicated. This represents a
further shift in preferred habitat away from the denser woodland frequented by
the Miocene ramapithecines.

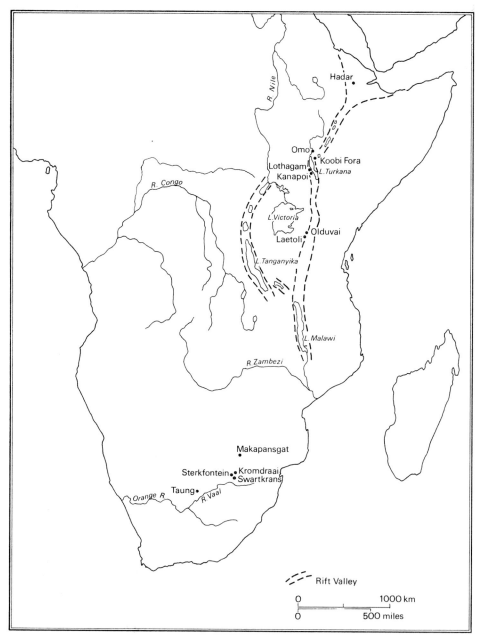

2.6 The principal sites at which *Australopithecus* and *Homo habilis* fossils have been
discovered.

It is important to realise that in both South and East Africa, but especially in the latter region, the majority of the fossil discoveries have been made within recent years. Study of many is as yet at a preliminary stage, and there is often considerable controversy about their attribution to named species and, on occasion, their dating. Likewise, new finds are steadily being announced, and these may mean the modification or abandonment of existing theories. Any account of the current state of research must, therefore, be both tentative and provisional.

The earliest hominid fossils are very fragmentary and come from Miocene and early Pliocene sites west and south of Lake Turkana in northern Kenya. At Lothagam a jaw fragment is dated to some 5.5 million years ago, while the Chemeron Formation near Lake Baringo has yielded a skull fragment from a somewhat more recent context. Little can confidently be said about this scanty material, but it is similar to specimens of rather later date which are attributed to the genus *Australopithecus* (Howell, 1982).

Additional, more abundant, remains attributed to *Australopithecus* of between 4.0 and 3.0 million years ago (Walter and Aronson, 1982) come from two sites in eastern Africa: Hadar in the Afar Triangle of Ethiopia 500 km north-north-east of Addis Ababa, and Laetoli (formerly known as Laetolil) on the western side of the Rift Valley in northern Tanzania. The larger collection comes from Hadar where lacustrine and river-delta deposits are separated by a series of volcanic tuffs: at one locality the remains of thirteen early hominids, including four juveniles, were found together. The most informative discovery, however, is a 40 per cent complete skeleton of a female, popularly known as Lucy. Her pelvis and leg bones indicate a well developed upright posture. Her original height was probably about 1.2 m (Taieb *et al.*, 1974; Johanson *et al.*, 1978; Johanson and White, 1979; Johanson and Edey, 1981). At Laetoli, aeolian tuffs have yielded remains which consist mainly of jaws and teeth, allowing detailed comparisons to be made (M. D. Leakey *et al.*, 1976; Johanson and White, 1979). The same deposits included layers of hardened ash-covered mud in which were preserved a remarkable series of footprints of hominids and other creatures (fig. 2.7). The hominid spoor provides further evidence for a fully bipedal gait (M. D. Leakey and Hay, 1979; White, 1980).

Because of their physical similarity and near contemporaneity, it seems likely that the Laetoli and Hadar hominid fossils should be regarded as representatives of the same species. Conflicting attributions have been proposed, but several researchers now agree that these finds belong to *Australopithecus afarensis*, a relatively lightly built or gracile species showing several features, principally in the teeth and face, which serve to distinguish it from the later australopithecines (Johanson and White, 1979; Day *et al.*, 1980). The Hadar discoveries are additionally important as providing by far the most extensive sample of postcranial remains belonging to any australopithecine population.

No artefacts have been recovered from the Laetoli deposits, but at Hadar small numbers of apparently artificially flaked cobbles (fig. 2.8) are reported in contexts provisionally dated to some 2.6 million years ago (H. Roche and Tiercelin, 1980). These specimens and their associations await full investigation; should preliminary accounts be confirmed, these occurrences are by a substantial margin the earliest known incidence of hominid-made artefacts, although it should be emphasised that they are not associated with, and are considerably more recent than, the Hadar hominid fossils. (See also Kalb *et al.*, 1982.)

To this same general period belongs the beginning of the long sequence of fossil-bearing deposits in the Omo Valley of southern Ethiopia (Howell, 1976; Howell and Coppens, 1976). The Omo River, flowing into the northern end of Lake Turkana, has exposed a complex series of deposits that were laid down at intervals during the last 4.0 million years in a variety of lakeside and riverine

2.7 The trail of hominid footprints discovered at Laetoli and dated to about 3.8 million years ago. The footprints are interpreted as those of two upright-walking hominids, one larger than the other.

environments. These deposits have yielded abundant fossil material, mostly very fragmentary. The hominid remains consist for the most part of isolated teeth. The oldest of these specimens are probably almost as ancient as those from Laetoli, but they are of relatively little value in illustrating the evolution of the various hominid species.

In the Omo Valley, artificially chipped stone tools in deposits which may be dated to just before 2.0 million years ago are especially interesting. These

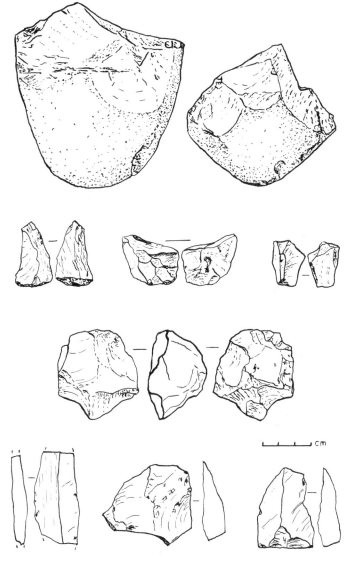

2.8 Stone artefacts: top row from Hadar (after Roche and Tiercelin, 1980); remainder from the Omo Valley (after H. V. and J. P. S. Merrick, 1976).

specimens, the earliest artefacts known from the Lake Turkana basin, are simple flakes struck from small nodules of quartz, which was the only suitable material available in the area. The nature of the specimens unfortunately precludes any detailed study of, or insight into, the technology of their makers (fig. 2.8).

Olduvai and Koobi Fora

Somewhat later in date, but of great richness and importance, are the discoveries from the Koobi Fora area on the north-east shore of Lake Turkana (M. G. and R. E. Leakey, 1978; Coppens *et al.*, 1976). Lake Turkana lies in a closed basin and has no outlet except an overflow channel to the Nile, which functions only when its waters reach a very high level (Butzer, 1980; Harvey and Grove, 1982). The height and size of the lake have thus fluctuated considerably; it and its feeder rivers have laid down a deep and complex series of sediments in which hominid and other fossils are exceptionally well preserved. The sediments with which we are here concerned have been named the Koobi Fora formation, and they are divided into a lower member and an upper member separated by a horizon of consolidated volcanic debris known as the KBS tuff. Although formerly the subject of much controversy, the age of the KBS tuff is now well established at about 1.8 million years, and the Koobi Fora formation as a whole appears to span the period from rather more than 2.0 million until about 1.2 million years ago. Detailed studies of the deposits have succeeded in demonstrating the local circumstances in which they were laid down, and thus the immediate environments where the various species represented in the fossil assemblages lived and died. Living sites and artefacts are also preserved at Koobi Fora, but unfortunately they are rarely in direct association with the hominid fossils (fig. 2.9).

Million years ago	Stratigraphy	Principal discoveries
	Guomde formation	
1.3	Chari/Karari Tuff	
	Upper member, Koobi Fora formation	Karari industry 3733 *Homo erectus*
1.8	KBS Tuff	KBS site and stone industry
	Lower member, Koobi Fora formation	1470 *Homo habilis*
3.2 (?)	Suregei Tuff	
	Kubi Algi formation	

2.9 Summary of the stratigraphy and principal discoveries at Koobi Fora.

At least two, and almost certainly three, hominid lines are represented at Koobi Fora (Walker and Leakey, 1978; M. G. and R. E. Leakey, 1978). There is a robust form of *Australopithecus, A. boisei,* and possibly the gracile species *A. africanus.* The genus *Homo* also occurs throughout the sequence. The early form, which some would attribute to a large-brained form of *H. habilis,* is best represented by the fossil skull generally known by its registration number, 1470. Virtually complete, the skull comes from a context in the lower member of the Koobi Fora formation which is securely dated to about 2.0 million years ago. The rounded skull-vault with a well-developed forehead housed a brain which, at about 800 cubic centimetres, was some 70 per cent larger than those of the contemporary robust australopithecines. The skull crest and massive muscle attachments of the latter species were likewise not present in 1470. Robust australopithecine remains are relatively rare below the KBS tuff; subsequently they become significantly more common, representing about half of the total hominid sample. By about 1.5 million years ago, an even more advanced hominid is attested in the fossil record of the upper member of the Koobi Fora formation by two skulls which may confidently be attributed to *Homo erectus.* These creatures, further discussed in chapter 3, had even larger cranial capacities than their predecessors, and thus presented a striking contrast with the robust australopithecines, their only hominid contemporaries, the gracile form having by this time become extinct. There may be a tendency at Koobi Fora for remains of *Homo* to occur predominantly in old lakeside environments, and those of *Australopithecus boisei* in riverine situations (Behrensmeyer, 1976).

Further confirmation for the existence, side by side, of early *Homo* and a robust australopithecine comes from the famous site of Olduvai Gorge in northern Tanzania (fig. 2.10). Here, natural erosion has exposed a deep series of superimposed beds which contain abundant artefact and fossil assemblages covering the greater part of the last 1.8 million years (L. S. B. Leakey, 1965; M. D. Leakey, 1971; Hay, 1976). In the lowest horizon, Bed I, laid down in lakeside conditions around 1.75 million years ago, are found the remains both of the gracile but large-brained *Homo habilis,* and of the robust *Australopithecus boisei.* Both have been found on presumed living sites in association with stone tools. Both hominids are unlikely at the same time to have been engaged in the manufacture of identical tools; and we assume that the artefacts were the work of *H. habilis,* who was physically, and presumably also intellectually, the more advanced of the two species.

Only at Olduvai and Koobi Fora have living floors of the earliest tool-making hominids been investigated *in situ.* A typical example is the KBS site at Koobi Fora, dated to about 1.8 million years ago (Isaac et al., 1976; Isaac and Harris, 1978). Artefacts have occasionally been found in even earlier contexts, in the lower member of the Koobi Fora formation. The KBS site appears to have been originally located in the sandy bed of a seasonal stream and its area was perhaps restricted by the availability of shade. Shortly after the site's brief occupation, volcanic activity covered the area with a thick deposit of fine ash, thus ensuring its preservation in a virtually unmodified state. The traces of hominid activity cover an area 12 to 15 m across. It may be calculated that between 400 and 500 stone artefacts were originally abandoned on the site. The assemblage contains a few core-tools – choppers, discoid cores and a scraper – but most of the artefacts are flakes, up to 6 or 7 cm long, very few of which showed any signs of intentional trimming. The presence of very tiny chips and splinters shows that the tools were made on the spot, not brought to the site from elsewhere, although the lava from which they were made must have been carried from about 5 km away. Broken animal bones were also discovered on the site, including those of porcupine, pig, waterbuck, gazelle, hippopotamus and crocodile. An interesting feature of this list is that it includes animals obtained as prey or carrion from several different environments: hippopotamus from the lake, and gazelle from the drier inland plains, for example. This seems to

2.10 Olduvai Gorge.

indicate that the early hominids used the site as a home-base and brought back to it carcases or joints of meat that they obtained elsewhere, from more than one source. This observation is of great importance, for it suggests that one of the most basic features of human behaviour, the transport of food in order to share it, had probably already been developed (Isaac, 1976; 1978).

If the KBS site was a home-base, this was not the only type of site that has been left behind by the earliest tool-making hominids of the Koobi Fora area. Only 1 km to the south, in a similar ash-filled stream channel, were found many bones representing the remains of a single hippopotamus. These were mixed with over a hundred stone artefacts, mostly flakes, essentially similar to, but less varied than, those from the KBS site. Whether or not the hippopotamus was killed by hominids, there can be little doubt that it was butchered, and that stone tools were manufactured on the site for this purpose. Here, then, was a second type of site, showing that the early hominids on occasion made use of temporary butchery sites for the dismemberment or consumption of carcases too large to be transported entire to their home-base. Similar butchery sites, but incorporating elephant skeletons, have been investigated in Bed I at Olduvai (fig. 2.11).

Several sites at Olduvai in Bed I and the lower part of Bed II provide evidence for the former existence of some simple type of shelter. This evidence takes two forms, the more obvious being a setting of stones which may have served as the foundation of some kind of windbreak and which enclosed the densest part of

2.11 Reconstruction of an early hominid butchery site at Koobi Fora.

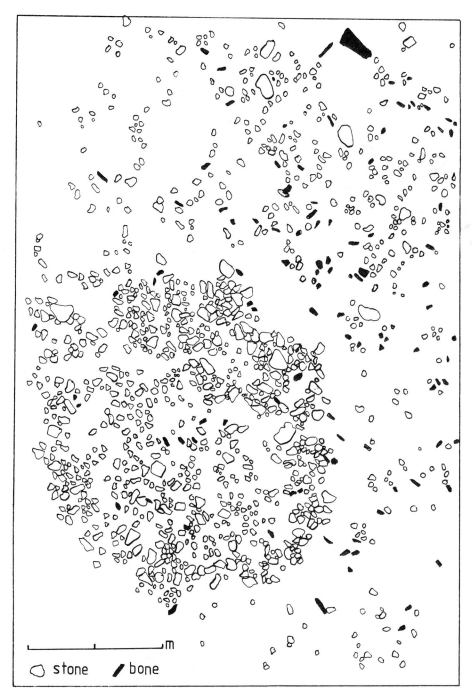

2.12 Plan of a stone circle on an occupation horizon at site DK in Bed I at Olduvai Gorge (after M. D. Leakey, 1971). This may represent the base of a shelter constructed of branches.

the artefact scatter on one particular site (fig. 2.12). A similarly confined scatter is suggestive of such structures also on other sites, where no other traces have survived.

The artefacts from the lower part of the Olduvai sequence clearly bear a close technological resemblance to those from the KBS and contemporary sites at Koobi Fora. There are, however, some significant differences. Whereas unretouched flakes predominate at Koobi Fora, at Olduvai there is a higher proportion of cores or core-tools, including cobbles from which a few flakes have been removed as if to produce a cutting or chopping edge. Flake tools, some of remarkably small size, are also a feature of assemblages from Olduvai (fig. 2.13). The very simple stone-working represented at Olduvai Bed I and other sites described in this chapter has been designated 'mode 1' in J. G. D. Clark's (1969) comparative study of stone-tool technology.

Faunal material from the Olduvai sites includes a high proportion of remains of small creatures and fish, the collecting of which may have been a major subsistence activity. However, the previously held belief that such small

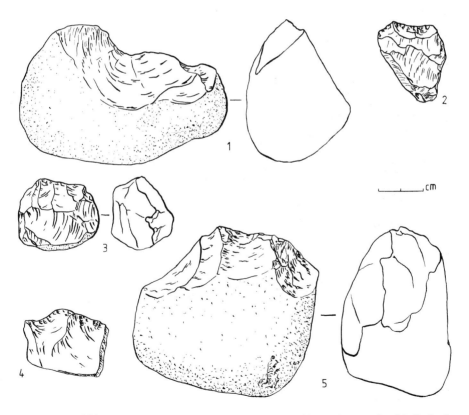

2.13 Oldowan artefacts from site DK in Bed I at Olduvai Gorge (after M. D. Leakey, 1971): 1 – unifacial chopper/core, 2 – flake scraper, 3 – light-duty chopper, 4 – utilised flake, 5 – bifacial chopper/core.

creatures were more abundantly represented in the oldest sites at Olduvai, being then gradually supplanted by larger species, is not supported by recent investigations. The nature of the available evidence unfortunately does not allow us to evaluate the importance of vegetable foods in the Oldowan diet.

South Africa

Remains of *Australopithecus* have been found at five sites in South Africa. The sites are all limestone caves where fossil bones have become incorporated in earthy deposits which have since hardened to produce the hard rock-like material known as breccia. The first discovery was made during quarrying operations at Taung, near the Harts River north of Kimberley, in 1924. It consisted of a magnificently preserved complete skull of a juvenile hominid who had perhaps been about six years old at death. Publication of the find (Dart, 1925) stressed the view that the specimen belonged to a previously unknown creature intermediate between apes and man. It was on the basis of this single, immature specimen that *Australopithecus africanus* was named. Its discovery made surprisingly little impact upon archaeological thinking at that time, because south-east Asia and Europe were believed to have been the main areas where the early stages of human evolution had taken place. A further problem was that, at Taung, there were no associated finds other than animal bones and, given the state of knowledge at that time, there was no way in which the absolute age of the site could be estimated (cf. Peabody, 1954; Butzer, 1974b).

From 1936 onwards, however, further discoveries began to be made in South Africa, first at the sites of Sterkfontein, Swartkrans and Kromdraai in the Blaawbank Valley near Krugersdorp, and then at Makapansgat in the northern Transvaal (Brain, 1958; 1976; J. T. Robinson and Mason, 1962; Sampson, 1974 and references; Inskeep, 1978 and references). Between them, these sites have yielded the remains of well over one hundred australopithecines. Although over the years a bewildering variety of species and genera has been proposed, it is now generally believed that they all belong to the two species *A. africanus* and *A. robustus* (Tobias, 1978b).

There has been considerable controversy over the precise nature of these Transvaal sites and how the bone concentrations, amongst which the australo-pithecine remains occurred, came to be accumulated there. It was at one time believed that many of the animal bones had been selected and taken to the sites by *Australopithecus* for use as tools (Dart, 1957). This argument was based upon the apparently very uneven representation of different body parts and upon the seemingly standardised fractures on many of the bones. This view, which involved acceptance of a tool-making status for *Australopithecus*, is not generally held today; for the breakage patterns may be paralleled at other sites where there is no possibility of hominid agency (Brain, 1967). The differential repre-sentation of body parts is also equivalent to that which occurs at leopard lairs, where carcases are often deposited in trees, out of reach of scavengers, for consumption at leisure. In the same way, over prolonged periods, bones – including those of the australopithecines – probably accumulated gradually in the Transvaal caves (Brain, 1969a; 1978; 1981).

Despite several attempts and experiments, no satisfactory method has yet been devised for directly dating the South African australopithecine sites. There are no volcanic deposits such as have yielded potassium/argon dates for the early hominid sites in East Africa. On the basis of comparisons of the faunal assemblages as a whole with those of the relatively well dated East African sequence, it has however proved possible to show that the South African sites fall within the period between 3.0 and 1.4 million years ago (fig. 2.14). The earliest occurrences are those at Makapansgat and in the earlier part of the Sterkfontein (Type Site) sequence. Significantly, in both these deposits *Australopithecus africanus* is the only hominid represented, and there are no stone tools. An age of about 3.0 million years seems probable for this material. After what may have been a substantial gap in the South African sequence come the occurrences at Sterkfontein Extension Site and in the Older Breccia at Swartkrans. Here, *A. robustus* is the only australopithecine species present; there are also traces of a creature who has been attributed to the genus *Homo*, possibly *H.*

Million years ago	Makapansgat	Sterkfontein	Swartkrans	Kromdraai	Taung
0.5					
1.0					⋮ ?
1.5		⋮	⋮	⋮	
2.0		⋮	⋮	⋮	
2.5		⋮	⋮		
3.0	⋮	⋮			
3.5	⋮				
4.0					

2.14 Chronological chart showing the probable ages of the South African australopithecine sites.

habilis. Both these sites have yielded a few fractured stones (further discussed in chapter 3) which are accepted by most archaeologists as artefacts akin to those of Bed II at Olduvai. The finds from Kromdraai also probably belong to this same general period – perhaps about 1.5 million years ago or shortly thereafter. By this time *Australopithecus africanus* was almost certainly no longer present in South Africa (Tobias, 1976). The Swartkrans Younger Breccia is much younger again, and need not be discussed here. Considerable uncertainty surrounds the date of the Taung site; its age may be as recent as slightly less than 1.0 million years (Peabody, 1954; Tobias, 1976). Should this prove to be correct, the identification of *A. africanus* there is doubtful, although with such an immature specimen precise affinities are always difficult to ascertain (Tobias, 1978b).

Conclusions: the earliest tool-makers

As has been shown, incontrovertible archaeological evidence for the earliest recognisable stages of human culture comes almost exclusively from eastern Africa, and dates to between 3.0 and 2.0 million years ago. Broadly contemporary sites in South Africa have yielded hominid fossils but no conclusive evidence for tool-making. The picture is made more complex by the presence in both regions at this time of different hominids which most authorities believe to represent more than one genus. It is clearly important to determine whether *Australopithecus* or *Homo* (or both) was the maker of the earliest artefacts.

Olduvai is the only site where hominid fossils and very early stone tools have been found in direct association with each other (M. D. Leakey, 1978), but it should be noted that from about 1.8 million years ago onwards such tools only occur on sites where the presence of early *Homo* is also indicated. In fact, the sole plausible candidates for pre-*Homo* artefacts are at the earliest occurrences at Hadar and in the Omo Valley. It may thus be argued that neither the gracile nor the robust variety of *Australopithecus* was a stone-tool-maker. (Such a hypothesis would explain the absence of stone tools on the earliest South African hominid sites, for there only *Australopithecus* has been found.) There is, of course, every probability that tool-using long preceded the first production of recognisably artificial tools, and also that the first made tools were of wood or other perishable substances which have not survived.

Our knowledge of the early hominids is, and will presumably always remain, very incomplete. We can learn something of these creatures' appearance and physical abilities from their fossil remains. We can learn about the places where they lived and the food that they ate. Their tools, when made of imperishable materials, can tell us something about their technology. Taken together, these factors allow us to reconstruct a very limited view of their life. The list of what we do not know is far longer. What was the social basis for the groups that inhabited home-bases such as the KBS site? Was there any socio-political unit larger than such a group? Were such associations permanent? How did they exploit the seasonally shifting and changing resources of their African home-land? To all these questions, as to the all-important ones of intellect and communication, we can only guess the answers, aided perhaps by very tentative comparisons (Lancaster, 1975) with studies of recent non-human primates.

CHAPTER 3

THE CONSOLIDATION OF BASIC HUMAN SKILLS

The Acheulian techno-complex in Africa

This chapter deals with one of the most remarkable and least understood phenomena of world prehistory: the enormously wide distribution, both in time and space, of people who made stone-tool industries of the type conventionally known to archaeologists as 'Acheulian'. These industries first appeared in the archaeological record, in East Africa, about 1.5 million years ago; and they seem to have survived in some areas until little more than 100,000 years ago. As well as in Africa, Acheulian industries are found in Europe and Asia, from Spain and Britain in the west and north, to India in the east. In many parts of the Old World the Acheulian is the oldest known manifestation of human settlement. It takes its name from Saint Acheul in the Somme Valley of northern France, which is one of the places where its characteristic stone artefacts were first recognised.

Despite the apparent uniformity of the Acheulian stone industries, there are good reasons to believe that this long period was one during which important human behavioural developments took place in the conceptual, linguistic, social and organisational fields, as well as in the technology which is far more directly represented in the archaeological record. The evidence for these processes is essentially circumstantial and difficult to interpret with precision. However, the time-span of the Acheulian industries was evidently one during which the geographical distribution of tool-makers was greatly expanded. This, together with the larger numbers of known later sites must indicate a substantial increase in human population. Adaptation to varied environmental conditions is also attested, with the ability to obtain food and safety in circumstances markedly different from those of the restricted areas known to have been occupied by the earliest hominids. Tool-making techniques were adapted to utilise different raw materials, with notable skill. There are some indications, as will be shown below, for group activities that may have involved linguistic communication for their organisation. The picture remains incomplete and open to differing interpretations, but there can be little doubt that, by the time of the latest Acheulian industries, mankind had developed many abilities and characteristics that earlier hominids had lacked.

The Acheulian has conventionally been defined by the presence, with variable frequency, of the enigmatic stone implements known as hand-axes or bifaces. These are characteristically pear-shaped in outline and biconvex in cross-section, usually 12 to 20 cm in length and flaked over at least part of both surfaces (fig. 3.1). A fairly sharp edge may be restricted to the area of the more pointed end, but more commonly it extends around all or the greater part of the implement's periphery. The earliest hand-axes tend to be crudely shaped, fewer than a dozen flakes having been removed from them: the scars which mark the position of these flakes are deep, suggesting that a simple stone hammer was used to detach them. These hand-axes are usually thick in relation to their breadth. In later assemblages, although crude examples may continue, there are also much more finely flaked specimens with shallow scars such as may have been produced by use of a soft (wood or bone) hammer or by indirect percussion.

In many Acheulian assemblages, particularly in Africa, there are also found implements known as cleavers. Similar in size and mode of production to the hand-axes, these are often made on large flakes and have a straight transverse cutting edge in place of the point.

So ubiquitous and numerous are these hand-axes and cleavers in Acheulian assemblages that it seems they may have been used for several different

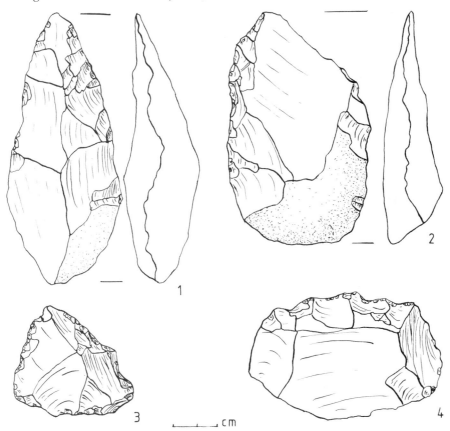

3.1 Acheulian stone implement types: 1 – hand-axe, 2 – cleaver, 3 – trimmed flake, 4 – scraper. These examples are from Montagu Cave, South Africa (after Keller, 1973)

purposes. Although we still call these implements 'hand-axes' and 'cleavers', they may have been used differently from the ways their names suggest. Experiments have shown that the cleaver is remarkably effective as a butchering instrument, and for skinning large game. Hand-axes were probably particularly versatile, and may have been used for digging or woodworking, as weapons or missiles, and for numerous other purposes. In some instances tools have been found in association with a particular activity, such as butchering a carcase, and then it is possible to see how these tools were used. But generally we have no definite knowledge of this, although studies of edge-wear (e.g. Keeley, 1980) are beginning to produce useful results.

Although hand-axes and cleavers are generally regarded as the most characteristic features of an Acheulian industry, they are not the only types of implement which such industries contain. Numerous flakes – both those removed in the course of hand-axe production and others – were used untrimmed as cutting and scraping tools, or were retouched into a variety of relatively unstandardised scrapers, piercers and the like. Cores sometimes include types which resemble Oldowan ones and may have been used as choppers.

Artefacts of Acheulian type have been found in most parts of Africa (J. D. Clark, 1967). They have not, however, been recorded from the densely forested regions of West Africa and the Congo basin; and this probably reflects a genuine discontinuity in their distribution rather than lack of research. It thus seems that it was the makers of the Acheulian artefacts who were responsible for the first human settlement of much of the continent away from the eastern savanna, to which the earliest stone-tool industries were apparently restricted. Just when this major expansion took place cannot yet be ascertained, but such evidence as is available suggests a date of about a million years ago. Throughout Africa and, indeed, in many other regions of the Old World, Acheulian stone tools are remarkably standardised technologically. They also show relatively little consistent change through time, for the Acheulian remained the dominant tool-making tradition for some 1.3 million years.

Despite this standardisation, it would not be prudent to regard the Acheulian as a single industry, using that term in the same sense as has been applied for more recent periods. Acheulian artefact assemblages are chronologically and geographically very widely distributed; and they are sometimes very different in composition (as will be shown below), with their main diagnostic components (the hand-axes and cleavers) varying so much in frequency and, presumably, in function, that they are best regarded merely as belonging to the same techno-complex. In other words, the Acheulian should not be regarded as an entity on grounds other than general technological similarity. It is too early, in the present state of knowledge, to assume any stronger affinity among its makers or specific details of their way of life. Acheulian stone-knapping corresponds to J. G. D. Clark's (1969) 'mode 2' lithic technology (cf. p. 58, below).

In most areas there is a marked variation in the proportions in which hand-axes and other tool types are represented in Acheulian assemblages. There are other assemblages from which hand-axes and cleavers are largely or completely absent, and there is considerable controversy (to be discussed below) as to whether or not these should be regarded as belonging to the Acheulian techno-complex. The causes for this variation are not yet properly understood. Most likely a number of factors were all partly responsible, such as style, personal or group preference, raw material availability, and the range of activities that were undertaken at the different sites. These activities may in some cases be linked with season, environment or subdivision within the social group. It is therefore not surprising that archaeologists have not been able to recognise significant patterning in this variation, either between different geographical areas or through time.

An important technological development which arose within the Acheulian tradition was the so-called Levallois technique, illustrated in fig. 3.2. This

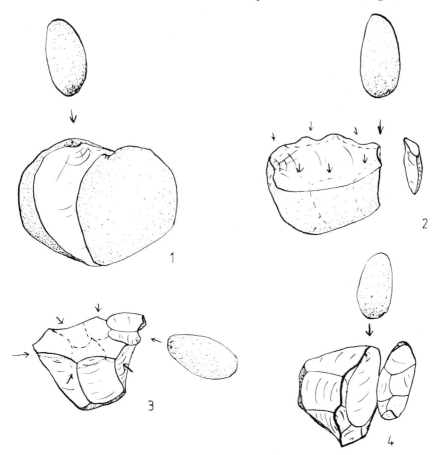

3.2 The Levallois technique whereby a flake of predetermined shape is struck from a prepared core

involved the production of a flake whose shape was predetermined by careful preparation of the parent core. By means of this technique standardised flake tools could be produced without extensive marginal trimming. Although inherent to hand-axe production, it became particularly common in later Acheulian industries of certain areas and survived, often in modified form or highly developed, into subsequent periods.

Acheulian artefacts are extremely common in certain areas of Africa, but sites where they may be found undisturbed in their original contexts are relatively few. As with the earlier periods, a high proportion of our evidence of this time

3.3 Air view of the Victoria Falls on the Zambezi River. The Falls are 2 km wide and almost 100 m high. Downstream of the present falls a series of zig-zag gorges marks the positions of former waterfalls. Gravel deposits now preserved near the edges of the gorges were laid down on the bed of the river and have been exposed by its subsequent down-cutting. Study of stone artefacts preserved in these gravels (J. D. Clark, 1950) enabled a sequence of industries to be proposed and correlated with the processes of back-cutting of the Victoria Falls

comes from East Africa. Proximity to water appears to have been an important factor in determining areas suitable for settlement; and some of Africa's great river valleys are thus particularly rich in Acheulian remains. Noteworthy in this respect are the Vaal (van Riet Lowe, 1952; Partridge and Brink, 1967; Butzer *et al.*, 1973; Helgren, 1980), the Zambezi (J. D. Clark, 1950), and the Nile Valleys (Sandford, 1934; Sandford and Arkell, 1933). As these rivers have developed and their rates of flow fluctuated, most of the early sites on their banks have been disturbed or destroyed, and the artefacts which they contained have been moved and incorporated in fluviatile deposits (fig. 3.3). Although in certain circumstances the artefact contents of successive river deposits may give us some information about the local archaeological sequence, this disturbed material is now recognised as being of very limited value; research emphasis has shifted to the location and excavation of undisturbed settlement sites.

Koobi Fora, Olduvai and the earliest Acheulian

The first appearance of Acheulian industries in East Africa is not easy to pinpoint. A first sight it appears that the archaeological record at this time – about 1.5 million years ago – presents a confusing complexity of different artefact assemblages; and the situation is made worse by the names conventionally used. It is important to find out the extent to which these new industries represent separate cultural developments – perhaps being the work of different groups of hominids – rather than variations of a common tradition. Archaeologists are far from agreement concerning the significance of this diversity, but there is now increasing support for the view that it represents facies of a single tradition.

Somewhat later than the KBS industry east of Lake Turkana (p. 24), and occurring in the upper member of the Koobi Fora formation, are the numerous sites which have yielded the distinctive and more advanced stone artefacts attributed to the Karari industry (J. W. K. Harris and Isaac, 1976; Isaac and Harris, 1978). So far known only from Koobi Fora, the Karari industry occurs on a number of sites stratified between the Okote Tuff of 1.6 to 1.5 million years ago and the 1.25 million-year-old Chari Tuff. Like the earlier ones, these sites are mostly located near ancient stream-courses. Karari artefacts include numerous core-tools, such as heavy-duty scrapers and choppers, some of which were bifacially worked. Trimmed flake scrapers are also represented. A good level of stone-working skill is evidenced and some types closely resemble artefacts once thought to be characteristic of much later periods (fig. 3.4). At other upper-member sites, such as that code-named FxJj 50 (Bunn *et al.*, 1980), the simpler artefacts of KBS type continued to be made.

The Karari industry thus appears largely to have replaced the KBS industry of the early Oldowan tradition at Koobi Fora by about 1.5 million years ago. It represents a major advance in man's tool-making ability as illustrated both by the manual dexterity and control of stone-flaking technique which the artefacts demonstrate, and by the ability to visualise and then to produce a standardised artefact type whose final shape bore little or no resemblance to that of the initial piece of raw material. The Karari industry was but one of several parallel developments which appear in the archaeological record at approximately this time.

At Olduvai Gorge differing artefact assemblages of this age, first occurring in the middle part of Bed II, are designated respectively Developed Oldowan and Acheulian (M. D. Leakey, 1971; 1975; 1976). They show both a greater variety of tool types and greater standardisation than do the Bed I industries (p. 26). Developed Oldowan assemblages contain a few simply flaked bifacial tools which recall the more numerous and – generally – more competently flaked hand-axes and cleavers of the assemblages attributed to the Acheulian (fig. 3.5).

From the middle of Bed II onwards, the Olduvai sequence (fig. 3.6) thus contains varied assemblages which some archaeologists would interpret as representing two parallel traditions. It is, however, hard to envisage how two distinct traditions could have maintained their separate identities for the enormously long period – over half a million years – which this view requires,

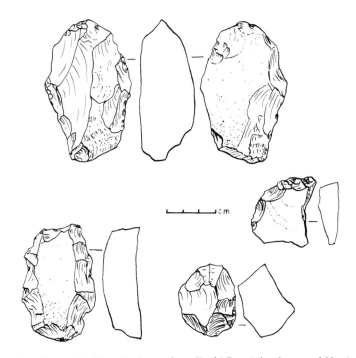

3.4 Artefacts of the Karari industry from Koobi Fora (after Isaac and Harris, 1978)

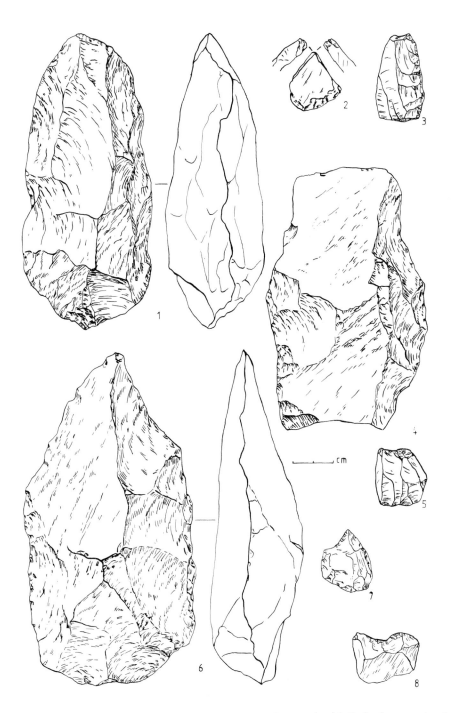

3.5 Stone implements from Bed II at Olduvai Gorge (after M. D. Leakey, 1971): 1,6 –
hand-axes; 2 – burin or graver; 3,8 – scrapers; 4 – cleaver; 5 – scaled piece; 7 – awl

even if (as some have suggested) they were the work of different hominid species existing at the same time and in the same place (Isaac, 1982). A more economical hypothesis, therefore, is that these assemblages represent different aspects of a single Acheulian complex, such as continued also into far more recent times.

In the middle and upper parts of Bed II at Olduvai, stone tools are more numerous relative to the faunal remains than was the case in the lower levels. The same is true for Beds III and IV. It is also noteworthy that large animals, such as rhinoceros and giraffe, are more commonly represented on the later sites: the two observations may well be interconnected. By this time the Bed I lake had largely dried up and an open grassland environment is indicated. It has been argued that the majority of the hominid sites at Olduvai represent dry-season encampments (Speth and Davis, 1976).

The first appearance of the Acheulian in East Africa, as exemplified at Olduvai Gorge, is puzzling. The former view, that there was a demonstrable development from the Oldowan, into Developed Oldowan, into Early Acheulian, is now disproved stratigraphically and has few adherents. In contrast, some archaeologists now believe that the first appearance of the Acheulian at Olduvai may represent an intrusion into the sequence of a stone-tool-making tradition, the earlier stages of which had taken place elsewhere. Perhaps the most reasonable interpretation of the currently available facts is that the Acheulian represents the dominant surviving technological tradition which prevailed after a period of varied experimentation. Such periods of accelerated development separated by consolidation and continuity have been recognised as recurrent features of world prehistory (cf. Spaulding, 1960). At Olduvai, it appears that

Million years ago	Bed		Stone industry	Hominids
	IV			
0.7			Acheulian / Developed Oldowan	Homo erectus
	III			
	II	upper		
1.6		middle		A. boisei / Homo habilis
		lower	Oldowan	
1.8	I			

3.6 Summary of the archaeological sequence in Beds I – IV at Olduvai Gorge. The Acheulian and Developed Oldowan are believed by many to be facies of the same tradition

both *Homo erectus* and *H. habilis* were present at this time (represented by the middle and upper levels of Bed II), as well as the robust australopithecine, *A. boisei*. If only one hominid type was responsible for the stone industries, this was probably *Homo erectus* (fig. 3.7). This tallies with evidence for the hominids responsible for the earlier Acheulian in other parts of Africa, as will be discussed below (p. 54).

A further early East African Acheulian occurrence is at Peninj, beside Lake Natron, near the Kenya–Tanzania border north-east of Olduvai (Isaac, 1967). Two *in situ* Acheulian horizons have been located in deep deposits that indicate a lake-shore environment similar to that of the present time. The finely preserved lower jaw of a robust australopithecine was found in a context somewhat earlier than the Acheulian horizons, which are dated by potassium/argon analysis to about 1.4 million years ago (Isaac and Curtis, 1974).

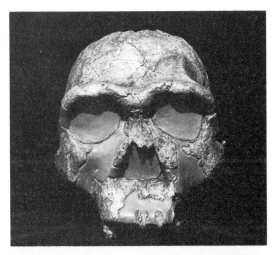

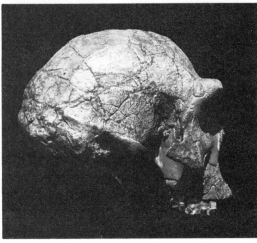

3.7 Skull of *Homo erectus* from Koobi Fora

Probably somewhat later, about one million years old, is the first evidence for Acheulian-related occupation of the Ethiopian plateau. This comes from two areas. At Melka Kunture near Addis Ababa (Chavaillon, 1976), a long series of occurrences, including some which have been attributed to the Oldowan, are under investigation. One of these Acheulian occurrences has yielded a jaw fragment of *Homo erectus* type. On the Gadeb Plain to the south-east, early Acheulian material is of particular interest as it provides evidence that raw material for tool-making was carried over a substantial distance (J. D. Clark and Williams, 1978). This perhaps indicates an improved capacity for planning as human groups learned to exploit their environment over a wider area and in a more comprehensive fashion (fig. 3.8).

Olorgesailie

One of the most informative Acheulian sites in Africa is at Olorgesailie in the Kenyan Rift Valley, some 50 km south-west of Nairobi (Isaac, 1977). Here, several major concentrations of hand-axes, cleavers and other stone artefacts occur in an area which formerly bordered a small lake (fig. 3.9). It is evident that the places most favoured for settlement were either on a low rocky promontory which jutted out into the lake, or on patches of sand which generally occurred in the channels of seasonal streams draining into the lake. Acheulian man seems to have preferred to camp in these dry watercourses rather than on the shore of the lake itself. Comparison with modern Rift Valley lake basins suggests reasons for these preferences: the stream beds provided open sandy ground in an area elsewhere covered with hummocks of coarse grass, and the trees lining the channel supplied welcome shade that was absent on the lake-shore. Water from holes dug in the bed of the channel was likely to be less saline than that of the lake. The rocky promontory could be used in the wet season, when the streams were flowing, and when the extra height provided relief from mosquitos.

Most of the Olorgesailie Acheulian occurrences are believed to have suffered some degree of sorting or movement as a result of water action since the sites were abandoned. However, even if the artefacts were not recovered absolutely in their original positions, it was possible to estimate from the extent of artefact scatter that the camp areas were generally between 5 and 20 m across. The larger scatters may represent areas of successive shifting use, or the presence of groups larger than a single nuclear family.

Bone was not always well preserved at Olorgesailie. No hominid fossils have been found there. At one locality remains of many baboons were discovered, and these may represent a troop that was attacked whilst sleeping in the trees overgrowing the site. The presence of many stones, which must have been carried to the site from elsewhere, and which were of a suitable size and shape for use as missiles, lends support to this suggestion.

Many of the Olorgesailie artefacts are made of types of stone which must have been brought there from some distance away. The scale of this transport makes it seem highly likely that, by this stage in their development, people had invented some sort of bag for carrying their possessions from one place to another. This simple invention would have had far-reaching implications for their mobility, adaptiveness, range of material culture and, most important,

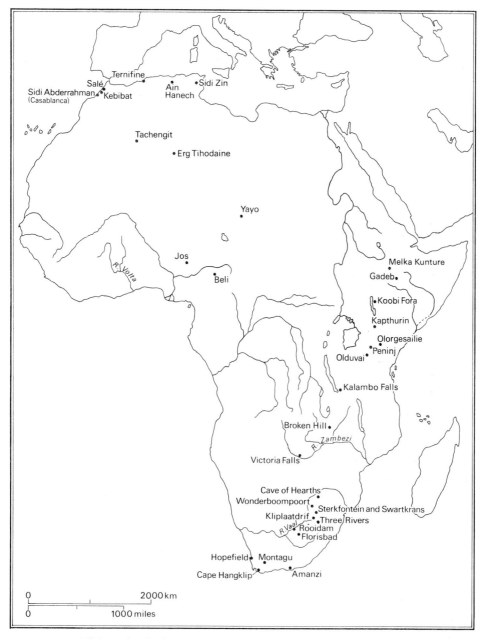

3.8 Principal Acheulian and related sites in Africa

ability with forward planning to keep things to use at some future time. While it seems highly probable that the Acheulian inhabitants of Olorgesailie, like their counterparts elsewhere, collected and made much use of vegetable foods, no firm evidence for this has been preserved.

A particularly noteworthy feature of these stone-tool assemblages is the range of their variation, both in composition and style. In some, hand-axes and cleavers were the most frequent tool types; in others they were virtually absent. While in some instances size-sorting of the artefacts by water action may have contributed to this variation, it cannot have been the major cause. Also, in the same area and at the same time there is a great range in quality of workmanship and other stylistic features within the same artefact categories. It seems reasonable to suppose that this variation was primarily due to differences in the skill and preferences of individual toolmakers or social groups, as well as to the intended uses of the artefacts. These factors provide an eloquent warning against attempts at arranging Acheulian assemblages in chronological sequence on the basis of their typology or refinement.

The various Acheulian occurrences at Olorgesailie are all contained within a single geological formation, although they are scattered through about 40 m of its vertical thickness. It is therefore probable that they were deposited at intervals over a substantial period of time. Unfortunately, it has not proved possible to date the site very precisely. The best interpretation of potassium/argon dates for pumice contained in the Olorgesailie formation suggests an age

3.9 Acheulian hand-axes and other artefacts preserved as discovered at Olorgesailie

between 500,000 and 400,000 years ago. This is not contradicted by other lines of investigation, such as faunal comparisons with dated sites elsewhere in East Africa.

Kalambo Falls

A much later Acheulian site, which is of particular importance because of the preservation of plant remains, is at Kalambo Falls near the southern end of Lake Tanganyika (fig. 3.10). The Kalambo River, which here forms the border between Tanzania and Zambia, flows over the edge of the Rift escarpment as a spectacular 220 m single-drop waterfall. Immediately above the waterfall the Kalambo Valley is very narrow; successive blocking and unblocking of this stretch has on several occasions caused the formation of a small lake in the wider section of the valley further upstream. In the silts and shore deposits of these ancient lakes abundant traces of prehistoric occupation have been preserved, in both primary and secondary contexts (J. D. Clark, 1969; 1974). The earliest such traces so far recovered are late Acheulian, but earlier material may be hidden below the modern water level.

At an early stage in the research at Kalambo Falls, radiocarbon dates were obtained which indicated an age for the Acheulian horizons there of about 55,000 to 50,000 years ago. These results were at the very furthest end of the radiocarbon dating method's time-range; and more recent work has shown that they were probably too young. New radiocarbon and amino-acid racemisation tests indicate a true age of more than 61,000 – perhaps as much as 190,000 – years (C. Lee *et al.*, 1976). Broadly similar Acheulian deposits preserved at a riverside situation at Isimila, in southern Tanzania some 300 km east of Kalambo, are probably of comparable antiquity (Howell, *et al.*, 1962; Hansen and Keller, 1971).

On several horizons at Kalambo abundant Acheulian artefacts were recovered, apparently not having been disturbed since they were originally laid down by their makers on banks of sand and gravel beside the river, presumably during the dry season. The artefact-bearing horizons cover substantial areas but probably represent shifting foci of occupation rather than extensive settlements. The implements show a very high standard of workmanship, the effect of which was aided by the fine-grained raw material that was abundantly available. Bone was not preserved, but wood did survive; and several pieces show signs of having been cut or shaped deliberately. Traces of burning on some of the wood indicate the presence of fire, but there is no way of knowing whether this fire was used and controlled by the site's inhabitants, or merely derived from naturally generated 'bush' fires. In this context it may be significant that none of the Acheulian areas investigated presented features which could plausibly be interpreted as hearths.

Particularly interesting is an arc of stones enclosing an area of about two square metres which, it has been proposed, represents the base of a simple shelter or windbreak. Two hollows filled with compressed grass may have been sleeping places. Seed pods and the remains of fruit show that a range of vegetable foods was exploited.

The silts which incorporated the Acheulian horizons at Kalambo Falls contained pollen grains which have been identified to provide a reconstruction of

3.10 The 220 m high Kalambo Falls. The Acheulian and later archaeological sites are in the small lake basin through which the Kalambo River flows above the falls

the local vegetation. Conditions warmer and drier than those of today are initially attested, with swamps and riverine gallery forest in the valley but dry woodland beyond. The final Kalambo Acheulian appears to have been associated with a cooler, damper climate, with a type of forest which today only survives in this part of central Africa at considerably higher altitudes; the composition of the artefact assemblages from these horizons shows trends towards some of the typological features characteristic of later periods (J. D. Clark, 1964). Further climatic change may also provide the background for post-Acheulian developments in the Kalambo Falls sequence: these are described in chapter 4.

Broken Hill mine, Kabwe

A cave at the Broken Hill mine near the town of Kabwe on the central plateau of Zambia is of great potential significance because of the discovery there, during mining operations in 1921, of human remains of at least four individuals, including a superbly preserved cranium attributed to *Homo sapiens rhodesiensis*. Unfortunately little was recorded concerning the precise circumstances of the discovery, and its true archaeological associations are consequently uncertain (J. D. Clark *et al.*, 1950; J. D. Clark 1959). However, as will be shown below, there is some evidence that the Broken Hill cranium belongs to the same time-span as the latest Acheulian industries, and the site is therefore discussed here.

The majority of the artefacts recovered from the Broken Hill cave, although not necessarily in direct association with the cranium, are flakes and retouched flakes, some of which were struck from prepared cores. In the absence of hand-axes, cleavers or other core-tools, they were originally attributed to the post-Acheulian industry now known as Charaman (p. 67). A true Acheulian occurrence with hand-axes has subsequently been located in the vicinity and, as has been shown above, other assemblages lacking hand-axes are now known from the Acheulian time-span. Of the large animal species represented in the abundant faunal collection from the cave, a quarter are now extinct, suggesting an age at the end of the Middle Pleistocene or an early stage of the Upper Pleistocene (Klein, 1973). This attribution has recently been strengthened by an amino-acid racemisation test on hominid bone from the site, indicating a probable age of some 110,000 years.

The Broken Hill cranium (fig. 3.11), with its pronounced brow ridges and receding forehead, has a capacity of 1,280 cubic centimetres, which is well within the range shown by modern populations. It is attributed to a no-longer extant sub-species of *Homo sapiens* which probably occupied a position in hominid evolution intermediate between *Homo erectus* and *Homo sapiens sapiens*, and one akin to that occupied by the neanderthaloid (*Homo sapiens neanderthalensis*) populations of North Africa, Europe and the Near East. Despite the uncertainties about its age and archaeological associations, the specimen is of major significance as one of the very few hominid fossils from sub-Saharan Africa which may represent the makers of the later Acheulian industries.

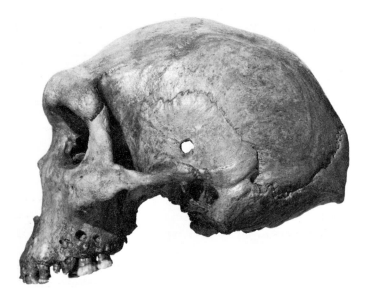

3.11 Skull of *Homo sapiens rhodesiensis* from Broken Hill mine, Kabwe

Southern Africa

Despite the large mass of Acheulian artefacts that has been recovered from south of the Zambezi, the amount of reliable information which it yields is disappointingly meagre. The absence of volcanic activity during the Pleistocene period in southern Africa means that none of this material has been dated by the potassium/argon method. The region provides good evidence for major fluctuations in climate during the Middle and Upper Pleistocene but it has not yet proved possible to provide these with a reliable absolute chronology. There is only a single plausible determination, by the thorium/uranium method, of between 190,000 and 150,000 years for a late Acheulian lakeside site at Rooidam in the Vaal Valley near Kimberley (Butzer, 1974a).

The only stone artefacts from the Transvaal australopithecine sites described in chapter 2 are occasional specimens from the more recent parts of the Sterkfontein and Swartkrans sequences. These include crude hand-axe-like bifacial tools and choppers; the closest East African parallels are from Bed II at Olduvai, but opinion is divided as to whether there is greater resemblance with the assemblages there dubbed Developed Oldowan or Acheulian (M. D. Leakey, 1970; Mason, 1976). This disagreement is perhaps a further reason for regarding the former industry as merely a facies of the latter, as proposed above. It is noteworthy that, at these sites, stone artefacts occur only in those contexts demonstrably contemporary with hominid fossils attributed to the genus *Homo* (Brain, 1976; Hughes and Tobias, 1977).

Among other South African Acheulian sites, the few which are thought on geological or typological grounds to be early are all in river gravels or other disturbed contexts: these include Kliplaatdrif and Three Rivers in the southern Transvaal (Mason, 1962). In the same region, at Wonderboompoort, large quantities of Acheulian artefacts accumulated in a natural defile which was evidently used for trapping game. Elsewhere, the most informative occurrences are in caves: the Cave of Hearths (Mason, 1962) in the Transvaal and Montagu Cave (Keller, 1973) in the Cape.

In parts of the South African interior the final Acheulian assemblages contain small well-finished hand-axes with rounded butts and concave sides, formerly regarded as representing a distinct 'Fauresmith industry'. It is now realised that these artefacts are almost always found in those areas where lydianite was the preferred raw material for tool manufacture (Humphreys, 1970).

Further sites of note, all in the Cape, are those in spring deposits at Amanzi near Uitenhage (H. J. Deacon, 1970), where vegetable remains including worked wood fragments are also preserved, on an 18 m raised beach at Cape Hangklip (Sampson, 1974), and in eroding sands at Hopefield, north of Cape Town. The Hopefield deposits (Singer and Wymer, 1968) have also yielded a hominid skull-vault with pronounced brow ridges, variously attributed by earlier writers to *Homo erectus* or to an early form of *H. sapiens*, but which is now generally regarded as a further example of *H. s. rhodesiensis*, and, on the evidence of the associated fauna, somewhat earlier in date than the type-specimen from Broken Hill mine. There is no reason to believe that any of these Cape occurrences is older than about 400,000 years.

West Africa and the Sahara

The archaeological evidence for the earliest human settlement of West Africa is still very poorly understood. It is likely that this area was not inhabited by the very earliest hominids, such as are known from the eastern part of the continent; but it is nevertheless possible that such remains have not been preserved or are yet to be discovered. What has been claimed as the oldest hominid fossil from this general region comes from water-lain sands at Yayo in northern Chad, some 400 km south of the Tibesti massif, and consists of the front part of a skull, including the face (Coppens, 1965). Animal remains found nearby suggest an age in the general order of 700,000 years, but the hominid specimen could be much more recent. Unfortunately, no stone artefacts were associated, nor are the affinities of the skull (whether australopithecine or *Homo*) certain. Further archaeological remains of this or even earlier periods may still be discovered in the Chad area, where lake deposits are known to extend to great depths.

Davies (1964; 1967) has provided surveys of West African occurrences, mostly in disturbed or poorly documented contexts, of artefacts attributed to modes 1 and 2. Stone choppers akin to those of the early Oldowan industry have been found at a number of places in West Africa, most notably at Beli in north-eastern Nigeria. These discoveries come from disturbed contexts such as river gravels which cannot be dated precisely. Choppers of this type remained in use for a very long time, so it cannot be assumed that these West African examples are as ancient as the Oldowan.

There can, however, be no doubt from the presence of the far more diagnostic hand-axes that true Acheulian industries were made in West Africa, although there is as yet no convincing demonstration of their age. The most notable occurrences are along the Volta River in Ghana, and on the Jos Plateau in Nigeria (fig. 3.12). In the latter area (Soper, 1965), river gravels mined for tin extraction have been found to contain numerous hand-axes, cleavers and other Acheulian artefacts, as well as specimens which are clearly of much more recent date. Here, again, there are no occurrences of Acheulian material in its primary position.

Similarly, in the Sahara, although Acheulian artefacts have been found in many places, there are few assemblages that have been carefully excavated from undisturbed situations (J. D. Clark, 1980). The few collections that appear on typological grounds to be early are all from secondary contexts, most notably in southern Morocco and central Mauritania. Apparently Acheulian material is more widely distributed. Where its original geological associations can be ascertained, these indicate conditions wetter than those of the present; and this is confirmed both by study of the faunal remains and by pollen analysis. It

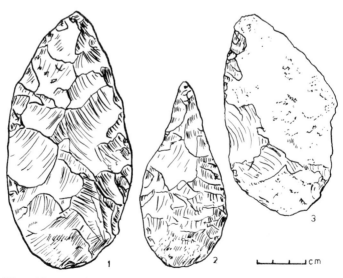

3.12 West African Acheulian implements from the Jos Plateau (after Shaw, 1978): 1,2 – hand-axes; 3 – cleaver

appears that there were major fluctuations in the Saharan climate during the time-span of the Acheulian. Only local studies of these have so far been undertaken and no overall picture has yet emerged. As in other areas, waterside locations were clearly preferred. A typical Saharan site is at Erg Tihodaine, in southern Algeria between the Tassili and Hoggar massifs, where presumably late Acheulian artefacts occur in the clays of a former swamp, together with bones of extinct types of elephant and buffalo and other creatures which cannot survive in the area today (Arambourg and Balout, 1955).

Several regional technological and stylistic variants may be recognised in the Saharan Acheulian. For instance, there is an incidence of developed prepared-core Levallois technique in the Wadi Saoura of central Algeria, as at Tachengit: prepared cores were made to yield large flakes requiring only minimal trimming to produce effective cleavers. There is, however, little chronological control, so we cannot be certain whether these variants were in fact contemporary with one another.

North Africa

Parts of North Africa have yielded evidence for a long sequence of Acheulian industries, as well as indications of pre-Acheulian human occupation typified by chopper and flake industries akin to the Oldowan. Unfortunately direct dating of these North African sites has not proved possible. The tentative chronology originally proposed was based upon faunal correlations with the European sequence and upon connexions with high sea levels which, it was believed, could be attributed to phases of the northern hemisphere glacial succession. Both methods, especially the latter, are tenuous and now merit little reliance; comparisons with the dated East African material are thus difficult to establish.

The most complete picture for North Africa comes from the Casablanca area on the Atlantic coast of Morocco (McBurney, 1960; Biberson, 1961). The detailed subdivision of this sequence into technological phases, as originally proposed, is now felt to lack adequate support. The earliest traces of human activity in this region are associated with beach deposits about 100 m above the modern sea level. It is generally believed that this beach was formed during a period of warm climate at a relatively early phase of the Pleistocene. Two series of stone artefacts have been recognised in these deposits, distinguished mainly on the basis of their physical condition. The rolled series, evidently derived from still earlier deposits, consists of pebbles from which flakes have been removed in one direction only. The second series, which is in fresher condition, has had flakes removed in two directions so as to produce a jagged cutting or chopping edge. Unfortunately, there are very few artefacts in either of these series, and it must be emphasised that they have not been recovered from their original positions, being disturbed by wave action, soil slip and other natural agencies.

The first appearance of hand-axes in the Casablanca sequence is in deposits which may be linked with a later sea level between 60 and 70 m above that of the present day. The most generally accepted dating for this episode is approximately 500,000 years ago. If this order of magnitude is supported by future research (and it must be admitted that the chronology at present remains extremely tentative) then the development of the Acheulian in Morocco must have lagged

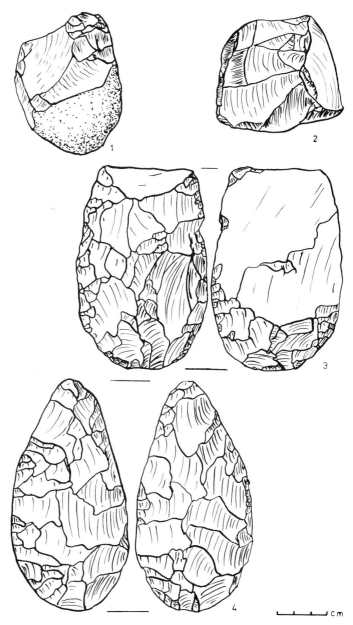

3.13 North African artefacts (after McBurney, 1960): 1,2 – spheroids from Ain Hanech; 3,4 – cleaver and hand-axe from Sidi Zin

far behind the corresponding events in East Africa. On the basis of the same correlation, the earliest occurrence of humanly chipped pebbles at Casablanca may not be much more than 1.0 million years old. It is clear that human occupation of North Africa and Europe covers a significantly shorter time-span than the corresponding East African sequence (Isaac, 1972).

Some degree of confirmation for the presence of pre-Acheulian stone industries in north-western Africa comes from the site of Ain Hanech near El Eulma in Algeria, where the faunal remains, including many species now extinct, suggest an age at the beginning of the Middle Pleistocene (about 700,000 years ago), if not earlier (Arambourg and Balout, 1952; McBurney, 1960). The Ain Hanech artefacts (fig. 3.13) are flaked to a roughly spherical shape, with jagged edges; they resemble in some respects objects which are frequent in East African Developed Oldowan assemblages. There is some doubt as to whether a few hand-axe-like objects from Ain Hanech are correctly associated with the main assemblage.

The Casablanca sequence of Acheulian industries is best exposed at the Sidi Abderrahman quarry (fig. 3.14). Whilst the sea was retreating from a high level of undetermined maximum height, Acheulian material was laid down upon the beach and subsequently buried beneath a massive sand dune which, as the sea level dropped still lower, accumulated on the old shore-line. (It is this beach, consolidated into sandstone, which is sought by the quarrymen whose activities have been responsible for unearthing much of the Casablanca sequence.) Later, the sea rose once again and cut back the dune to form a cliff, in which several caves came into being. Beach deposits in these caves are at 27–30 m above modern sea level which enables their formation to be correlated provisionally with some part of a prolonged interglacial period around 300,000 years ago, to which many important European Acheulian occurrences also belong. Two of these caves exposed at Sidi Abderrahman, the Grotte de l'Ours and the Grotte

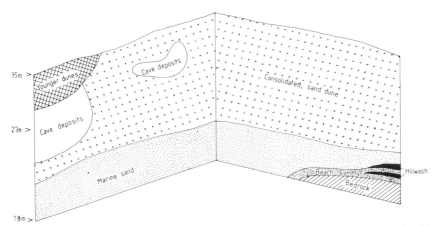

3.14 The deposits exposed in the walls of Sidi Abderrahman quarry near Casablanca (after McBurney, 1960). The figures on the left give heights above mean sea level

des Littorines, are of particular significance because they were occupied by man soon after the formation of the 30 m beach. Abundant well-made hand-axes, cleavers, flake tools and other artefacts were recovered; many of both the hand-axes and the cleavers were made on flakes struck from remarkably massive cores. Several successive Acheulian horizons occur in these caves and, in one of the upper ones at the Grotte des Littorines, part of a lower jaw attributed to *Homo erectus* was recovered. The specimen is closely similar to somewhat earlier examples from Ternifine in Algeria and from Rabat. The final Acheulian industries at the Sidi Abderrahman caves have superbly finished hand-axes with a twisted, S-shaped, profile and flakes struck from carefully prepared Levallois cores.

Probably somewhat more ancient than the *Homo erectus* fossil from Sidi Abderrahman is another similar mandible from the nearby Thomas quarry (Sausse, 1975), also associated with a sparse Acheulian occurrence. Another specimen from the Thomas quarry, like other Moroccan fossils showing *H. erectus*-like features (discussed on p. 55), is apparently of more recent date.

The Ternifine site, not far from Oran in north-western Algeria, lies beside a spring whose deposits contained abundant faunal remains of early Middle Pleistocene type, demonstrably later in date than those from Ain Hanech. The Ternifine artefacts appear to belong to a fairly early stage of the North African Acheulian (Balout *et al.*, 1967). Three human mandibles and a skull fragment, all exceptionally well preserved, are of *Homo erectus* type (fig. 3.15).

To the east, the Libyan coastland has yielded no informative Acheulian sites; and such information as we possess about the Acheulian of north-east Africa comes from the Nile Valley and its immediate environs. Here there are numerous occurrences in the Wadi Halfa area which may pre-date the Nile's capture of its southern tributaries. Where this material is in an undisturbed context, it appears to represent quarry or workshop sites rather than settlements (Chmielewski, 1968). There is no evidence for the absolute age of this material, or of that recovered from the alluvial terraces of the Egyptian Nile Valley (J. D. Clark, 1980; Hassan, 1980).

The makers of Acheulian industries

There can be little reasonable doubt that the earlier African Acheulian industries, in the wide sense of that term here proposed, were the work of hominids akin to *Homo erectus*. As we saw, fossil remains attributed to this species have been reported from South, East and North Africa and illustrate a relatively large-brained (800–1,200 cubic centimetres) hominid with heavy brow ridges and a low cranial vault (Howells, 1966). In the postcranial skeleton only minor differences are apparent between *H. erectus* and modern man.

After the period when tool-makers experimented with different tool types, in industries such as those named Karari, Developed Oldowan and early Acheulian, the stability and uniformity of the later Acheulian is good testimony for the strength of cultural tradition which developed about 1.2 million years ago and was maintained for the best part of a million years. During this prolonged period considerable evolution took place among the hominids that were responsible for the Acheulian industries. Prior to about 700,000 years ago no hominid more advanced than *Homo erectus* is attested anywhere in the world. From the succeeding Middle Pleistocene there is a marked dearth of informative hominid fossils from well-dated African contexts. European evidence suggests that some Middle Pleistocene hominids in that continent had evolved physical features already indicative of *Homo sapiens*.

Some North African specimens, unfortunately insecurely dated, may be interpreted as demonstrating a similar process (Howell, 1982). The relevant fossils are fragmentary skulls from Salé (Jaeger, 1973), Kebibat near Rabat

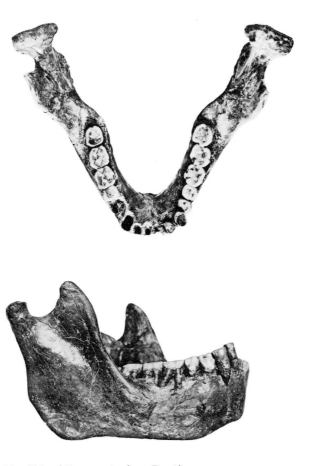

3.15 Mandible of *Homo erectus* from Ternifine

(Saban, 1977) and the later of two specimens from Thomas quarry, Casablanca (Ennouchi, 1972), all in Morocco.

Similar developments may be discerned in East Africa, as at Kapthurin near Lake Baringo, Kenya, where a hominid mandible is claimed to be associated with an Acheulian industry showing use of a well-developed Levallois technique (M. Leakey et al., 1969). An age of about 200,000 years has been suggested, but there are indications that this may be too young. A fragmentary skull from Lake Ndutu, not far from Olduvai Gorge in northern Tanzania, may occupy a comparable position (Mturi, 1976; R. J. Clarke, 1976).

In more southerly latitudes, it is only from the final Middle Pleistocene that hominid fossils have been preserved. The Hopefield and Broken Hill specimens have been noted above. In both, Homo sapiens features are dominant and they are attributed to an extinct sub-species, H. s. rhodesiensis. Fossils from Florisbad in the Orange Free State and from the Cave of Hearths, Transvaal, may be related and broadly contemporary (Singer, 1958; Howell, 1982).

Few anthropologists would now disagree that Homo sapiens evolved from H. erectus during the long Middle Pleistocene time-span represented in the archaeological record by the later Acheulian industries. The African Acheulian also saw major cultural developments. Acheulian man eventually spread to most parts of Africa except those most densely forested, and the highest mountain ranges; but his sites were almost invariably located beside or in easy reach of water. For the first time there is evidence that caves were occasionally occupied. Although the evidence is inconclusive, controlled use of fire may have been learned by Acheulian tool-makers (Gowlett et al., 1981). The extent of such few settlement sites as have been fully investigated suggests that population groups may have numbered between twenty and fifty individuals. As in earlier times, these home-base sites (which seem often to have seen more intensive or long-lasting settlement than their Oldowan/KBS counterparts) were supplemented by sites used for a specific activity, such as butchery or tool manufacture. In the former case it is generally impossible to distinguish between kills and carrion; although where large numbers of carcases of a single species occur together, as at Olorgesailie and Olduvai, several individuals must have hunted together in a group. Such a level of organisation implies that they had developed the use of language. Thereafter, the individuals who were most successful, in the evolutionary sense, were those with communicative and co-operative skills. The preservation of the evidence of hunting almost certainly tends to overemphasise the importance of meat in the Acheulian diet at the expense of vegetable foods, traces of which have rarely survived.

The progressive standardisation and elaboration of tool types and processes of manufacture observed in later Acheulian assemblages may also be interpreted as a further indication that their makers could talk to one another. The extraordinary and, in functional terms, probably unnecessarily fine finish of some hand-axes suggests the existence of basically aesthetic standards, in turn implying that cultural values now extended into non-utilitarian spheres. Acheulian man may thus be seen as having differentiated himself from his unthinking animal kindred to an extent probably not achieved by the makers of the Oldowan industries (Butzer and Isaac, 1975; J. D. Clark, 1976).

CHAPTER 4

REGIONAL DIVERSIFICATION

The 'Middle Stone Age' and the 'Late Stone Age'

Developments in Africa in post-Acheulian times (from rather more than 100,000 until about 8,000 years ago) show a steady shift away from the broad cultural uniformity which was described in the last chapter, and the establishment of distinct regional traditions. These may most readily be traced in the archaeo-logical record by study of stone-tool typology; but it is important, wherever possible, to go beyond artefact studies in an attempt to find out the nature of the ancient societies which, to an increasing extent, may be regarded as ancestral to recent African populations.

Despite this increasing diversity, developments seem to have followed a roughly parallel course in different parts of Africa and, indeed, in other regions of the Old World (J. G. D. Clark, 1977). The reasons for this are not yet fully understood; and the various developmental stages were not reached at the same time in different areas. With this proviso, it is appropriate to give a brief overall summary before discussing the individual regional sequences.

The period with which we are concerned in this chapter has conventionally been divided by archaeologists of sub-Saharan Africa into the 'Middle Stone Age' and the 'Late Stone Age', although the distinction between these two stages has never been very clearly defined. Broadly speaking the industries of the 'Middle Stone Age' display a stone-tool-making technology which is clearly derived from that of the later Acheulian, being often based upon elaborations (eventually with reduced size) of the prepared-core or Levallois technique. This is the 'mode 3' technology of J. G. D. Clark (1969). 'Late Stone Age' industries generally show a further reduction in artefact size, and the resultant tiny tools (microliths) were often fitted into handles, several sometimes being used together as a composite tool. This innovation, which characterises Clark's 'mode 5' technology, involved devising a new way of trimming the flake edges steeply in order to blunt them, so that they did not split their hafts or cut their users' fingers. This blunting retouch, or backing, also served to provide a key for the mastic that was used to hold the stone inserts in place in their hafts. Studies of edge-wear and mastic remains have provided some indications of the various ways in which such artefacts may have been used (D. W. Phillipson, 1976); and in rare instances complete hafted specimens have survived, as at certain South African caves (J. D. Clark, 1958; H. J. Deacon, 1966) and at Columnata in

Algeria (Cadenat and Tixier, 1960). Ancient Egyptian specimens (J. D. Clark
et al., 1974) are also informative in this connexion (fig. 4.1).

In North Africa, the Sahara and the Nile Valley archaeologists have conventionally referred to stone-tool industries with a terminology akin to that used in
Europe. Mode 3 industries are here frequently designated 'Middle Palaeolithic',
and mode 5 ones 'Epipalaeolithic' or 'Mesolithic'. In some parts of North and
north-eastern Africa there occur industries which belong to Clark's mode 4,
based upon the production of long parallel-sided blades from prismatic cores;
the term 'Upper Palaeolithic' is sometimes applied to these North African
industries, as it usually is to their European counterparts.

The 'Middle Stone Age'/'Middle Palaeolithic' and the 'Late Stone Age'/'Upper
Palaeolithic'/'Epipalaeolithic' of the conventional terminology are in this book
discussed together, rather than as two separate stages. This is because, as will be
shown, there is now widespread and increasing evidence for continuity
throughout this period in many parts of Africa and, as a result, the distinctions
formerly proposed are now seen to be far from clear.

Similarly, it should be emphasised that the named stone-tool industries
described here are not always clearly defined. A number of assemblages occur
which seem to be typologically intermediate between more than one named
industry. To a large extent archaeologists have recognised compartments in
what is really a continuous range of variation through both time and space.

Throughout the period covered by this chapter, man in Africa remained a
hunter and a gatherer, obtaining his food from wild sources. His material culture
became more elaborate and regional specialisation became increasingly apparent, tendencies which may be attributed, at least in part, to man's progressive
mastery of his natural environment and his development of more efficient
methods of exploiting the wild sources of food which it supplied. Different

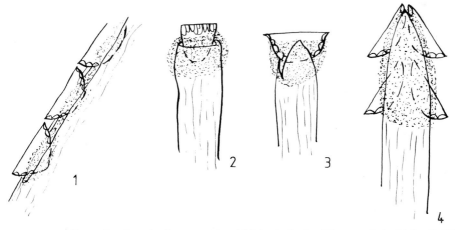

4.1 Reconstructions to show ways in which backed microliths were hafted (after D. W.
     Phillipson, 1976): 1 – as knife or sickle, 2 – as adze, 3 – as transverse arrow-head,
     4 – as barbs on a spear

situations offered varying potential, and distinct technologies were developed to exploit these. Despite increasing inter-regional diversification, it will be seen that technological development followed broadly parallel courses throughout the continent. Chapters 5 and 6 will discuss how, in the northern half of the continent, the later makers of microlithic (mode 5) industries eventually developed the food-producing economies which formed the basis for future developments throughout Africa.

The precise identity of the hominids responsible for the first post-Acheulian industries remains obscure. It is clear that they belonged to the species *Homo sapiens* for, as seen in chapter 3, there is now increasing evidence that this species, in the form of *H. sapiens rhodesiensis*, was already present in southern Africa in late Acheulian times. There are, surprisingly, far fewer well-preserved and adequately documented human fossils from African contexts associated with mode 3 industries than there are from late Pliocene and early Pleistocene times. Nevertheless, the earlier mode 3 industries appear to have been the work of *Homo sapiens* types which retained rhodesioid characteristics or, as in North Africa, were akin to *H. s. neanderthalensis* of Europe. Fully modern man, *H. s. sapiens* was present, at least in southern Africa, more than 100,000 years ago; and most if not all mode 5 industries appear to have been his workmanship. Far more human skeletons have been recovered from sites of the last 20,000 years than are available for earlier periods; and we are able to make a very tentative attempt at recognising the ancestors of some of Africa's recent populations (see chapter 5).

With the passage of time, human culture became more complex, and its archaeological remains are consequently more varied as well as more abundant. Furthermore, as man developed a life-style closer in many ways to our own, the surviving traces of his activities are easier for us to interpret. The thought-processes and beliefs that lie behind these activities may, for these more recent periods, occasionally be illustrated in the archaeological record through the investigation of graves or rock paintings, for example. Such clues will be touched upon at appropriate places in the regional survey which follows.

Southern Africa

It is convenient to begin this survey in southern Africa. Not only is the prehistoric sequence there relatively well known (though many important gaps in our knowledge remain), but there are indications that the major cultural developments of this period took place at least as early as did their counterparts elsewhere in the continent or, indeed, in other parts of the world.

In southern Africa, the end of the Acheulian is particularly ill-defined. There is, regrettably, no site which provides evidence for the change from the Acheulian industries to their immediate successors. At those rare places, such as the Cave of Hearths in the Transvaal (Mason, 1962) or Montagu Cave in the Cape (Keller, 1973), where Acheulian deposits are overlain by later material, a long gap separates the two phases of occupation. The date of the first post-Acheulian industries is also uncertain, although it is now clear that such industries have a far greater antiquity in South Africa than was, until recently, considered possible. At Klasies River Mouth on the south coast, 40 km west of Cape St Francis, the earliest occupation, retaining no trace of Acheulian technology, is associated with the retreat of the sea from a height 6–8 m above its present level and dated, by a combination of amino-acid racemisation and correlation of oxygen isotope composition of shells with similar evidence derived from deep-sea sediment samples, to *c.* 120,000 years ago (Singer and Wymer, 1982). At Border Cave in northern Natal, Butzer *et al.* (1978) have argued that the post-Acheulian sequence extends back to almost 200,000 years ago. The earliest industry at Klasies River Mouth is of mode 3 (fig. 4.2), based on

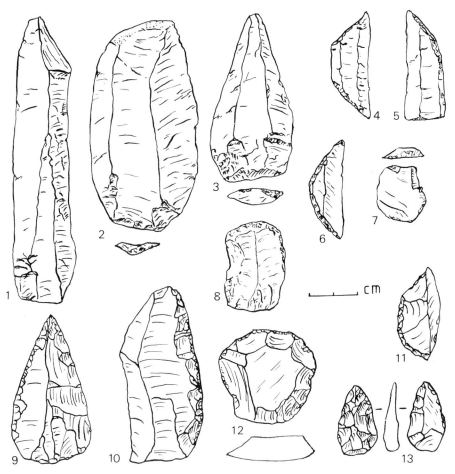

4.2 Artefacts from Klasies River Mouth (after Singer and Wymer, 1982): 1–4 – from the lowest horizon, 5–8 – from the Howieson's Poort industry. Implements of the Bambata and Tshangula industries (after Sampson, 1974): 9,10 – Bambata-type industry from Cave of Hearths, 11–13 – Tshangula industry from Pomongwe

the production of parallel-sided flake-blades from prepared cores. Details of the oldest Border Cave industry have not yet been published, but the excavators' use of the term 'Pietersburg' (see below, p. 64) in this connexion implies that it, too, may be of this same general type.

The remarkable sequence of industries at Klasies River Mouth, supplemented, where necessary, with evidence from other sites on the South Cape coast, may be used as a framework for an account of the stone-tool industries of south-ernmost Africa during the past 100,000 or more years (Klein, 1974; Singer and Wymer, 1982). Investigation of this cave complex (fig. 4.3) has revealed a total depth of archaeological deposit of more than 18 m, ranging in age from *c.* 120,000 years (see above) to *c.* 1,000 years ago. The greater part of this sequence is occupied by mode 3 industries, the makers of which produced parallel-sided and pointed flake-blades from the local quartzite beach-cobbles. A small proportion of the pointed flake-blades were retouched unifacially and may, along with unretouched specimens, have been hafted for use as spear-points. On a number of examples the bulb of percussion was flaked away, as if to make

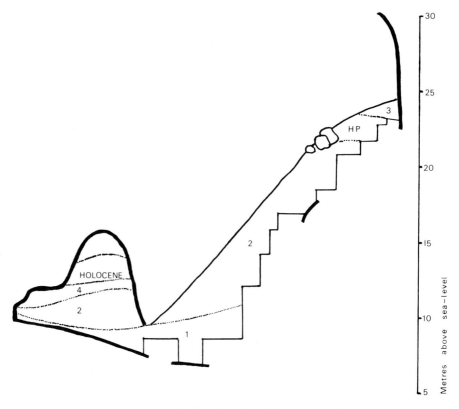

4.3 Composite section through the archaeological deposits at Klasies River Mouth (after Singer and Wymer, 1982). Nos. 1–4 refer to stages of the mode 3 industry, HP to the Howieson's Poort horizon

hafting easier. Other retouched tools included scrapers and a number of burins, or gravers (fig. 4.2). This stone industry at Klasies River Mouth continued, with one notable interruption which will be described below, for an enormously long period of time, perhaps as much as *c.* 80,000 years. Throughout this period both terrestrial and marine creatures were exploited for food, although fishing as opposed to shellfish-collecting was evidently rarely practised. Initially, large land animals such as eland and buffalo were the preferred prey, suggesting that hunting was conducted in a mixed forest–grassland environment. Subsequently, somewhat colder conditions are attested both by changed representation of shellfish species and by increased numbers of smaller antelope. Eventually, the sea fell below its present level, so that the caves overlooked broad coastal plains, now again inundated. Only casual occupation of the Klasies River Mouth sites is attested from this time, which was followed by a prolonged period of total abandonment until the caves were re-occupied about 3,000 years ago.

A phase at Klasies River Mouth which marks a pronounced discontinuity in the development of the mode 3 industry is particularly interesting. A markedly distinct stone industry was produçed, of a type known at several other South African localities and named after the site of Howieson's Poort. Its age remains uncertain, but is probably in excess of 50,000 years, perhaps as much as 90,000 years, which accords with evidence from Montagu and Border Caves (Singer and Wymer, 1982).

The Howieson's Poort industry has large numbers of very small blades, often trimmed by steep backing into crescentic or trapezoidal forms anticipating, by tens of thousands of years, the microlithic implements of the last few millennia. Small scrapers, gravers and notched pieces are also represented. The local quartzite was mostly unsuitable for making such small delicate tools, and finer-grained materials were carefully sought and collected. Not surprisingly, the makers of the Howieson's Poort industry appear to have hunted more of the smaller antelope, such as the steenbok, than had their more heavily armed predecessors. Seafood was still collected, although the shoreline was probably retreating. It is significant, however, that the makers both of the Howieson's Poort and of the earlier industry exploited broadly similar ecosystems; and it does not seem plausible to attribute the development of microlithic technology to a response to changed environmental conditions in the south coast area itself. Indeed, Singer and Wymer (1982) conclude that the introduction of the Howieson's Poort industry into the Klasies River Mouth sequence was due to the arrival of a new human group which had invented its distinctive technology elsewhere. After the Howieson's Poort interlude, Klasies River Mouth was re-occupied, albeit less intensively, by people whose mode 3 stone industry was essentially the same as that of the initial occupation.

The South African Howieson's Poort industry is probably the earliest yet known anywhere in the world to be based upon a mode 5 technology. Parallel technological developments took place in several regions of Africa in later times.

Possible explanations for these phenomena are discussed in a later section of this chapter (pp. 75–8).

Fragmentary human fossils have been recovered from Klasies River Mouth in association with the mode 3 industries; they are attributed without exception to *Homo sapiens sapiens* (Rightmire, 1978; Singer and Wymer, 1982). The presence of this type of hominid near the base of the Klasies River Mouth sequence may represent its earliest known attestation anywhere in the world. Regrettably, no human remains have been recovered from the Howieson's Poort horizon.

Further sites in southernmost Africa add to the data provided by the Klasies River Mouth research. At Mossel Bay (Keller, 1969), the evidence of early excavations demonstrates a sequence parallel to that at Klasies River Mouth some 200 km to the east. Between them, Nelson Bay Cave at Plettenberg Bay (Klein, 1974; J. Deacon, 1978) preserves a mode 3 industry overlain, after a gap in occupation, by successive occurrences of the Robberg and Albany industries (dated respectively from 19,000 to 12,000 and 12,000 to 8,000 years ago) which are further discussed below. Inland, at Boomplaas Cave in the Cape Folded Mountains, a similar sequence shows Robberg and Albany industries overlying a long succession of blade-based occurrences which have not yet been described in detail (Inskeep, 1978; H. J. Deacon, 1979).

It now appears that mode 3 technology based upon the production of flake-blades, such as is present in the earliest levels at Klasies River Mouth, was widespread in South Africa, representing the earliest post-Acheulian developments. In the Transvaal, such industries, known as Pietersburg, are best seen in the long sequence at the Cave of Hearths, Makapan (fig. 4.2). Here, Pietersburg material overlies the final Acheulian but, as noted above, the two industries are separated by a thick sterile deposit representing a period of unknown length when the site was unoccupied. The Pietersburg industry is typified by large numbers of long, parallel-sided flake-blades, often with trimming or use-wear along their edges. Disc-cores and triangular points are both relatively rare. It is noteworthy that the latest Acheulian assemblages from the Cave of Hearths show a tendency towards the production of elongated flake-blades; and the Pietersburg may represent a Transvaal development from a local Acheulian ancestor. Industries of Pietersburg type seem to have continued in use for tens of thousands of years: at least the earlier phases are beyond the range of radiocarbon dating (Mason, 1962; Sampson, 1974).

Perhaps even longer is the stratified sequence of industries at Border Cave in northern Natal, on the frontier with Swaziland (Beaumont, 1973). As noted above, it has been claimed that the succession of stone industries at this site may extend back as far as 195,000 years (Butzer *et al.*, 1978). The first half of this enormous time-span is occupied by horizons containing an industry of Pietersburg type. It was succeeded by an occupation represented by artefacts, described as 'Epi-Pietersburg', which appear to be analogous to those of the broadly contemporary Howieson's Poort further to the south. Tentatively dated between 80,000 and 50,000 years ago is the later mode 3 industry of which different authorities stress the Pietersburg and Bambata (p. 68) affinities. By about 38,000 years ago an essentially microlithic industry was being produced at Border Cave. Although full details of this site await publication, of particular interest are the fossil human remains (Beaumont *et al.*, 1978; Rightmire, 1979), which attest the presence of *Homo sapiens sapiens* since pre-Howieson's Poort times, as is also indicated at Klasies River Mouth.

Assemblages similar to those of the Pietersburg industry come from a number of recently investigated sites in the Orange Free State and northern Cape Province, of which the most informative is an undisturbed open site at Orangia (fig. 4.4). Here, at least six semicircular settings of stones two to three metres across and all open to the west are clearly the remains of some sort of artificial shelters (Sampson, 1968). The ground inside each shelter had been scooped out to form a hollow, perhaps for sleeping. It is estimated that approximately half the site had been destroyed by erosion before it was archaeologically investigated, so perhaps the whole site originally provided accommodation for about two dozen people. Orangian artefacts show strong resemblances to their Pietersburg counterparts, but their morphology was influenced by the preferred raw material – lydianite – that was quarried in large quantities at several outcrops in the middle Orange basin and traded over a wide area.

Possibly contemporary with this Pietersburg-related industry is a human skull from spring deposits at Florisbad in the Orange Free State, dated to at least 50,000 years ago. With brow ridges significantly less pronounced than those of the Broken Hill specimen (see p. 47), this is best regarded as belonging to an early form of modern man, *Homo sapiens sapiens* (Sampson, 1974 and references cited).

Further blade-based occurrences are reported from rockshelters in the mountains of Lesotho, at Ha Soloja, Sehonghong and Moshebi's, dating from more than 43,000 until about 30,000 years ago (Carter and Vogel, 1974). The blades show a progressive diminution in size, and backed retouch is clearly attested. In later times true microlithic industries were produced. Clearly, the role played by this cold high-altitude region in the development of southern African mode 5 industries requires further investigation.

In most areas of South Africa it appears that the Pietersburg and other industries based on flake-blades were followed by assemblages with sub-triangular points and scrapers made on flakes removed from prepared cores, bearing some resemblance to the Bambata material from Zimbabwe, discussed below. The Transvaal sequence is well seen at the Cave of Hearths (Sampson, 1974) and at Mwulu's Cave near Potgietersrust (Tobias, 1949). In the Cape broadly similar industries are recorded, but they are from poorly documented contexts and their position in the general sequence of mode 3 industries is unclear; possibly they belong to the period between *c.* 40,000 and 20,000 years ago, when sites such as Nelson Bay Cave and Klasies River Mouth were unoccupied.

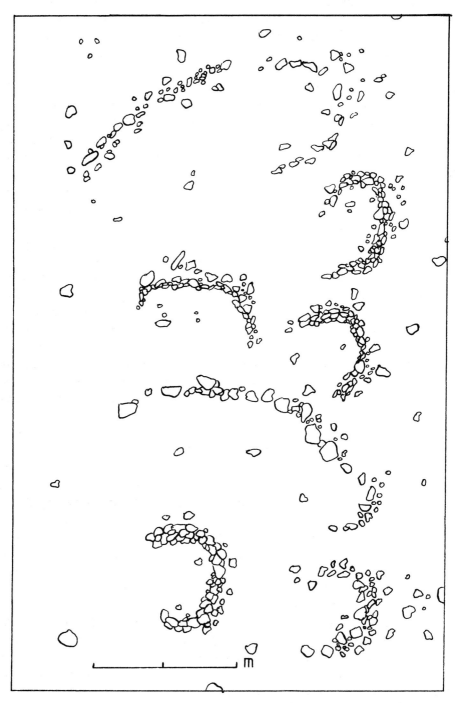

4.4 Stone settings from a site of the Pietersburg complex at Orangia (after Sampson, 1974)

North of the Limpopo, the post-Acheulian archaeology of the region centred on Zimbabwe and south-western Zambia differs in important respects from that of the Transvaal and other parts of South Africa. In these more northerly areas the stone-tool assemblages which occur in contexts apparently immediately following the final local Acheulian are characterised by crude triangular-sectioned picks, thick hand-axes or core-axes and a variety of small flake-tools, notably scrapers. These components occur in very variable frequencies. The heavy core-tool element is generally dominant at sites which occupy river-valley situations or thickly wooded environments; assemblages of this type have conventionally been attributed to a Sangoan industry, named after Sango Bay on the western shore of Lake Victoria. In more open-plateau situations, notably in Zimbabwe, the light-duty flake-tool element dominates the assemblages, which have been regarded as belonging to a Charaman industry taking its name from an open site in north-western Zimbabwe.

Detailed study of these Sangoan and Charaman industries has been hampered by the fact that the only unmixed unsorted assemblages from stratified dateable contexts are either of small size, like those of Charaman type from the basal horizons of Bambata and Pomongwe caves in the Matopo Hills of Zimbabwe (Cooke, 1963; 1969); or lacking in associated faunal material, like the Sangoan material from Kalambo Falls in northern Zambia (J. D. Clark, 1964; 1969; 1974). At both Kalambo Falls and Pomongwe, radiocarbon analyses indicate an age in excess of 40,000 to 50,000 years. At least at the former site there are indications that the true age may be in the order of 80,000 to 100,000 years (J. D. Clark, 1982a). Clearly, these occurrences are therefore at least broadly contemporary with the Pietersburg and related industries of South Africa.

It has often been argued that several of the typical Sangoan tool types were used for woodworking, and that the development of the Sangoan was a response to a wetter climate and a resultant spread of forest cover. Although plausible, such an argument rests upon very slender foundations, for we have no direct information about the uses to which individual artefacts were put; and the evidence for a shift to wetter conditions at this time is less convincing than was once believed. More persuasive is the suggestion (J. D. Clark, 1982a) that the assemblages formerly attributed to distinct Sangoan and Charaman industries were, in fact, facies in a continuum of variation comparable with that noted in the Acheulian assemblages described in chapter 3. The scarcity of sealed and well-studied assemblages precludes a more detailed consideration of this problem, although related phenomena in other regions of Africa will be discussed below. Unfortunately no comprehensive faunal assemblages come from demonstrably Sangoan or Charaman contexts, nor are there any associated hominid fossils. (The Broken Hill skull from Kabwe in Zambia, formerly believed to be associated with a Charaman industry, is now regarded, as noted on p. 47 above, to be of earlier date.)

In Zimbabwe and southern Zambia, the Sangoan and Charaman facies eventually gave way to stone-tool assemblages which display a well-developed mode 3 technology and which are generally known as Bambatan after Bambata Cave in the Matopo Hills near Bulawayo. Informative occurrences have been investigated also at Pomongwe (Cooke, 1963), at Redcliff in central Zimbabwe (Cooke, 1978) and at Kalemba in eastern Zambia (D. W. Phillipson, 1976). Unifacially trimmed sub-triangular points were produced, with occasional bifacial forms, together with a variety of flake scrapers. These tools may well have served functions similar to those of their counterparts in the more southerly (and probably earlier) Pietersburg industries, but they clearly belong to a different technological and stylistic tradition. At Redcliff, Pomongwe and Kalemba the Bambata levels are dated by radiocarbon to between 45,000 and 30,000 years ago: but this is probably the minimum age of the industry. The faunal remains from the cave sites suggest that the Bambata hunters exploited a wide range of animal species for their food. At several sites there is evidence that the climate was becoming progressively wetter during the Bambata occupation (Brain, 1969b). Particularly interesting is the discovery, within the Bambata industry, at three widely separated sites in Zimbabwe, of horizons marked by a proliferation of small blades (Cooke, 1971; 1973). These occurrences have (perhaps minimum) ages of some 40,000 years and it is tempting to regard them as counterparts of the more southerly Howieson's Poort.

Little is known about the archaeology of Namibia between the end of the Acheulian and the appearance of mode 5 industries. Surface occurrences suggest the presence of industries of Pietersburg and Lupemban (p. 78) types (MacCalman, 1963; MacCalman and Viereck, 1967). The only long excavated sequence is in the extreme south of the territory, at the 'Apollo 11 Cave', where a long mode 3 sequence underlies a scraper industry of about 12,000 years ago (Wendt, 1972; 1976). As will be shown below, this site is of particular importance because it has evidence for rock art at a very early date.

It is in the context of the Bambata-related industries of Zimbabwe and South Africa that we see the first widespread local evidence for the development of techniques of backed-microlith manufacture. In most areas these industries show, with the passage of time, a significant reduction in mean artefact size. Flakes and blades with partial backing occur in most Bambata-related assemblages; in the later industries these artefacts become more numerous, the backing is more extensive and crescent-shaped segments of blade with continuous backing along the curved edge regularly occur. A similar sequence is probably present at Mumbwa Cave in central Zambia (J. D. Clark, 1942). In Zimbabwe these later industries have been named Tshangula after a cave site in the Matopo Hills. Broadly similar occurrences are known in several areas of south-central Africa, and they are generally dated to various periods with the general time-span 25,000 to 14,000 years ago (e.g. Cooke, 1963; D. W. Phillipson, 1976). It seems that the development of microlithic technology proceeded at differing speeds in the various regions of southern Africa.

North of the Zambezi the earliest true backed-microlith industry had developed by about 19,000 years ago as seen, for example, at Kalemba rockshelter in eastern Zambia (fig. 4.5). Tiny pointed backed bladelets and varied scrapers are the characteristic tool types of these Nachikufan I industries, together with bored stones, the larger examples of which resemble objects which are known to have been used in later periods as weights for digging sticks (S. F. Miller, 1972; D. W. Phillipson, 1976). Broadly contemporary with this Zambian material is the Robberg industry of southernmost South Africa, dated to between 19,000 and 12,000 years ago at sites such as Nelson Bay Cave (Klein, 1974; J. Deacon, 1978) and Boomplaas (H. J. Deacon, 1979). Few details of the Robberg industry have yet been published, but it apparently comprises many tiny bladelets with few standardised retouched tools. Its makers, like their predecessors, hunted the grassland fauna of the coastal plains. Similar microlithic industries are now known from more northerly areas, as in Lesotho (Carter and Vogel, 1974) and at Bushman Rock in the Transvaal (Beaumont and Vogel, 1972), but in the intervening regions, such as Zimbabwe, the Tshangula industry seems to have survived without interruption.

4.5 Kalemba rockshelter in course of excavation

Between about 12,000 and 8,000 years ago several widely scattered sites distributed southwards from Zimbabwe and southern Namibia to the Cape show occupation by makers of a poorly understood industry with many large scrapers, from which microliths and backed pieces are totally absent. In the Cape this industry is named Albany, in Zimbabwe, Pomongwan. At Nelson Bay Cave the abrupt change from the Robberg to the Albany industry appears to coincide with the rise of sea-level to its post-glacial height, with a corresponding change in faunal availability.

Subsequently, microlithic industries became virtually ubiquitous in southern Africa. At coastal sites this development correlates with the final rise of the sea to approximately its present level, and there is evidence that marine food resources were once again intensively exploited. Exceptional areas included the greater part of the Kalahari, which seems to have been largely uninhabited from c. 9,500 until c. 4,500 years ago (J. Deacon, 1974), and the upper Zambezi Valley, where the open grassy plains saw a later persistence of mode 3 stone-working techniques (L. Phillipson, 1978). Elsewhere, most of the microlithic industries were characterised by geometrical backed forms, chiefly lunates, which replaced the single-pointed types of Nachikufan I and its counterparts. These industries show considerable regional variation, the significance of which is not yet apparent. In some local industries, such as those of the southern Cape coast, small convex scrapers far outnumber the backed microliths; and when a number of these assemblages are compared a great range in the frequencies of specific tool types is to be observed. Despite this variability, there has been a tendency among archaeologists to put most of these industries under the generic name Wilton, after a site near Alicedale in the eastern Cape (J. Deacon, 1972; H. J. Deacon, 1976). This has helped to obscure the very real differences between most of the assemblages so designated, while exaggerating the idiosyncracy of those, such as the later Nachikufan phases of northern Zambia (S. F. Miller, 1972) and the Kaposwa from Kalambo Falls (J. D. Clark, 1974), which have been given different names. It now appears that temporal, economic, cultural and regional factors all influenced the types of tools that were used. At sites with a stratified sequence of microlithic industries, there has been noted a general decrease in artefact size with the passage of time (D. W. Phillipson, 1977a).

A large proportion of the dated archaeological occurrences of this period in southern Africa are from cave or rockshelter sites where little has been preserved apart from the stone artefacts and, on occasion, associated faunal remains. Only rarely has vegetable matter survived, leading to an unbalanced representation of the tool-kits and diet of the people. The dry cave deposits of southernmost Africa (H. J. Deacon, 1976) and the few waterlogged sites, such as those at Gwisho hotsprings in southern Zambia (Fagan and van Noten, 1971), where there has been excellent preservation of organic materials, are therefore particularly important (fig. 4.6). From these sites we can see that, at least in some areas, wood was used for bows, arrows, digging sticks, pegs and wedges. Bark was used for trays. Bags and clothing were made of sewn leather. Leaves were used as a wrapping material for valuables; while grass and soft undergrowth were collected for use as bedding. Vegetable foods were varied and often assumed considerable importance in the total diet, as they do among most modern tropical hunter-gatherer groups. Remains of plant foods have also provided important information about the seasonality of settlements, confirming the often less detailed evidence of the faunal remains. In the south-western Cape, for example, it now seems that some hunter-gatherer groups moved regularly between their coastal winter settlements and summer haunts further inland (Parkington, 1972). Seasonal movement is also indicated in the eastern Cape and in the highlands of Lesotho.

A substantial number of graves have been found, and these show a variety of burial customs. Generally, the dead appear to have been buried within the settlement area, whether this was a cave or rockshelter or in the open air

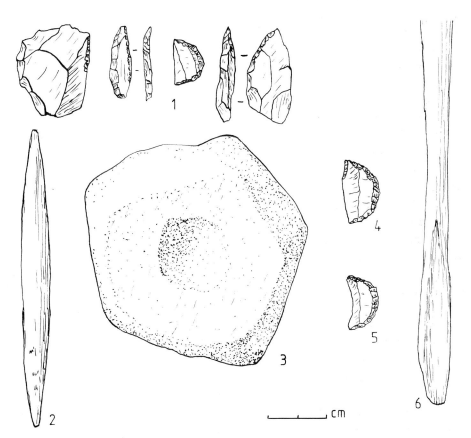

4.6 Artefacts from Kalemba and Gwisho: 1 – early mode 5 examples from Kalemba (after D. W. Phillipson, 1976): 2–6 from Gwisho (after Fagan and van Noten, 1971): 2 – wooden linkshaft from an arrow, 3 – grinder, 4,5 – backed microliths, 6 – tip of wooden digging stick, not to scale

(fig. 4.7). Grave goods in the form of tools, items of adornment or other personal belongings are often present and perhaps indicate a belief that the dead would have some use for such objects. Trophies such as antelope horns or warthog tusks were also sometimes buried with the dead. As will be shown below painted gravestones were in vogue in the south coastal area.

Items of personal adornment are frequently encountered on settlement sites and in graves. Beads and pendants of bone or shell are widespread. Rock paintings suggest that such beads were sometimes sewn onto clothing or worn in the hair, as well as being threaded in strings. Ochre and other colouring matter was probably used for cosmetic purposes as well as for mural decoration; its incidence in southern African sites extends into far earlier periods, where it is associated with mode 3 industries (Dart and Beaumont, 1968).

No account of the later prehistory of southern Africa would be complete without reference to the remarkable rock art – both paintings and engravings – that is so abundantly preserved there (cf. Summers, 1959; Willcox, 1963; D. N. Lee and Woodhouse, 1970). It is generally difficult to establish the age and authorship of such art, but until this is done we cannot hope to be able to make full use of this potentially most illuminating evidence, which relates to aspects of prehistoric life that would otherwise remain unknown (figs. 4.8; 4.9).

Virtually all southern African rock art occurs on the walls of shallow caves or rockshelters or on rock outcrops in the open air. It thus invariably suffers some degree of exposure to the elements (unlike European palaeolithic paintings,

4.7 A human burial of *c.* 2000 B.C. at Gwisho, in the characteristic contracted position

which are in deep caves), and it is inherently unlikely that any extant examples, at least of the paintings, will be more than a few thousand years old at the most. Painted stone slabs, however, which throw some light on the earlier phases of the art, have been excavated from southern African sites. At 'Apollo 11 Cave' in southern Namibia, detached slabs bearing naturalistic paintings of animals occur in levels dated as long ago as 28,000 years, associated with a late mode 3 industry, indicating that some southern African rock art has an antiquity comparable with that of its European counterpart (Wendt, 1976). Rather later in date, but showing much greater variety, are the painted stones found in graves of the makers of microlithic industries in caves on the south Cape coast, as at Coldstream Cave and Klasies River Mouth (Singer and Wymer, 1969; Rudner, 1971).

Despite the difficulty in dating the art which remains unburied on site walls, it is often possible to ascertain the order in which differing styles were practised by study of superimpositions, where one motif has been painted over another. In this way the earliest extant styles can be isolated. In Zimbabwe, cultural elements associated with metal-using farming peoples are first represented in the third of six styles and it is therefore reasonable to conclude that the first two styles belong to the period before the advent of such peoples in the first millennium A.D. These paintings, and their counterparts in South Africa, Namibia and Zambia, depict wild animals and, on occasion, human beings, the latter often in the guise of hunters. They show an artistic quality that was not

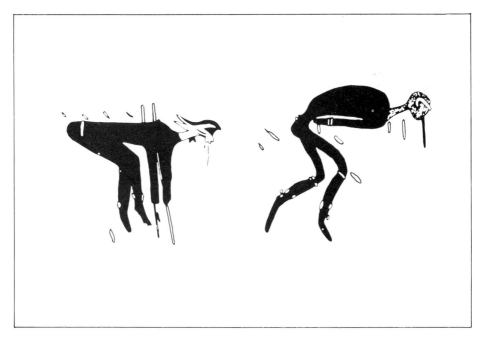

4.8 Rock paintings showing people in trance (after Lewis-Williams, 1983)

subsequently maintained north of the Limpopo; although further to the south the finest development of the painting tradition came in later times. It is to this final expression that most of our data regarding the meaning and significance of the art relates; but it is pertinent to cite such evidence here since it provides at least some indication of the original function of the more ancient art.

Several writers, viewing southern African rock art from a primarily foreign viewpoint, have stressed its undoubted aesthetic qualities and suggested that the painters' main object was to create a thing of beauty. This 'art for art's sake' explanation can no longer be accepted in view of detailed comparisons that have been made between, on the one hand, the arrangement and subject matter of the paintings and, on the other, ethnographic records relating to southern San-speaking peoples in the nineteenth and twentieth centuries (Vinnicombe, 1976; Lewis-Williams, 1981). The eland is the animal most frequently shown in the paintings but not, by contrast, in the food debris represented by faunal remains on occupation sites. The same species occupied an important place in the belief

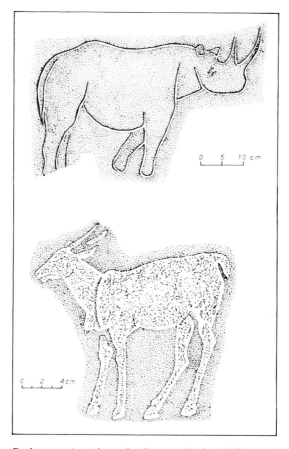

4.9 Rock engravings from the Transvaal (after Willcox, 1963): top – at Doornkloof, bottom – at Sweitzer Reneke

systems and symbolism of the San. Close parallels may be drawn between certain painted scenes and rites practised by San on occasions such as puberty and marriage. Many paintings have otherwise inexplicable features that may readily be understood in terms of trance, which occupied an important role in the lives of the southern San. Only three examples need be cited. Paintings of human figures in the Cape and Natal provinces of South Africa often show lines descending from the nostrils: trance among the San is frequently accompanied by nose-bleeding. A strange, forward-leaning, half-crouching stance, not infrequently represented in the paintings, is identical to that adopted by San dancing while entering trance (fig. 4.8). San emerging from trance have described their experience as feeling like riding on the back of a serpent; and paintings in the Matopo Hills of Zimbabwe show an enormous serpent, sometimes double-headed, with numbers of people standing on its back. Independent studies attribute an analogous significance to schematic rock art further to the north, as will be described in chapter 7. It thus seems appropriate to conclude that rock art can only be interpreted adequately with reference to the belief systems of the artists; and it is fortunate that some of the southern African art was executed by societies sufficiently recent for these systems to be understood.

In southern Africa, as this section has shown, recent research has demonstrated the archaeological sequence of mode 3 and mode 5 industries to be of considerable length and complexity. If we can believe the very early date proposed for the start of the Pietersburg sequence at Border Cave, comparison with evidence cited in chapter 3 for a late Acheulian occurrence at Rooidam suggests that the post-Acheulian technological traditions began at an approximate time-depth of 200,000 to 150,000 years. This emergence may have taken place regionally at different times, as was the case with the later development of mode 5 technology.

The earliest post-Acheulian stone industries are now seen to have depended to a far larger extent on the production of flake-blades than was previously believed. Much research relating to these industries has not yet been published in detail, but the Cape excavations at Klasies River Mouth have provided important information on hunting strategy, with its emphasis on the young of certain species, notably buffalo (Klein, 1978). The extent to which vegetable foods were exploited at this time remains to be demonstrated.

The early appearance and development of mode 5 industries is particularly interesting. Their oldest attestation is in the Howieson's Poort horizons at Klasies River Mouth and, probably, Border Cave. At the former site it has been suggested that this industry was introduced by a distinct population moving in from a source area elsewhere. Such a source area, if it existed, has not yet been located. In the south-eastern highland areas there is evidence for continuous occupation by makers of industries comprising small blades with backed retouch for most of the last 45,000 years and perhaps longer. By 30,000 years ago these industries show features recognised as ancestral to the later mode 5 traditions.

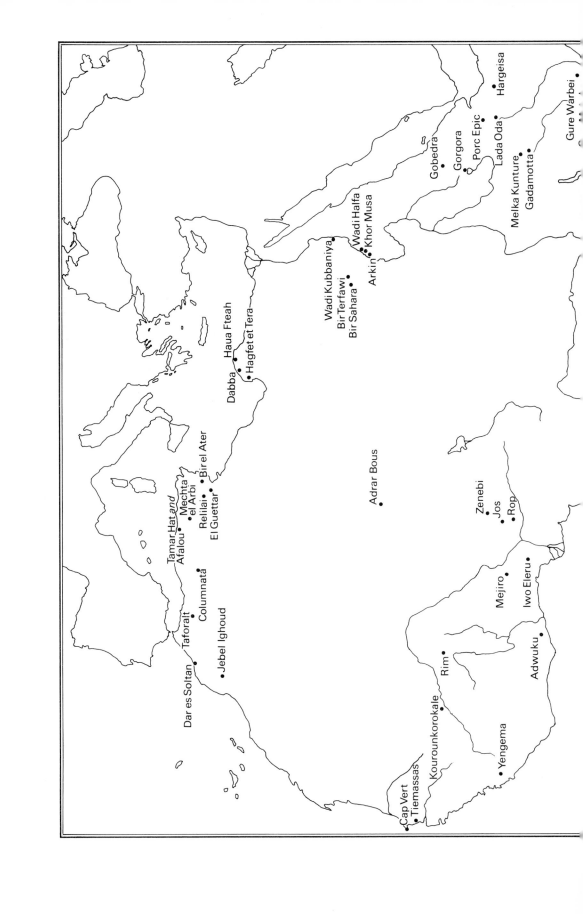

4.10 Occurrences of post-Acheulian stone industries discussed in chapter 4

The following place names appear on the map:

Kagera · Nderit Drift · Lukenya
Nasera · Olduvai · Kisese
L Eyasi · Singida · Kondoa
Kalambo Falls
Mwanganda
Nachikufu
Luangwa Valley · Kalemba
Broken Hill · Zombepata
Mumbwa · Redcliff
Gwisho · Makwe
Victoria Falls · Bambata · Pomongwe
Tshangula
Gombe Point, · Mufo
Malebo Pool · Dundo
Musolexi
Mwulu's Cave · Bushman Rock
Border Cave
Pietersburg, · Sehonghong
Cave of Hearths · Ha'Soloja
Doornkloof · Florisbad
Schweitzer Reneke · Moshebi's
Fauresmith · Howieson's Poort
Orangia · Wilton
Montagu · Boomplaas · Klasies River Mouth
Mossel Bay · Coldstream
Nelson Bay Cave
'Apollo II'

2000 km
1000 miles

This technology is not firmly attested in post-Howieson's Poort contexts in the Cape until some ten millennia later, but this period remains poorly known as several major sites were not then occupied.

In several areas there is evidence that the appearance of mode 5 technology accompanied a shift in hunting preference towards smaller game species, in contrast to the larger gregarious creatures that were often the prey most sought after by the makers of the mode 3 industries. Clearly, no rigid cause-and-effect relationship may be proposed between the two trends, but the observation does help our understanding of why the development of mode 5 technology proceeded at such disparate speeds in different areas of southern Africa. Although the southern African sequence is better known than those in other parts of the continent, further consideration is best presented in a later section of this chapter.

Central Africa

In most of Angola, northern Zambia and Malawi (as well as in parts of East Africa) the stone-tool assemblages immediately following the Acheulian are of Sangoan type (fig. 4.11). In much of Zaire and adjacent parts of the Congo basin, Sangoan-type assemblages are the earliest trace of human settlement yet found (Mortelmans, 1962a; van Noten, 1982). They appear to belong to a time when the equatorial forest was less widespread and dense than it had been previously.

By about 40,000 years ago, if not before, more evolved industries were being produced, of the type known as Lupemban. Lupemban artefacts are character-ised by refined bifacial stone-working techniques, especially on core-axes and on long double-ended points which may perhaps have been mounted for use as spear-tips. They are found abundantly in the area of the Plain of Kinshasa beside the Malebo (Stanley) Pool (van Moorsel, 1968), and also in the river gravels of the Dundo area in northern Angola, which have in recent years been mined extensively for diamonds (J. D. Clark, 1963). In the latter area, at Mufo, the Lupemban is dated to more than 30,000 years ago. It appears to have continued for some 15,000 years or more, with a gradual reduction in artefact size. A similar age is indicated at Kalambo Falls, where Lupemban artefacts overlie the Sangoan horizons. Unlike the earlier material at Kalambo, the Lupemban does not occur on undisturbed floors; the artefacts are instead incorporated in a thick layer of rubble (J. D. Clark, 1964; 1982a). Here and at several north-east Angolan sites pollen has been preserved which suggests that the Lupemban vegetation and climate did not differ significantly from those of the present time. Also provisionally attributed to the Lupemban, although the characteristic bifacial points are not represented in this specialist context, is an elephant-butchery site at Mwanganda in northern Malawi (J. D. Clark and Haynes, 1970). The implements, scattered among the bones of a single elephant, consist almost exclusively of scrapers, with a few core-axes.

Recent research has shown that there is no adequate basis for the multi-phase sequence of post-Acheulian industries formerly proposed for the Kinshasa area

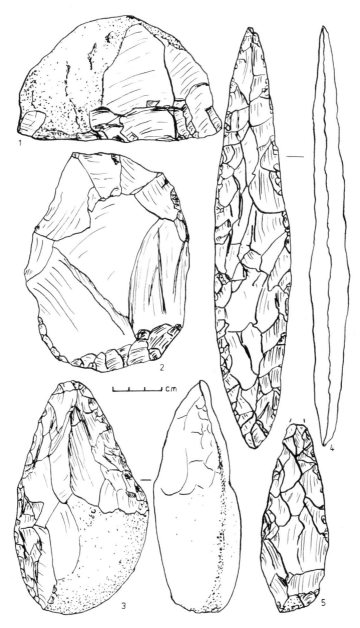

4.11 Sangoan implements from the Luangwa Valley, Zambia (after J. D. Clark, 1950): 1 – 'push-plane' or core, 2 – flake scraper, 3 – pick. Lupemban implements from Musolexi, Angola (after J. D. Clark, 1963): 4,5 – bifacial points

(Cahen, 1978). The artefacts occur in poorly stratified sands, as at Gombe Point, and it is now clear that considerable mixture has taken place, both between specimens originally deposited at different levels, and of the materials sampled for radiocarbon dating. Consequently, neither the typological composition of the industries nor their chronology may be regarded as securely established.

The development of microlithic technology in central Africa is best considered in two regional subdivisions. In the savanna regions such as those in much of Zambia and southern Angola, on the one hand, true mode 5 industries appeared at an early date, as noted on p. 69, having their roots in the earlier Bambata/ Tshangula tradition. An early microlithic occurrence at Matupi in the extreme north-east of Zaire (see also p. 82) is best considered in this connexion. On the fringes of the equatorial forest, on the other hand, a local largely microlithic industry known as the Tshitolian gradually developed from the preceding Lupemban tradition. This process, best seen in the Dundo sequence after about 14,000 years ago, involved a general decrease in artefact size and a gradual shift in emphasis from flakes struck off prepared cores to parallel-sided blades. Backed microliths appear, especially the flared triangular form known as *petits tranchets* that may have been hafted as transverse arrowpoints (fig. 4.1), becoming smaller and more numerous with the passage of time. Small core-axes and picks continue, as do leaf-shaped points. In southern Zaire it is noteworthy that sites in the more densely forested river valleys contain a higher proportion of backed microliths; while assemblages from the more open plateaux contain the larger bifacially worked tools. The distribution of comparable industries extends northwards into Congo, Gabon and Cameroon.

Studies of the archaeology of central Africa are hampered by the sparseness and uneven coverage of research, by the total lack of hominid fossils and the almost complete absence of faunal and floral remains. In addition, as has been shown above, doubt has been cast upon the stratigraphic integrity of many of the open-air Kalahari Sand sites which formed the basis for much of the sequence previously proposed.

Eastern Africa

In contrast with the abundant and widely distributed sites from this period that have been investigated in southern Africa, further to the north in East Africa our knowledge remains very incomplete. Some small areas, notably in Kenya, have been intensively examined but elsewhere enormous regions remain virtually unexplored by archaeologists, whose attention has tended to be concentrated on the very rich sites in this region belonging to the earliest Stone Age periods.

Two localities in eastern Africa have yielded stone-tool industries which may be regarded as developments of the late Acheulian leading to the appearance of true mode 3 industries; unfortunately both sites are at present incompletely documented. At Melka Kunture near Addis Ababa, horizons stratified above the

Acheulian material noted in chapter 3 contain a series of industries in which bifacial tools became progressively rarer and smaller, being gradually replaced by sub-triangular points and side-scrapers made on flakes (Hours, 1973). Full details of these discoveries have not yet been published, nor are any age determinations available. It is, however, relevant to note potassium/argon dates of *c.* 150,000 and *c.* 180,000 years ago for a mode 3 factory site on obsidian outcrops at Gadamotta near Lake Zwai, some 70 km south of Melka Kunture (Wendorf and Schild, 1974). The second locality is very poorly understood: a site on the Kinangop Plateau of central Kenya has yielded a potassium/argon date of *c.* 400,000 years for an industry of small hand-axes, flake points and side-scrapers (Evernden and Curtis, 1965). If the great age of this material is substantiated by future research, it indicates that technological trends leading to the development of mode 3 industries can be traced much further back into the Acheulian time-span than had previously been believed (cf. M. Leakey *et al.*, 1969).

Mode 3 industries, characterised by the presence of scrapers and sub-triangular points made on flakes, often struck from prepared cores similar in general terms to those from southern Africa attributed to the Bambata industry, are widely distributed in most regions of eastern Africa except the Lake Victoria basin. Their chronology and economy await detailed investigation, but appear to have been broadly analogous to those of their counterparts further to the south. Industries of this type have been described in Somalia (J. D. Clark, 1954) and in Ethiopia, where they are associated with a neanderthaloid human mandible at Porc Epic cave near Dire Dawa (J. D. Clark and Williams, 1978). At Olduvai Gorge such material occurs overlying Bed IV in the Ndutu Beds, where its age may exceed 100,000 years (M. D. Leakey *et al.*, 1972). At nearby Lake Eyasi an industry of this type is associated with fragmentary human crania which show morphological features akin to those of the *Homo sapiens rhodesiensis* specimen from Broken Hill, Kabwe. Many further occurrences, especially in southern Kenya, await detailed publication (cf. Anthony, 1972). Related mode 3 industries also occur in the early stages of several of the local sequences which have been established on the basis of cave or rockshelter excavations, notably those at Nasera (Mehlman, 1977) on the eastern edge of the Serengeti Plain in northern Tanzania and Lukenya Hill (Gramly, 1976) near Nairobi in southern Kenya.

The area around Lake Victoria, which was for much of this time an internal drainage area with no outlet to the north, belonged to the well forested zone where the immediately post-Acheulian industries were of Sangoan type. Particularly abundant remains of this period occur in the valley of the Kagera River, west of the lake, on the modern border between Uganda and Tanzania. All, however, occur in disturbed river-gravels; and East Africa has so far yielded no undisturbed Sangoan horizons comparable with those from Kalambo Falls. Likewise undated, but presumably later, are Lupemban-type industries, best known from sites such as Yala Alego in the Winam Gulf area of south-western Kenya (O'Brien, 1939; Cole, 1964). This sequence is paralleled by abundant discoveries in Rwanda and Burundi (Nenquin, 1967; van Noten, 1982). Throughout this area the published data are unfortunately virtually restricted to typological descriptions.

In some parts of eastern Africa, as in some more southerly regions, the techniques of bladelet production and of backing retouch can be traced back to far earlier periods than were previously considered relevant. For example, at Matupi Cave in the extreme east of Zaire a quartz industry displaying these features extends back for at least 30,000 years (van Noten, 1977). Elsewhere, however, its appearance was considerably later, as at Nasera where a very long sequence of mode 3 industries shows no sign of backed bladelets until about 22,000 years ago.

By about this time, as in northern and eastern Zambia, there is evidence that microlithic industries containing quantities of backed bladelets and some geometrical microliths were widespread in the highlands of Tanzania and southern Kenya. The best-described occurrences are at Kisese rockshelter in central Tanzania (Inskeep, 1962) and at Lukenya Hill (Gramly, 1976), where such artefacts are associated with a fragmentary human skull showing, it is claimed, features resembling those of recent negroid populations (Gramly and Rightmire, 1973). A similar but rather later industry comes from Buvuma Island in Ugandan waters of Lake Victoria (van Noten, 1971). Broadly contemporary material from the Naisiusiu Beds near the top of the Olduvai Gorge sequence probably owes its distinctive appearance to the fact that many of its artefacts are made of obsidian (M. D. Leakey et al., 1972).

In the more northerly parts of eastern Africa, there are very few dated sequences that can be compared with those noted above. At Laga Oda in the escarpment of the south-east Ethiopian plateau near Dire Dawa, a backed microlith industry was established at least 16,000 years ago (J. D. Clark and Williams, 1978). Elsewhere, industries of mode 4, based on the production of large blades from prismatic cores, intervene between the mode 3 and the backed-microlith industries. A blade industry of this type in northern Somalia, known as the Hargeisan, has not been dated (J. D. Clark, 1954). In northern Ethiopia, at Gobedra rockshelter near Axum in Tigre, a mode 4 industry was replaced by a microlithic one some 10,000 years ago (D. W. Phillipson, 1977b).

The best known of these eastern African blade industries is also the most southerly. The Eburran industry, formerly known as the Kenya Capsian, is restricted to a small area near Lake Nakuru in the eastern Rift Valley of south-central Kenya. It is best represented at Gamble's Cave and Nderit Drift, and is dated between 13,000 and 9,000 years ago (Isaac et al., 1972; Ambrose et al., 1980). The fine large artefacts of the Eburran – it is typified by large backed blades, crescent-shaped pieces, end-scrapers and gravers (fig. 4.12) – probably

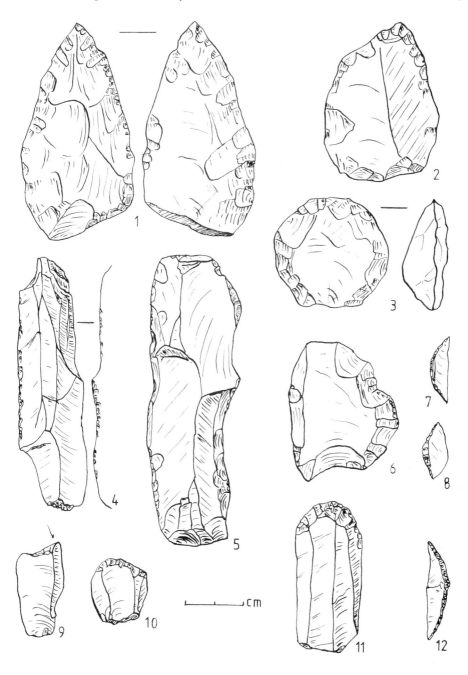

4.12 1–3 – mode 3 artefacts from Hargeisa (after J. D. Clark, 1954), 4–8 – modes 4 and 5 from Gobedra (after D. W. Phillipson, 1977b), 9–12 – Eburran from Gamble's Cave (after L. S. B. Leakey, 1931)

owe much to the quality of the obsidian from which they are made, and the similarity with the more northerly blade industries may thus be fortuitous.

By 10,000 years ago backed-microlith industries appear all over eastern Africa. These industries, despite their overall similarity, show a confusing complexity of variation; and no really convincing and meaningful classification of them has yet been proposed. In the north our knowledge comes from widely scattered localities: Gobedra and Laga Oda in Ethiopia, for example, as well as from Gorgora near Lake Tana (L. S. B. Leakey, 1943). In northern Somalia, such an industry succeeded the Hargeisan at an unknown date; in the south and east of that country its counterpart, known as Doian, has unifacial and bifacial points alongside the backed microliths, as at Gure Makeke and Gure Warbei (J. D. Clark, 1954). Further to the south, the specialised fishing settlements of this period beside Lake Turkana are discussed in chapter 5. Elsewhere, except in the parts of the Rift Valley where obsidian was plentiful (and whence it was sometimes evidently traded to less fortunate neighbouring areas), the micro- lithic industries are generally of quartz and of rather informal character. The longest and best documented sequences are those at the Lukenya Hill, Kisese and Nasera sites noted above. Similar material comes from northern and western Uganda (e.g. Nelson and Posnansky, 1970).

The makers of the microlithic industries of between 5,000 and 2,000 years ago were probably responsible for the earliest extant East African rock paintings. Such paintings are only surely known from north-central Tanzania and have fairly close stylistic parallels with their counterparts in southern Africa. Isolated naturalistic animal figures and stylised humans are the most frequent motifs, shown either in outline or flat monochrome. The best known sites are in the Kondoa and Singida areas (Fosbrooke et al., 1950; Masao, 1979). The naturalistic art tradition did not continue here into such recent times as it did in South Africa, and its interpretation is thus more problematic. In general terms, however, it is possible that it fulfilled much the same function; certain features, such as the frequency of eland representations, are common to both areas, and there is, furthermore, linguistic evidence for the recent use of Khoisan-related languages in Tanzania.

Although the data are from widely scattered sites in quite different environ- ments, and although long detailed sequences are so far lacking, the succession of post-Acheulian stone industries in eastern Africa is now seen to have been much the same, and lasted for about as long, as that revealed by more intensive research further to the south. There is, however, no evidence for any early appearance of mode 5 technology such as that represented by the Howieson's Poort industries south of the Limpopo. The earliest post-Acheulian industries are not based to the same extent on flake-blade production but, in contrast to the situation in the south, true mode 4 industries are attested in the more northerly parts of eastern Africa. The reasons for these distinctions will not be properly understood until comprehensive data relating to the economy and life-style of this period have been recovered from eastern African sites.

West Africa

As with the Acheulian, the subsequent stone industries of West Africa have not been thoroughly investigated, although abundant remains are known to exist (fig. 4.13). We have virtually no reliable information relating to the chronology of this material. At least the more easterly parts of West Africa appear to fall within the zone of Sangoan-type industries similar to those found further to the south and east, although certain features serve to differentiate the West African finds from their neighbours. Sangoan artefacts occur at numerous localities in the gravels and terraces of the major rivers of Nigeria and Ghana (especially the Volta) and in the coastal regions of Ghana, where drier conditions would have caused contraction of the forest. With the exception of a few finds near the head-waters of the Gambia River in southern Senegal and Guinea, Sangoan artefacts have not been convincingly reported from west of the Ivory Coast; but this absence may to some extent reflect the vagaries of research emphasis (Davies, 1967; Wai-Ogusu, 1973).

Considerable confusion surrounds the sequence of West African stone industries in later times because so much of our information is based upon undated collections from disturbed contexts or surface exposures. However, there can be little doubt that in several areas, such as Cap Vert (Senegal), south-western Mali and central Guinea, there existed an industry typified by large lance-shaped points akin to, but generally cruder than, those of the central African Lupemban.

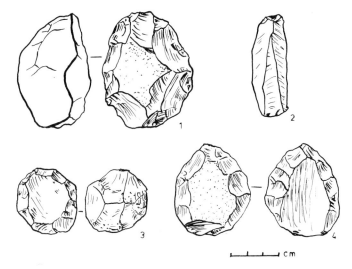

4.13 Sangoan and mode 3 artefacts from Nigeria (after Shaw, 1978)

It is difficult to be certain about the true distribution of this industry, because of the superficial similarity between some of its artefacts and those of much later times. More clearly defined are the mode 3 industries based on prepared cores and flakes, made into points and scrapers rather like those from more easterly and southerly regions, and also showing affinities with Levalloiso-Mousterian material (see p. 90) from further to the north. These are widespread in river-gravel deposits in Nigeria, notably on the Jos Plateau, where they belong to a later cycle of erosion and deposition than does the local Acheulian. A particularly rich occurrence is in the outwash gravels below Zenebi Falls; a very late radiocarbon date for this material probably does not represent its true age, which remains unknown since no undisturbed assemblage of this type has been excavated *in situ* anywhere in West Africa (Soper, 1965; Shaw, 1978).

There has been more research into later periods, at least in some areas, and a rather fuller picture may therefore be drawn. No sequence has yet been established which shows when backed-microlith industries began in West Africa; but at the rockshelter of Iwo Eleru in the now forested zone of south-western Nigeria such an industry was established by 12,000 years ago (Shaw, 1969). This early horizon also yielded a human burial which is stated to show negroid physical features (Brothwell and Shaw, 1971). The stone industry, which included a very low proportion of intentionally retouched tools, was characterised by crescent-shaped, triangular and trapezoidal microliths. It continued with only minor change for some 9,000 years. Around 5,500 years ago, pottery and ground stone artefacts made their appearance. (These late

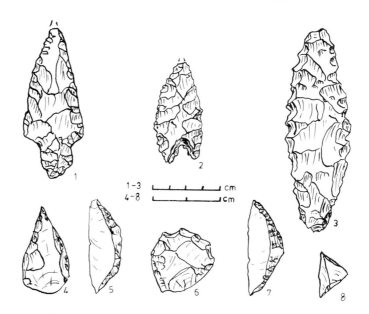

4.14 West African mode 5 implements: 1–3 – bifacial points from Tiemassas (after Dagan, 1956), 4–8 – microliths from Rop (after Shaw, 1978)

pottery-associated industries are described and discussed in chapter 6.) Comparable microlithic industries without associated pottery are known elsewhere in Nigeria, as at Mejiro near Old Oyo (Willett, 1962) and at Rop on the Jos Plateau (B. Fagg *et al.*, 1972).

Elsewhere in West Africa, the earlier microlithic industries, before the start of pottery manufacture, have only been found in a few areas, but were probably originally widespread (Shaw, 1981a). Such an occurrence at Rim in Upper Volta has an age of over 5,000 years. In Ghana there are numerous surface finds which probably belong to this period, as at Adwuku, but none has been dated precisely. By contrast, sites in Guinea and Sierra Leone, such as Yengema (Coon, 1968), have yielded crudely flaked pick- and hoe-like artefacts, flake-scrapers and a few backed blades. Such material (like analogous finds from the Congo basin) often represents an adaptation to forest life; but the presence of a true backed-microlith industry at Iwo Eleru remains to be explained, unless that site's surroundings have become only recently afforested. Material from Kourounkorokale near Bamako is described in chapter 5. In the far west, in Senegal, the lagoonside Tiemassas site 80 km south of Dakar yielded a pre-pottery microlithic occurrence. Crescents and backed blades are large and crude: they are associated with bifacially flaked leaf-shaped points (fig. 4.14). More than one phase of occupation is probably represented in these extensive exposures for which, unfortunately, no radiocarbon dates are available (Dagan, 1956; 1972).

Despite the very incomplete nature of our evidence, the following tentative conclusions can be made. It is clear that microlithic technology in West Africa began at least 12,000 years ago. For many millennia prior to this date the Sahara was largely uninhabited, and so the microlithic industries to the south, as in other areas of sub-Saharan Africa, were probably indigenous developments. However, in some densely forested regions of West Africa, such as south-eastern Nigeria, Sierra Leone and Guinea, non-microlithic industries continued until the last few millennia (Shaw, 1981a). The characteristic artefacts of these industries are crude core-tools, hoe-like or axe-like in form, perhaps, used for forest clearance and for digging. Cultivation of tubers may have begun at an early date in those West African areas where yams are today the staple food. The plausibility of such a contrast more than 2,500 years ago, between an essentially hunting life-style in the West African savanna and a vegecultural one in the forests, will be further explored in chapter 6.

North Africa and the Sahara

The archaeology of the northernmost parts of Africa has for the most part been studied, because of the region's geographical position, in an essentially Mediterranean, rather than an African, context. The terminology and the conceptual framework conventionally employed thus differ in some important respects from those used in other parts of the continent. In the present work it is the African aspects and connexions that are stressed; and North Africa will thus be shown to have occupied a more central and innovative place in prehistory than some earlier accounts would suggest.

The Acheulian in the Sahara appears to have been followed by an arid phase when many previously inhabited areas were abandoned. Sites in Morocco which have yielded very small hand-axes and cleavers as well as flake tools appear to belong to this arid period: similar artefacts also occur at a few places in the Sahara, notably in south-eastern Libya (Biberson, 1967; Arkell, 1964; J. D. Clark, 1980). With the return of moister conditions, about 100,000 years ago, settlement again became widespread. The industry then prevailing is of the type known as Mousterian or Levalloiso-Mousterian, after its closely similar and broadly contemporary European counterpart. Although small heart-shaped hand-axes occur in some of these North African Mousterian assemblages, light-duty tools are now the characteristic element, being made generally on flakes removed from prepared cores. Side-scrapers and sub-triangular points, perhaps for projectiles, are the most common implement types. This North African Mousterian is best known from the Algerian and Moroccan Maghreb; and it soon developed into its characteristic Saharan form, the Aterian, named after Bir el Ater, near Tebessa, Algeria (Camps, 1974; J. D. Clark, 1980).

The Aterian is most readily recognised by the presence of a variety of flake tools which possess a well-worked tang, which facilitates hafting (fig. 4.15). These include not only specimens which resemble projectile points, but also several scraper types and flakes with little intentional retouch other than that which forms the tang. Aterian assemblages are encountered throughout the Sahara proper, from the Atlantic coast almost as far east as the Nile. In the eastern half of this vast region, and in the south, as at Adrar Bous in Ténéré, bifacial points are a regular component of the Aterian tool-kit (J. D. Clark et al., 1973). Assemblages from later sites in both areas include numerous parallel-sided blades in addition to flakes struck from discoid cores: this marks a technological development parallel to, and perhaps connected with, the advent of mode 4 industries in Cyrenaica (see p. 90). These general observations apart, although several local versions have been recognised, regional and temporal variation within the Aterian complex have not yet been sorted out.

Chronologically, the Aterian period falls within the time-span of the last major northern hemisphere glacial period, when reduced temperatures prevailed in North Africa, resulting in glaciers on the High Atlas mountains and a general spread of vegation zones to lower altitudes. In the Sahara, evergreen vegetation, primarily of Mediterranean species grew in the highlands; and lower evaporation rates ensured that the rivers flowing from these highlands watered the adjacent parts of the otherwise relatively dry intervening plains (van Campo, 1975). In such a situation was the site of Bir Terfawi in the Western Desert of south-western Egypt where, about 44,000 years ago, Aterians living beside a shallow lake were able to hunt a variety of animals, including gazelle, warthog and ostrich (Schild and Wendorf, 1975). Species included ones which are now restricted to the Mediterranean zone as well as some of more southerly affinities: for rhinoceros remains were found on Aterian sites as far to the north as El Guettar in southern Tunisia (Camps, 1974).

From about 38,000 years ago steadily increasing aridity made much of the Sahara progressively unsuited to human settlement and few Aterian sites are

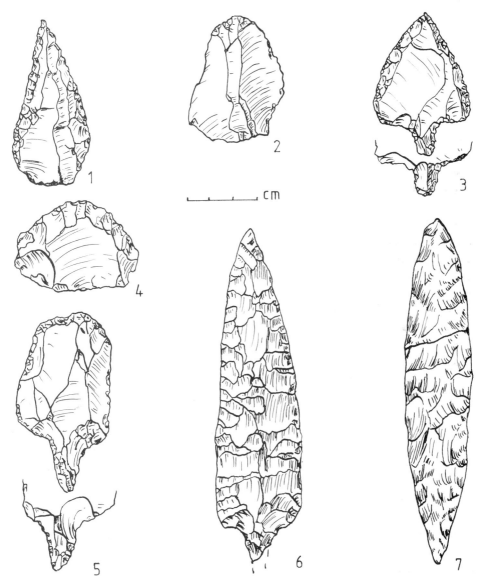

4.15 Aterian implements (after Camps, 1974): 1–5 – from Bir el Ater, 6,7 – from Adrar Bous

significantly later than this. Neither the Nile nor the Niger at this time attained their present courses or extent: the upper reaches of the Niger flowed north-eastwards into the present inland delta where its waters were lost by evaporation. Lake Chad was probably almost completely dry (Williams and Faure, 1980). These conditions, which coincided with the most severe period of glaciation in northern Europe, continued in the Sahara until about 13,000 years ago.

We do not know which human types were responsible for these North African and Saharan industries. At Jebel Ighoud in Morocco and at the Haua Fteah in Cyrenaica fossils akin to European finds of *Homo sapiens neanderthalensis* have been found in association with Levalloiso-Mousterian artefacts (Ennouchi, 1962; McBurney, 1967). By later Aterian times, however, a more fully modern population is attested – as at Dar es Soltan, also in Morocco – of the heavily built Mechta-Afalou type which continued to inhabit the Sahara until much later millennia (Chamla, 1968). The relationship between these two human types is not known, in the absence of any fossils clearly connected with the earlier Aterian industries. Continuity need not be assumed for, at the few sites (such as Adrar Bous in Niger or Bir Sahara in the Western Desert of Egypt) where Aterian occupation is stratified over one of Levalloiso-Mousterian type, there was once again an arid intervening period during which the site was abandoned.

Mention has already been made of the archaeological sequence of Cyrenaica. This part of northern Libya possesses, at the great cave of Haua Fteah, the most complete succession of Upper Pleistocene industries known from any part of North Africa (McBurney, 1967). The oldest levels have not yet been reached by excavation, but it is known that Levalloiso-Mousterian occupation of the cave was established by, at the latest, 60,000 years ago. This industry continued through the period when its counterpart in the Sahara further to the south was replaced by the Aterian. It was preceded, in the lowest levels at Haua Fteah so far reached by excavation, by an apparently quite distinct industry, which has been named the Libyan pre-Aurignacian, based upon the production of parallel-sided blades struck from prismatic cores (fig. 4.16). Its makers were accomplished hunters of wild cattle, gazelle and zebra; unlike their successors they also collected sea-food. This industry is not known from any other African site, although comparable technology is attested in South Africa at broadly the same time-depth. Fairly close parallels have also been suggested in Israel, Lebanon and Syria. Its local precursors in Cyrenaica remain unknown.

After the Libyan pre-Aurignacian phase, Levalloiso-Mousterian occupation of Haua Fteah continued for over twenty thousand years until about 40,000 years ago when it was abruptly replaced by a more developed blade industry, called Dabban after another Cyrenaican site. The Dabban clearly belongs with the great complex of broadly contemporary mode 4 industries in Europe and western Asia conventionally known as the Upper Palaeolithic. Its most characteristic features are backed blades, end-scrapers and chisel-like tools called burins. Here again, the closest connexions of this phase of the Haua Fteah sequence are with the Levant, but it should be noted that it first appeared in Cyrenaica at broadly the same time as the Saharan desiccation, which led to the eclipse of the Aterian. Cooler conditions at this time are also indicated at Haua Fteah. With relatively little change, the Dabban occupation continued until about 14,000 years ago when it was abruptly replaced, possibly with some overlap, by a mode 5 industry known as the Eastern Oranian, characterised by large numbers of small backed bladelets.

This Eastern Oranian, known also from other Libyan sites such as Hagfet et Tera, takes its name from its apparent close likeness to an industry of the Maghreb farther to the west. This latter Oranian industry, more generally known as the Iberomaurusian, is widespread in the North African coastland and hinterland from south of Rabat as far east as Tunis (Camps, 1974; 1975). It was at

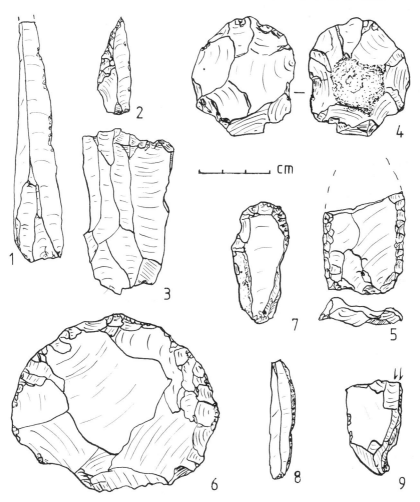

4.16 Artefacts from Haua Fteah (after McBurney, 1967): 1–3 – pre-Aurignacian, 4,6 – Levalloiso-Mousterian, 7–9 – Dabba industry

one time believed that the Iberomaurusian represented the reoccupation of the Maghreb after the period of abandonment following the final Aterian about 30,000 years ago. We now know, however, that the earliest Iberomaurusian of about 16,000 years ago at Taforalt in eastern Morocco was preceded by another blade industry, details of which have not yet been published (J. Roche, 1971). This discovery either indicates continuous human occupation of this part of the Maghreb after the Aterian, or that the Taforalt occurrences were a local ancestor for the Iberomaurusian. So far, the earliest Iberomaurusian occurrences are those located in Morocco and Algeria, for at Tamar Hat on the coast of eastern Algeria an occupation dated to *c.* 20,000-16,000 years ago is attributed to this industry (Saxon *et al.*, 1974).

Remains of the Iberomaurusians have been discovered in several extensive cemeteries, notably Taforalt (which has yielded the remains of 183 individuals), Columnata some 200 km south-west of Algiers, and Afalou bou Rhummel, adjacent to Tamar Hat, on the coast of eastern Algeria. They belong without exception to the Mechta-Afalou type of *Homo sapiens sapiens* which has a long ancestry in North Africa (Chamla, 1970; 1978). This is a further argument in support of a local origin for the Iberomaurusian industry. The Mechta-Afalou people were of medium height, robust build and large brain-size (average: 1650 cubic centimetres). They were buried in an extended or, at later sites, contracted position. At Columnata several skeletons were covered with settings of stones, in one case capped by horns of wild cattle, *Bos primigenius*. The presence in the grave of red ochre and perforated shells indicates, for the first time in the Maghreb, the practice of personal adornment (fig. 4.17).

During the Iberomaurusian occupation, species of pine and oak, which are at present restricted to high altitudes in the Atlas Mountains, were of more general distribution, indicating cooler climatic conditions contemporary with the final stages of the last glaciation. In this environment abundant animal species were available for hunting, and the organisation of this activity may be reflected in the survival of numerous small open-air sites, evidently briefly occupied, which contrast with the large, repeatedly re-occupied cave sites. Barbary sheep were intensively hunted and there is some evidence that, at Tamar Hat, the herds were managed by selective culling as the grazing on the coastal plain was curtailed by rising post-glacial sea levels (Saxon *et al.*, 1974). Land and water molluscs were also collected, particularly in later Iberomaurusian times, following the rise in sea level.

By about 10,000 years ago the Iberomaurusian unity had broken down and several local short-lived blade industries, such as that named Columnatan, are found in the Maghreb. Of particular interest is the so-called Typical Capsian, attested from about 8,500 years ago in a restricted area of the Algeria/Tunisia border country south of Tebessa, as at Relilai. It is characterised by the large size of its artefacts, among which burins and backed blades varyingly predominate. Many of its sites are shell-heaps. Far more widespread, being found as far afield as western Algeria, is the more microlithic Upper Capsian, which is somewhat earlier in date than the Typical Capsian (P. E. L. Smith, 1982). This industry, also, is frequently found on shell-midden sites. At Columnata it replaced the Columnatan about 7,500 years ago; at Relilai it overlay Typical Capsian a few centuries earlier. Crescentic, triangular and trapezoidal backed microliths, backed bladelets and notched or denticulated flakes are the most frequently encountered tool types, together with a variety of bone tools. Much artistic

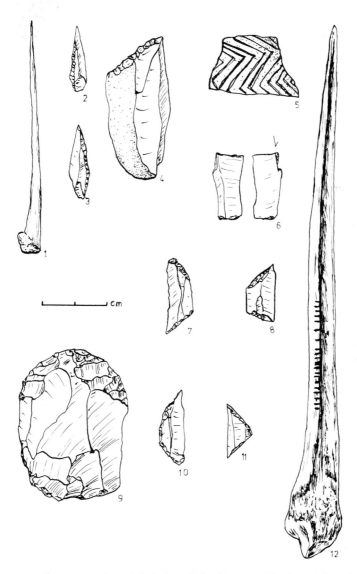

4.17 1–4 – Iberomaurusian artefacts from Taforalt, 5–12 – Capsian artefacts from Relilai and Mechta el Arbi (after Camps, 1974). 1 and 12 are bone points, 5 a fragment of decorated ostrich eggshell

ingenuity was applied to the engraved decoration of ostrich eggshells, and to the carving of stone. Hunting, as well as snail-collecting, is well attested, in an environment which shows the beginning of deforestation. Industries related to the Upper Capsian (which, like its predecessors, was the work of a Mechta-Afalou population, although some skeletons appear related to more recent Mediterranean peoples) are also found in the adjacent Saharan regions (Camps, 1974). This industry and its related variants (such as the Libyco-Capsian attested at Haua Fteah from about 10,000 years ago) continued until the inception of food-production, which will be described in chapter 6.

The Nile Valley

The archaeological sequence of the Nile Valley, even at this early period, differs sufficiently from those of neighbouring areas to merit separate discussion. Furthermore, investigations which originated as rescue operations prior to the flooding of much of Sudanese Nubia by the waters of Lake Nasser have led to a more complete understanding of the complexity of the local prehistory than is available elsewhere.

Post-Acheulian industries of Levalloiso-Mousterian type are best known from the area upstream of Luxor as far as Sudanese Nubia. Traces of its counterpart further downstream have presumably been destroyed by erosion or deeply buried by accumulations of silt. Several successive stages have been recognised of which the earliest – named Mousterian – shows considerable diversity with at least three variants that are believed to reflect different activities (Wendorf and Schild, 1976). In one of these variant Mousterian industries small hand-axes occur, although never in large numbers. Wild cattle (Bos primigenius) was the preferred prey at these sites, which are too old to be dated by the radiocarbon method.

Later Mousterian assemblages show some Aterian affinities and are presumed to be broadly contemporary with that complex in the desert to the west. These artefacts show accomplished use of the Levallois technique, with a few tanged pieces and also bifacial leaf-shaped points similar to those of the southern Saharan Aterian at Adrar Bous. At Arkin near Wadi Halfa are factory sites at the raw material outcrops, where the leaf-points were roughed out (Chmielewski, 1968). Nearby, at Khor Musa, is a contemporary occupation site where, for the first time, most of the food debris is the remains of fish (Wendorf, 1968). Further to the south, near Khartoum, a comparable industry has large, elongated foliate points akin to those of the Lupemban, which may indicate an extension of the equatorial forest environment along the valley of the White Nile at this time (J. D. Clark, 1980).

Another site at Khor Musa has given its name to the final phase of this group of industries, where the earlier artefact types are accompanied by blade tools and burins of the same general type as those in the Libyan Dabban industry. The Khormusan is broadly contemporary with the Dabban and with the period starting about 40,000 years ago when the Sahara became uninhabited (fig. 4. 18). This industry occurs on extensive sites where both fish and land mammals were eaten (Wendorf, 1968).

Following the Khormusan, about 25,000 years ago, began a period where the prehistory of the Nile Valley is characterised by numbers of even more diverse local industries of restricted distribution both in time and space. One of the

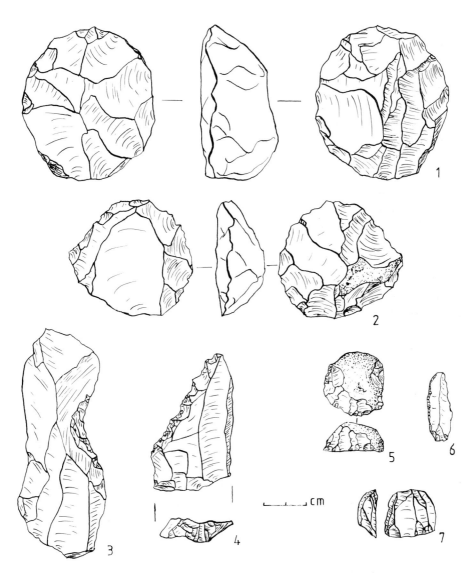

4.18 Artefacts from Nubia (after Wendorf, 1968): 1–4 – Khormusan, 5–7 – Halfan

earliest of such industries, the Halfan, is found on hunting/fishing camps in the Wadi Halfa area. Its tools, made on small blades, are in clear contrast with those of the Khormusan, which it eventually replaced (Marks, 1968). Downstream, in Upper Egypt, the time-span of the Halfan is taken by non-microlithic industries grouped under the name of Edfuan, in which blade technology accompanies a continuation of the Levallois technique. At Wadi Kubbaniya near Aswan, intensive use of vegetable foods is attested by about 18,000 years ago, although the claim for the early use of barley at this site (Wendorf *et al.*, 1980) has been disproved by subsequent research (Wendorf, 1984). From about 17,000 years ago the industries become progressively more microlithic, as with the Fakhurian which is contemporary with the later Edfuan and Halfan (Lubell, 1974).

These markedly disparate industries co-existing at the same time so close together suggest that we are dealing not merely with activity variants, but with the presence of distinct population groups. Perhaps, in the closely circumscribed habitat provided by the Nile Valley, pressure of numbers was already stimulating technological innovation as part of the competition for control of, or access to, resources. This same process may have stimulated social contact and reinforced group differentiations, identity and rivalry. This situation continued into the period from about 15,000 to 11,000 years ago when there was a rise in water level in the Nile contemporary with the high lakes in the Sahara and East Africa. These, and the important economic innovations which accompanied them, are the subject of chapter 5.

The foregoing survey of the post-Acheulian stone-tool makers in North Africa, the Sahara and the Nile Valley has brought out two main points. First, throughout the whole of this area except the Mediterranean littoral, the distribution and nature of human settlement has been largely dependent upon changing environmental conditions. Major manifestations of this dependence are that settlement apparently ceased in much of the Sahara during the arid period following the florescence of the Aterian, and the dense concentration of occupation in parts of the Nile Valley. Secondly, and in part causally related, at a remarkably early date a sidespread series of innovative practices evolved, in order to maximise the food-yielding capacity of the natural environment. These developments were intimately connected with the presence of closely circumscribed communities which, as is reflected in their material culture, showed considerable ingenuity in adapting their life-style to varied situations. In later times, as will be shown in chapter 5, similar developments are found over a far wider area.

Changing life-styles and technology

At first sight, this chapter has presented a bewildering mass of data of very varying quality, ranging from the results of modern, scientific excavations to details pieced together from observations of undated surface occurrences. It is now necessary to stand back from the details in an attempt to view the picture as a whole.

Despite obvious local variations, broadly speaking, technological developments followed parallel courses throughout Africa – as, indeed, in other parts of the Old World. The general course of this development has been outlined in the introductory section of this chapter and need not be repeated here. We should, however, note the distinctive industries of the Congo basin and adjacent densely forested regions. There, the Sangoan, Lupemban and Tshitolian industries preserved, long after its displacement elsewhere, the large-core-tool tradition which had its roots in the Acheulian. But, as chapter 3 has shown, the prepared-core or Levallois tradition which is characteristic of the contemporary industries of other parts of Africa can equally be traced far back in Acheulian times. Diversity through parallel evolution seems here, as in the later part of the time-span to which this chapter is devoted, to have been established. We are hampered by the absence of adequate information on the diet of the makers of the Sangoan and Lupemban. It is tempting to suggest that gathering and digging up vegetable foods was more important for these people than for those who lived in more open savanna lands, where hunting remained the mainstay of the economy.

More truly innovative, perhaps, was the eventually almost ubiquitous backed-microlith technology which involved far more economical use of raw material, and the facility to repair or modify tools without resorting to their total replacement. In parts of north and north-east Africa, as in the Near East and elsewhere, this is best and conventionally seen as a development from mode 4 blade industries in which techniques for making backed retouch were frequently practised. Further to the south in Africa, however, backed microliths appear in the Howieson's Poort industries at dates which are significantly earlier than those known for comparable technology elsewhere in the world. Archaeologists are still far from being able to explain why these parallel technological developments should have taken place; simple diffusion from a common source is unlikely.

These early southern African developments are accompanied by the oldest examples yet known of fossils attributed to modern man, *Homo sapiens sapiens*. In most other parts of the continent, human fossils and precise age-determinations are too few to allow us to compare local human evolution, but at least in North Africa it appears that the contemporary population included individuals of neanderthal type. The early emergence of *H. s. sapiens* in Africa, together with the general picture of post-Acheulian continuity noted above (p. 59), contrasts with the sequence in much of Eurasia, where a pronounced discontinuity in the archaeological record is generally associated with the first local appearance of fully modern man at least 60,000—35,000 years ago. Recent genetic research among modern populations (A. C. Wilson *et al.*, 1985) has suggested that *H. s. sapiens* spread from Africa into Eurasia at least 90,000 years ago. The implication that our species as a whole originated in Africa and expanded from there to replace or incorporate earlier hominid populations in other parts of the world is in accord with the archaeological interpretations here proposed.

In several areas where the development of backed-microlith technology may be pinpointed in the archaeological record, there may also be seen an accompanying shift to the hunting of smaller creatures, often more solitary species, such as frequent a more closed habitat than the larger gregarious herbivores that were preferred prey in earlier times. Such an association may be seen in Zambia at the time of the emergence of Nachikufan I and, later, with the appearance of the earliest Wilton industry of the south Cape coast of South Africa. In the Maghreb, the Iberomaurusian also appears at a time when wooded environments reached their maximum extent. Clearly, no single cause-and-effect correlation should be proposed here, but this is one explanation of the adoption of lighter hunting equipment such as that produced by backed-microlith technology. Later, of course, the very ubiquitousness of such technology shows that it could be used in a very wide range of environments.

Throughout the period discussed in this chapter the archaeological sites in most parts of Africa are both larger and more numerous than may be explained by the fact that they were preserved with less disturbance or obliteration than earlier sites. There is evidence that a wider range of environments was exploited by man, and that there was a progressive increase in the size of human populations both at a local and continental level (R. B. Lee, 1963).

In overview, during this period of African prehistory, virtually all parts of the continent were at least sporadically occupied by man, some of them for the first time. This in itself indicates that man had become more adaptable and consciously responsive to environmental and other pressures. The obvious result of this adaptability was the steady proliferation of local industries and the accompanying faster rate of cultural change that may be recognised in the archaeological record. Demographically, it led to increases both in the size of individual groups and in overall population levels. A corresponding acceleration in the development of non-material culture is indicated, for example, by the burial customs, artistic traditions and the personal adornment that has been preserved. By the end of this period many of the foundations for the diverse richness of later African cultures had already been laid.

CHAPTER 5

THE BEGINNINGS OF PERMANENT SETTLEMENT

The Nile Valley

With much of the Sahara being still unsuited for human habitation, the relatively favourable environment afforded by the Nile Valley some 18,000 years ago allowed the population to increase within a narrowly defined area. Competition for resources and socio-political demarcation were the largely inevitable result of such processes. We must now examine the relevant archaeological evidence in greater detail (fig. 5.1).

By this time, as shown in chapter 4, a number of localised lithic industries developed in the Nile Valley, suggesting the presence of distinct closely circumscribed communities with specialised and intensive exploitation of food resources. The best documented and also one of the earliest incidences of this development is at Wadi Kubbaniya near Aswan.

During the period of high Nile levels, which lasted from about 15,000 until about 11,000 years ago, one of several contemporaneous Nubian industries, the Qadan, shows a good deal of variation in the percentage frequencies of the various microlithic tool types found at different sites. This reflects the varied activities carried out by the population, who evidently fished, hunted wild cattle and other large ungulates, and also made considerable use of wild grains. This last food-source is indicated by the presence on Qadan sites of large numbers of grindstones and also by the fact that many of the microliths bear on their edges the characteristic polish known as sickle-sheen which, it has been demonstrated, may result from their being used to cut grasses (Witthof, 1967). The Qadan people buried their dead in cemeteries at one of which, Jebel Sahaba, a substantial proportion could be shown to have met violent deaths. This is perhaps a further indication of territoriality and inter-group conflict (Wendorf, 1968).

To the north, further downstream, other industries of this time, such as the Sebilian with its trapeziform microliths, and the Sebekian, present a similar picture of pronounced variability. On the plain of Kom Ombo, for example, at least three distinct groups are attested and the available food resources were comprehensively exploited: those of the plain itself, the surrounding desert, the river and its wooded fringe (P. E. L. Smith, 1967). Some Kom Ombo sites seem to have been occupied on a year-round basis and here, too, wild grasses were harvested. At Esna in Upper Egypt pollen analysis suggests that wild barley

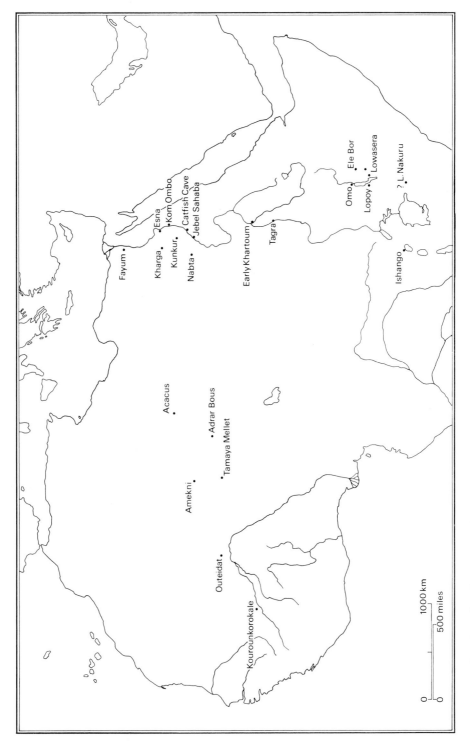

5.1 Location of settlement sites discussed in chapter 5

was, by 12,000 years ago, one of the varieties gathered on the flood plain (Wendorf and Schild, 1976). Several of the animal species whose bones are represented in the food debris from sites of this period would have had a circumscribed habitat and this may have enabled man to experiment with the development of management techniques over wild or semi-wild herds. These important innovations may be seen, at least in part, as responses to the concentration of population in the Nile Valley brought about by desiccation of the surrounding deserts.

The Nile Valley industries between 12,000 and 8,000 years ago are poorly illustrated by the research that has so far been undertaken. Thereafter the Nubian stone industry is of the microlithic type known as Shamarkian, which includes small numbers of Ounanian points – pointed bladelets with basal retouch – such as also occur in Saharan industries of this time, as will be shown below (fig. 5.2). By 7,000 years ago, at Catfish Cave near Abu Simbel in southern Egypt, a Shamarkian-like stone industry was associated with specialised fishing equipment in the form of bone harpoon heads barbed along one edge (Wendt, 1966). Such objects are widely distributed at sites in the Sudanese Nile Valley, in the southern Sahara and in parts of East Africa, and have received undue emphasis from some archaeologists (Sutton, 1974), who have suggested that they may indicate a unified 'civilisation' based upon the exploitation of aquatic resources. As has been shown above, these sites do not mark the beginning of intensive fishing; at least in the Nile Valley, this had already been practised for several thousands of years.

Nubia lay on the northern fringe of the area occupied by the harpoon-fishers. Very little is known about contemporary inhabitants of the Egyptian Nile Valley, but the Fayum Depression between 7,000 and 8,000 years ago was the scene of

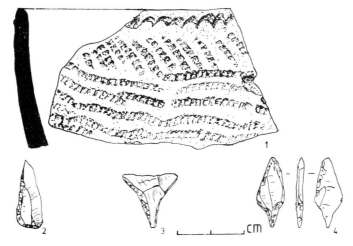

5.2 Artefacts from Nubia (after Wendorf, 1968): 1 – Khartoum-related pottery, 2–4 – Shamarkian microliths (4 is an Ounanian point)

lakeside camps of people who made microlithic artefacts, mounted fish jaws as points for arrows, and made their livelihood by a combination of hunting and fishing (Caton-Thompson and Gardner, 1934; Wendorf and Schild, 1976). This Qarunian occupation beside the extensive lake which formerly occupied the Fayum Depression provides examples of arrow-manufacturing techniques which continued in use in Egypt into dynastic times.

It is from the Khartoum area that we have our most detailed knowledge of the inhabitants of the Nile Valley at this time. By 8,000 years ago this part of the valley was occupied by hunters and fishers who made use of substantial base-camps, probably occupied for much of the year, such as that which is known as Early Khartoum (Arkell, 1949). (The local antecedents of its population remain unknown.) At Early Khartoum the stone industry included scrapers, backed microliths and larger tools, for which the name 'crescent adzes' has been proposed. They are thought to have been used for the shaping of spear- or harpoon-shafts or similar wooden objects. Bone harpoon heads, barbed on one

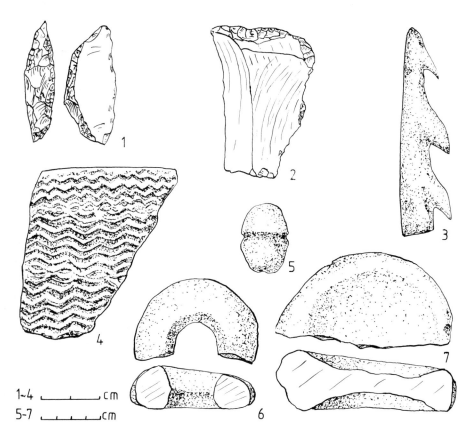

5.3 Artefacts from Early Khartoum (after Arkell, 1949): 1 – backed microlith, 2 – scraper, 3 – barbed bone harpoon head, 4 – potsherd with wavy-line decoration, 5 – grooved stone interpreted as weight for a fish net, 6 – stone ring, 7 – grindstone

side only, were also a characteristic part of the assemblage. Stone rings and other objects, best interpreted as weights for nets, suggest that harpooning was not the only method by which fish were taken. Pottery was common at Early Khartoum, generally decorated with multiple-grooved wavy lines, which may be duplicated experimentally by dragging a catfish spine over a surface of wet clay. During the later phases of the site's occupation, these designs were elaborated by jabbing the clay with a pointed object to produce a series of impressed dots (fig. 5.3).

Traces of sun-dried daub were recovered, suggesting that structures of some sort were erected there. Fishing and hunting were both important subsistence activities; and the presence of several swamp species in the faunal assemblage shows that Khartoum was significantly wetter than it is at the present time. The dead were buried, in contracted positions, in graves within the settlement. Early Khartoum was excavated before the development of radiocarbon dating techniques, so its age remains uncertain but probably falls between 6,000 and 8,000 years ago. A related but presumably earlier site with harpoons but no pottery, at Tagra on the White Nile some 200 km to the south, is dated to about 8,300 years ago (Adamson *et al.*, 1974).

To the north, in Nubia, pottery seems to have remained unknown until late Shamarkian times, around 6,500 years ago. There can thus be no reasonable doubt that, whatever the origin of the Early Khartoum pottery (and this will be discussed below), it does not represent a technology that spread up the Nile from Egypt. Comparable pottery does occur further to the south, despite a substantial gap in its known distribution between the Sudanese Nile Valley and Lake Turkana in northern Kenya.

East Africa

With one significant exception, the relevant East African sites are located around Lake Turkana and may be linked with the fluctuating high levels of its waters during the early Holocene (Butzer, 1971). The waters of the lake rose rapidly around 10,000 years ago to a level 80 m above the modern one, which gave it nearly twice its present surface area and maintained an overflow channel to the north-west which eventually connected with the Nile. Deposits in the Omo Valley of southern Ethiopia, which represent a major northerly extension of Lake Turkana at this time, have yielded bone harpoons from levels dated to between 8,000 and 10,000 years ago (Brown, 1975). More detailed information concerning the makers of these artefacts comes from several sites located near the 80 m beach lines on the north-east, south-east and south-west sides of the lake in Kenya (Robbins, 1974). At Lowasera (fig. 5.4) to the south-east, harpoons were in use by 9,000 years ago; there is evidence elsewhere for a brief period of significantly lower water levels between about 7,500 and 6,800 years ago (D. W. Phillipson, 1977c). Before this interval pottery was rare and of wavy-line type;

after it sherds are much more abundant and generally undecorated. In the Lake Turkana basin the earlier harpoons have a nick at the base for the attachment of the line. The later ones used several concentric carved rings for this purpose (fig. 5.5). The associated stone industry was, throughout, a mixture of backed microlithic elements and of large scrapers and choppers, with a few grindstones. Food remains consisted almost exclusively of the bones of fish, crocodile and hippopotamus. The second harpoon-fishing phase continued until after 4,500 years ago, by which time the waters of Lake Turkana were again falling; there are, indeed, indications that a similar life-style continued at Lopoy, west of the lake, until less than 1,000 years ago, when the lake stood at about 18 m above its present level (Robbins *et al.*, 1980). Elmolo people of the Lake Turkana littoral still fish by means of barbed harpoons, now with iron heads.

Apart from inconclusive hints from the Lake Nakuru basin in southern Kenya, the only other part of East Africa to have yielded evidence for harpoon fishermen is that around Lake Edward on the border between Uganda and Zaire. Here, we are concerned with a single site, Ishango on the north-western shore, which has preserved a long sequence of occupation, although its dating remains uncertain. Bone harpoon heads occurred throughout, at first barbed on both sides, latterly on one side only. The crude stone industry, of quartz, included scrapers and some backed microliths. There was no pottery. An age between 11,000 and 6,000 years ago appears likely, but is not proven. Conditions

5.4 Old beach deposits at Lowasera, 80 m above the present water level of Lake Turkana. The volcano, Mount Kulal, is in the background

wetter than those of the present are once again indicated by the animal bones that were preserved in the deposits; because of its outlet Lake Edward is less susceptible to changes in water level than is Lake Turkana, and its level at this time was only about 10 m above that which prevails today (de Heinzelin, 1957).

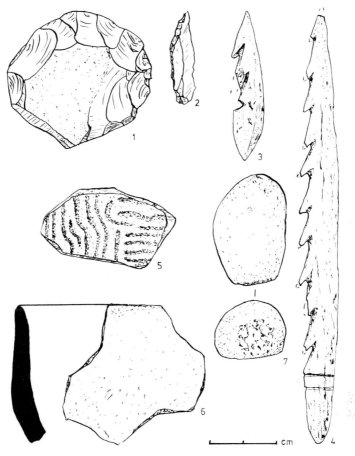

5.5 Artefacts from Lowasera (after D. W. Phillipson, 1977c): 1 – scraper, 2 – backed microlith, 3 – barbed bone harpoon head of early type with basal nick for attachment of the line, 4 – barbed bone harpoon head of later type with basal grooves, 5 – early potsherd with wavy-line decoration, 6 – later undecorated potsherd, 7 – hammerstone

The southern and central Sahara

It was noted in chapter 4 how the greater part of this area had little or no human settlement during the arid period which broadly corresponded with the coldest part of the last northern-hemisphere glaciation. There are clear geomorphological traces, such as now-consolidated sand dunes, which indicate that the desert at this time extended even further to the south than it does today.

Shortly after 12,000 years ago there was a remarkably rapid return to better watered conditions. Increased run-off from the highlands coupled, presumably, with higher rainfall and decreased evaporation resulted in the return of a regular flow of water to the long-dry wadis, the great enlargement of existing swamps and lakes – notably Chad – and the formation of many new ones (Street and Grove, 1976). There were corresponding changes in vegetation and in the distribution of wild animals. The reasons for these substantial changes are not fully understood. One of their most puzzling features is the rapidity with which they took place: the lakes appear to have reached their maximum heights as early as about 11,000 years ago.

Little research has yet been done on archaeological sites which may confidently be attributed to the first human settlement of the Sahara during these better climatic conditions. No such sites are yet known which are certainly more than 10,000 years old, but it will be surprising if earlier occurrences are not eventually discovered. From Mauretania to the Western Desert of Egypt, the earliest post-Aterian industries contain basally retouched Ounanian points akin to those noted above in Shamarkian contexts in the Nile Valley. Assemblages of this type from the Western Desert, as at Kunkur Oasis, also contain many roughly trimmed flake-scrapers but no backed microliths; though the latter artefacts are important components of contemporary assemblages at Nabta Playa and Kharga Oasis (Schild and Wendorf, 1977). At all these sites the presence of grindstones suggests that here, as at many Nile Valley sites of the same period, cereal grains – presumably wild – were harvested and prepared for use as food. A similar industry occurs at Adrar Bous in the Ténéré Desert of Niger. The degree of similarity between these Saharan industries and broadly contemporary material from southern Tunisia, such as the Upper Capsian, supports the view that the initial repopulation of the Sahara may have taken place from the north. Whatever the population source, it is clear that, although numerous and widespread, the Saharan sites of this time were individually of limited extent and briefly occupied, indicating a population of small mobile groups (J. D. Clark, 1980).

By 8,000 years ago significant changes had taken place. Fishing and the exploitation of other aquatic food resources now played a much larger part in the economy of a vast area of the central and southern Sahara from the Nile Valley at least as far to the west as Mali. Sites were now concentrated on the shores of rivers and lakes which were significantly higher and more extensive than those of today. Although at most sites hunting and grain-collecting were continued on a reduced scale, the pre-eminence of fishing now allowed larger populations to remain for longer periods of time at individual sites. Bone harpoon heads, as described above at Early Khartoum, were the characteristic artefacts indicative of this new development. Pottery is also present at most sites of this type: it usually bears the idiosyncratic wavy-line decoration which serves as another link with Early Khartoum. In the Sahara, such pottery may appear at a slightly earlier date than in the Nile Valley, being attested between 8,500 and 9,500 years ago, at Acacus in southern Libya, Tamaya Mellet west of the Air Mountains of Niger (A. B. Smith, 1980), and Amekni (fig. 5.6) in the extreme south of Algeria (Camps, 1969). Further to the west, in Mali, wavy-line pottery occurs also at Outeidat near Timbuktu (Gallay, 1966), and barbed bone harpoons at Kourounkorokale near Bamako (Szumowski, 1956).

The available radiocarbon dates indicate a strong possibility that this early Saharan pottery was a local invention, there being no reliable evidence for any earlier material in adjacent areas from which the necessary technology could have been derived. Such an interpretation is fully plausible, since the accompanying relatively settled life-style, also an independent development, would

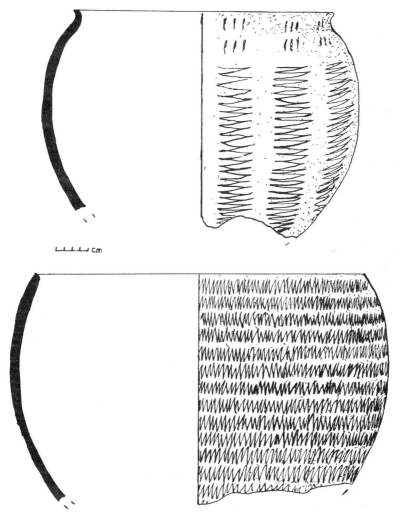

5.6 Pottery from Amekni (after Camps, 1974)

have made possible the adoption of heavy fragile receptacles. These were very useful in a semi-permanent settlement but would have been ill-suited to the more mobile life-style of earlier times.

Overview

These settled communities represent economic adaptations over a very wide area that parallel similar processes of environmental change. At least in the Nile Valley, there had been for some millennia previously a tradition of intensive exploitation of various food resources, including aquatic ones, in circumstances which sometimes encouraged prolonged settlement of a particular site. Nevertheless, the Nile Valley does not appear to have been the original homeland of the harpoon-fishing adaptation. On the evidence currently available the East African material of this type may have been the earliest, although unfortunately the Ishango site, with its early biserially barbed harpoons, cannot be dated precisely. There can likewise be little reasonable doubt that pottery, the earliest in Africa, was an independent invention of the harpoon-fishers, perhaps in the southern Sahara.

Many of the bone-tipped harpoons were used for fishing, but it cannot be assumed that this was invariably the case. At Daima, in north-eastern Nigeria, a bone harpoon head was found embedded between the bones of a human skeleton, so such weapons were, at least in later times, occasionally used against human targets (Connah, 1981).

Despite the basic typological similarity over a very wide area of both the bone harpoons and the pottery, the associated chipped-stone industries show considerable variation. They appear generally to be rooted in distinct local traditions which may be traced back into earlier times. For this reason it seems most satisfactory to regard these industries as representing a common adaptation (or parallel adaptations, with many shared features) to a common economic opportunity, rather than to consider them as belonging to a single uniform culture.

The fishing settlements, being concentrated in location, are the most readily recognised archaeological sites of this time. Their inhabitants were able to exploit enormously rich sources of food that was obtainable with very little effort. Other means of livelihood were, however, pursued both alongside fishing and on different sites, away from permanent water. Hunting and, probably, grain collection continued in the Sahara. In northern Kenya, as at Ele Bor, hunters maintained their traditional life-style without pottery long after this had been adopted on the lakeside fishing settlements (D. W. Phillipson, in press).

The full importance of the innovations represented by the harpoon-fishing adaptation and of the settled life-style that accompanied it can only be

appreciated fully when we consider the subsequent adoption of food-production. This will be discussed in detail in chapter 6.

Africa 10,000 years ago

This is an appropriate point to view the overall distribution of African prehistoric
communities at a single time, before effective food-production is attested in the
northern half of the continent. We will also examine the evidence for the
distribution of human physical types at this time and enquire to what extent we
can recognise populations that were ancestral to more recent ones (fig. 5.7).

The modern indigenous population of Africa comprises several varied physical types, the distinctions between which are frequently ill-defined. We will
briefly investigate the extent to which this diversity may be traced back in the
archaeological record. Several writers (e.g. Hiernaux, 1968; 1974) have stressed
the difficulty of defining discrete recent populations even on the basis of a
complete range of physical characteristics, including such features as finger
prints and blood groups. For past populations effectively our sole source of
information is fragmentary skeletal material. Furthermore, since African populations have lived in close contact with one another for many thousands of years,
it is inherently highly improbable that any population will have retained in
unmixed form the physical characteristics of any prototype which may formerly

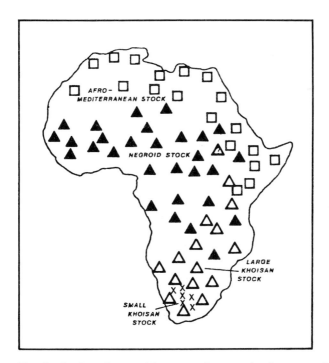

5.7 The distribution of recent African populations (after Brauer, 1978)

have existed. Yet it is such non-homogeneous populations which have, per-force, to form the basis for our recognition of the groupings concerned.

There are thus major problems not only of recognition but also of definition. These problems have led some authorities to ask whether it is reasonable for archaeologists to attempt to identify discrete human physical types ancestral or related to those of the present day. It is nevertheless widely recognised that there are metrical skeletal features, notably of the skull, which are generally more characteristic of one population than of another. Although observed ranges of variation frequently overlap, the ranges noted in a prehistoric population may show a close degree of fit with those of a particular recent group; the affinities of isolated individuals are correspondingly difficult to determine. Bearing these many hazards in mind, it is worthwhile to survey the views that have been proposed for the affinities of final Pleistocene/early Holocene African populations.

In the Maghreb the Iberomaurusian hunter-gatherers were replaced by the makers of the varied microlithic industries which eventually gave rise to the Capsian. It was presumably at this time also that people of proto-Mediterranean type first appeared in North Africa alongside the Mechta-Afalou folk, who seem to have been the sole inhabitants of the region during Iberomaurusian times. The skeletal features of these two populations are relatively well known from the remains preserved in the extensive cemeteries noted in chapter 4. The Mechta-Afalou people were probably a branch of an ancient African population; their successors are related to the recent caucasoid inhabitants of the circum-Mediterranean lands. These proto-Mediterranean people may have been at least partly responsible for the resettlement of the northern Sahara following the post-Aterian period of desiccation.

To the south, the harpoon-using fishermen of the central and southern Sahara, the Sudanese Nile Valley and parts of East Africa are represented by a few fragmentary skeletons from Ishango, Lothagam on Lake Turkana (Robbins *et al.*, 1980), Early Khartoum and elsewhere which are said to show negroid physical features. Similar characteristics occur in skeletons from the Qadan cemetery at Jebel Sahaba in Nubia (Wendorf, 1968), where Mechta-Afalou features have also been recognised. These remains may be from a population ancestral to present-day Nilotic negroids. Other authorities, emphasising the presence of features which are also seen in Khoisan and north-east African caucasoid populations, prefer to interpret this material as representing a more generalised 'ancestral African' physical type, which may be regarded as akin to a common ancestor of several more recent populations. This explanation also seems plausible for the varied human remains that have been recovered in association with broadly contemporary and rather later industries from southern Kenya (Rightmire, 1975).

The archaeology of this period in West Africa remains poorly understood, being covered by only one dated sequence, that of Iwo Eleru in south-western

Nigeria. In this area the hunter-gatherer people of the forest margin had adopted a backed-microlith technology akin to that of the neighbouring savanna. Elsewhere in the West African forest regions non-microlithic stone-tool manufacture continued. A single human skeleton (fig. 5.8), some 12,000 years old, from the lowest level at Iwo Eleru has been described as already showing specifically negroid features (Brothwell and Shaw, 1971). In other parts of West Africa, skeletal material has not been preserved. The same is unfortunately true of the whole of the Congo basin and adjacent forested regions where the distinctive Tshitolian industries had by this time developed.

On the southern savanna many areas had seen the practice of backed-microlith technology for many thousands of years. By 10,000 years ago related industries had been adopted by hunter-gatherers in most of the region except, it appears, in areas of the arid South African interior and parts of the upper

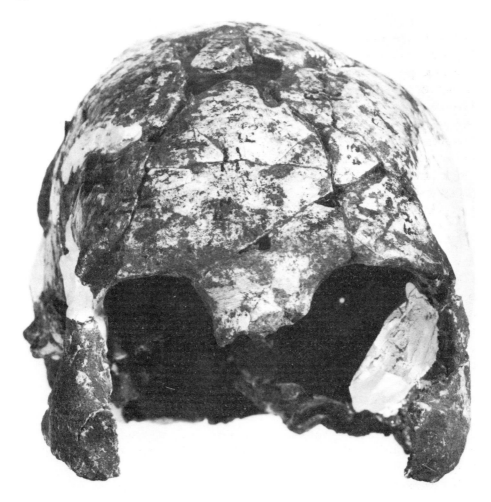

5.8 Human skull from Iwo Eleru

Zambezi Valley to the north. Substantial numbers of human skeletons have been recovered in association with these industries, particularly noteworthy (although late) being the group of 33 individuals of *c.* 5,000–3,000 years ago from Gwisho hotsprings in southern Zambia and a somewhat earlier series from graves in cave sites on the south Cape coast. There can be little doubt of the Khoisan affinities of most of this material. However, some skeletons, particularly from north of the Zambezi, are also stated to show features characteristic of recent southern African negroid populations (e.g. de Villiers in D. W. Phillipson, 1976). This observation serves to emphasise the difficulties in a continent where for many millennia few barriers to miscegenation have existed. Such links do little more than reinforce the view that both Khoisan and negroid stocks are derived from a single generalised African ancestral population (Tobias, 1978c).

By the early Holocene, it thus appears possible to make the first tentative correlations between communities represented in the African archaeological record and the ancestors of some modern populations. The principal physical types recognised in recent indigenous populations turn up in the archaeological material, where the distinctions between them are no more clear than they are between the modern groups. What we see in the incomplete archaeological picture so far available is the gradual process of differentiation of modern human types from ancestral populations that were genetically as mixed as those of the present day.

CHAPTER 6

EARLY FARMERS

Food-production

So far we have discussed the stages of human development during which man relied for his livelihood on the foods provided by his natural environment – on the meat of wild animals and fish, and on wild vegetable foods. In Africa, as in other parts of the world, man has been exclusively a forager for more than 99 per cent of his existence.

It has been shown in chapters 4 and 5 how, from as early as 12,000 years ago, some Nile Valley communities in Upper Egypt may have been making relatively intensive use of cereal foods. These practices may have been accompanied by care of wild grasses by such means as control of weeds, clearance of ground and, perhaps, occasional provision of water. Under these circumstances sowing might also have been employed to increase the density of growth in the tended places and to extend the areas colonised by the wild plants. With or without conscious selection for desired qualities, such practices would in due course have led to the development of crops morphologically distinct from their fully wild prototypes (cf. Zohary, 1969). By such means, some of the late Pleistocene peoples of the Nile Valley seem on occasion to have exploited wild cereals, but there is no evidence that true cultivation was developed at this time. These are among the earliest instances of intensive cereal utilisation that have yet been demonstrated anywhere in the world, and there can be no reasonable doubt that they were indigenous African achievements. But they did not lead to the widespread adoption of such practices at this early date. A later section of this chapter will offer some speculation as to why this was so.

Food-production did not become widespread in the northern half of Africa until about the sixth millennium B.C. By that time plant cultivation and animal domestication had both been long established in the Near East. Although it is not easy to show to what extent some early food-production practices in northern Africa were derived from the Near East, it is clear that many developments both here and further to the south were autochthonous (Harlan, 1982). In this context it is particularly illuminating to consider from where the wild forms of the various plant and animal species that were eventually domesticated came. It has for long been assumed that cultivated wheat, barley and flax were all introduced into Africa from the Near East, but it is now known that wild barley and einkorn wheat occur in several areas of Egypt where their food-value was recognised from very early times. If we exclude crops such as maize and cassava (manioc), which are known to have been introduced from the New World within the last five hundred years, and those such as bananas brought somewhat earlier across the Indian Ocean, most of the crops which are or have been cultivated in Africa are species that are indigenous to that continent and which must presumably have been first cultivated there. Examples are the more important types of yam, African rice, and the cereals sorghum, finger millet, bulrush millet and teff, together with the Ethiopian plants ensete and noog (fig. 6.1), all of which are derived from plants which grow wild in the sub-Saharan latitudes. It will be noted from this list that indigenous African food-crops fall into three primary categories: rice, other cereals, and vegetatively propagated plants such as yams and ensete. Each of these categories requires a distinct method of cultivation, and there is no reason to believe that the development of these horticultural modes was in any way interconnected. Much discussion of early African food-crops centres on the cultivation of cereals, because of the nature of the primary evidence and its greater chances of preservation, but cereals did not necessarily come first.

In the case of domestic animals the position is somewhat different. Sheep and goats have no African wild prototypes, for it has been shown that the Barbary sheep cannot have given rise to any known domestic types (Epstein, 1971). Cattle present more difficulties, and could be descended from wild forms in North Africa and/or the Near East. Perhaps in due course light will be thrown on this problem by bone studies more detailed than those which have so far been undertaken (cf. Carter and Clark, 1976). An added complication is that it is often difficult to differentiate between sheep and goats on the basis of the fragmentary bones that are recovered from archaeological sites, and references

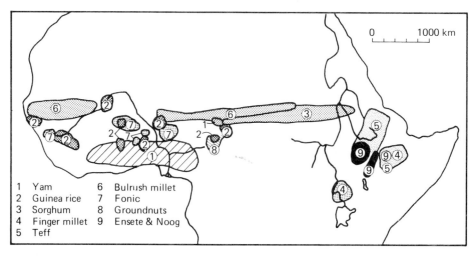

1 Yam   6 Bulrush millet
2 Guinea rice   7 Fonic
3 Sorghum   8 Groundnuts
4 Finger millet 9 Ensete & Noog
5 Teff

6.1 The probable areas of the initial domestication of indigenous African crops (after Harlan, 1971)

to 'sheep/goat' or to 'small stock' in later sections of this book will indicate remains which cannot be attributed with confidence to the correct species. It is, however, abundantly clear that none of the major domestic animals of sub-Saharan Africa are derived from species that are indigenous to that part of the continent; they must therefore have been introduced from elsewhere.

Here, it is appropriate briefly to evaluate the types of archaeological evidence that may be accepted as proof of ancient food-production. By far the most convincing are the actual remains of cultivated plants or domestic animals, or unequivocal artistic representations of them. Pollen grains or seeds may be preserved under appropriate conditions, or impressions of seeds may occur on pottery. Some food-plants, such as yams, will by their very nature hardly ever be represented in the archaeological record, and this leads, as noted above, to undue emphasis often being given to the better preserved evidence for cereal cultivation. Furthermore, plants generally will tend to be under-represented in comparison with animals, whose bones are relatively indestructible.

Domestication of both plants and animals eventually give rise to physical differences which serve to differentiate the domestic forms from their wild prototypes. The domestication process involves deliberate selection and control of breeding. For example, preference will be given to the largest yams or to cereals which do not shed their seeds as soon as they are ripe, but retain them when harvested. Animals of docile temperament, often of small size, will more readily be incorporated in controlled herds. Thus, after a few generations, significant physical differences will have been established. It follows from this that the initial stages of domestication are correspondingly difficult to recognise in the archaeological record. Furthermore, it now appears highly probable that the emergence of fully food-producing economies was the result of a far longer period of intensive exploitation and experimentation than was previously realised. The distinction between hunting and gathering on the one hand and food-production on the other is thus far from distinct.

Archaeological evidence for food-production, other than actual food remains, is far less convincing. The evidence of artefacts is often ambiguous: sickles and grindstones for instance could have been used for gathering and preparing wild cereals, or for different materials altogether.

Despite the elusiveness of the evidence, the importance of the adoption of food-production techniques should not be under-emphasised. Possession of such techniques gave man greater control than he had generally possessed over his own food supply. Although concentrated natural resources had in earlier times occasionally allowed him to maintain semi-permanent settlements, these were usually small. In several areas food-production seems to have been adopted in response to environmental deterioration and population pressure; and it in turn enabled populations to increase still further. The relatively settled life which is inherent to most forms of agriculture (but not, of course, to pastoralism) provided a stimulus for the accumulation of material possessions beyond those which could readily be transported. A sedentary life-style could also have facilitated increased child-bearing, as pregnancy and nursing are a hindrance to mobility. Communities could now more readily afford to maintain members who specialised in activities other than the obtaining of food. The increased sizes of these communities and the frequency with which they came into contact with their neighbours must often have necessitated the development of political structures more complex than those which had existed among the simpler societies of earlier times.

Such developments were not, of course, automatic. On the one hand they help to explain how such a complex civilisation as that of ancient Egypt arose apparently less than 2,500 years after food-production was first regularly adopted on a significant scale in the Nile Valley. On the other hand, in many areas of Africa, peasant communities have been able to maintain themselves without centralised state systems into recent times. Nor must it be thought that food-production, once adopted, led to the rapid abandonment of hunting and gathering. Both activities continued to play an important part in most pre-colonial African economies, while a few communities have maintained an exclusively hunting–gathering life-style. With low population densities, such as have prevailed in many parts of Africa until recent times, the natural resources are such that hunting and gathering provide a level of nutrition as high as, or higher than, that achieved by farming peoples (R. B. Lee, 1968). It is nevertheless true that food-production has provided the economic basis for most of the major technological, artistic and socio-political achievements of African culture during the past 7,000 years.

The Sudanese Nile Valley

Despite the evidence, described in chapters 4 and 5, for early experiments with cereals, the permanent adoption of food-production techniques in the Nile Valley is known only from a relatively late date. In the Khartoum area there is no indication that any form of food-production was practised before the early fourth millennium B.C. Recent research has shown that the settlement pattern at that time was one of unanticipated complexity.

The first relevant site to be excavated was that of Esh Shaheinab, 50 km north of Khartoum (Arkell, 1953). The industry represented is clearly a development of that seen at Early Khartoum (p. 102). The site had a river-bank location and fishing was evidently of major importance. Barbed bone harpoon heads were now pierced at the base for attachment of the line, and shell fish-hooks were also in use. Axes and adzes, finished by grinding, were fashioned from both bone and stone (fig. 6.2). Both the microlithic stone industry and the pottery resemble those from Early Khartoum, but the pottery was now burnished and also included new types resembling contemporaneous pre-dynastic Egyptian wares. Beads were made from amazonite which appears to have been traded from

Tibesti, over 1,700 km distant. The bones recovered, in addition to those of fish, were mostly of wild species, but a dwarf variety of domestic goat was also represented in very small numbers.

It is now known that food-production in the central Sudanese Nile Valley at this time was not restricted to the small scale suggested by the investigation of Esh Shaheinab. This is demonstrated, for example, at the nearby site of Kadero, which covered an area of 4 ha on the edge of the flood plain north-east of Khartoum (Krzyzaniak, 1978). Here, at the same time as the occupation of Esh Shaheinab, cattle were herded in very large numbers along with sheep and goats: about 90 per cent of the animal bones recovered from this site were of domestic species. There were enormous numbers of heavily used grindstones.

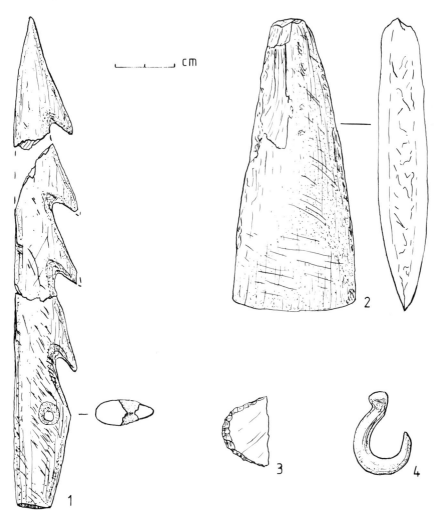

6.2 Artefacts from Esh Shaheinab (after Arkell, 1953): 1 – barbed bone harpoon head with pierced base, 2 – bone adze, 3 – backed microlith, 4 – shell fish-hook

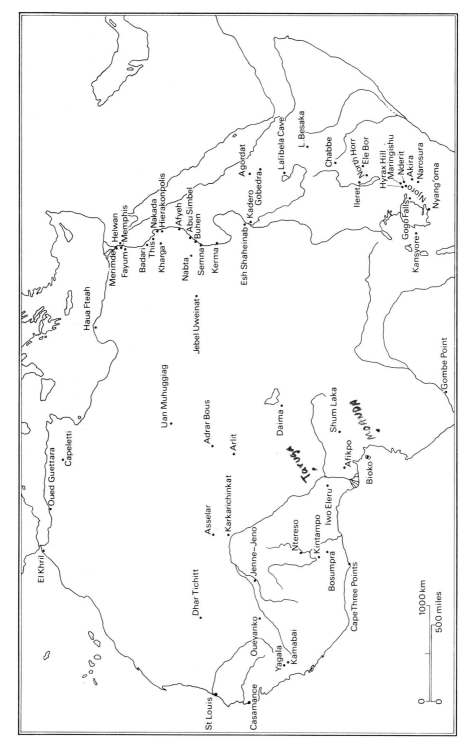

6.3 Location of sites with evidence for early food-production

Grain-impressions on pottery showed that sorghum, finger millet and panicum were the principal grains used. It is not completely clear whether sorghum and finger millet were cultivated, but in any case they were clearly gathered on a substantial scale. Hunting and fishing were both of marginal importance. The dead were buried within a circumscribed area. The Kadero site, by its size and evidence for prolonged use, may be regarded as a base settlement. Other sites in the locality were occupied by smaller groups on a seasonal basis, for different economic activities, including fishing. The overall picture which is emerging from current research is of a community which occupied several different sites on a seasonal cycle, using various food resources according to their availability, possessing large numbers of domestic animals and perhaps also cultivating cereals at some of their locations. This example provides an excellent demonstration of the dangers in drawing detailed conclusions from the investigation of single sites which may yield very incomplete pictures of ancient life-styles.

Downstream, pottery which seems to be related to that from Esh Shaheinab occurs at a number of sites in the Dongola region and extending into Nubia, where it is sometimes associated with the stone industry known as Abkan. In Nubia the earliest fully food-producing community is that known to archaeologists as the A-Group (fig. 6.4). The Abkan affinities of the stone artefacts found on A-Group sites, together with some features of their pottery, suggest that the A-Group was of indigenous Nubian origin; it was nevertheless greatly influenced by contact with the contemporary later pre-dynastic peoples of Egypt (p. 124). Trade between the two areas was extensive, with Egyptian flint and a wide range of manufactured goods including stone vessels, copper tools, palettes, amulets and the like finding their way southwards. It was presumably raw materials such as ivory and skins that went to Egypt in exchange. The A-group people are known mainly from their graves, which occur in large cemeteries and show burial customs similar to those which prevailed in Egypt. Sheep and goats were herded, with smaller numbers of cattle. Wheat and barley were cultivated; linen cloth was in use, but may have been imported from Egypt rather than made from locally grown flax. Fishing and hunting were both practised. Although many people lived in insubstantial shelters, others – perhaps an elite – were housed on a grander scale, as at Afyeh near the First Cataract, where an A-Group settlement consisted of rectangular houses with up to six rooms, dating to about 3000 B.C. (Adams, 1977). The reasons for the end of the characteristic A-Group settlement at about the time of the end of the First Dynasty in Egypt (*c.* 2900 B.C.) are poorly understood. For several centuries Egyptian contact with Nubia was at a reduced level, although a Fourth Dynasty raid (*c.* 2500 B.C.) is recorded as having resulted in the capture of 7,000 people and 200,000 domestic animals (Breasted, 1962).

From Sixth Dynasty times (*c.* 2300 B.C.) onwards Nubian archaeology is again better known. The indigenous population is known as the C-Group (Trigger, 1976). Particularly in the south, there is evidence for cultural continuity between the A-Group and the C-Group, but connexions have also been noted between the latter and people living east of the Nile, in the Red Sea hills. Although domestic cattle clearly occupied an important place in the lives of the C-Group, as shown by figurines and representations on pottery, faunal remains suggest

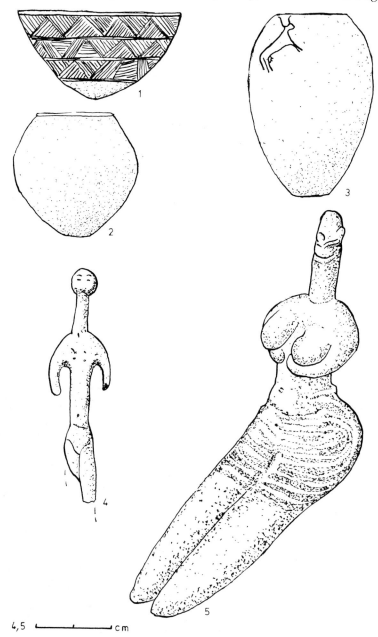

6.4 A-Group artefacts from the Wadi Halfa area (after Nordström, 1972): 1–3 – types of pottery vessels, not to scale, 4,5 – human figurines

that their herds also included numerous small stock. Settlements were initially small and consisted mainly of large circular houses with the bases of their walls built of stone. More complex structures are attested in later times. Egyptian luxury goods were imported, but on a moderate scale.

In Middle Kingdom times (2000–1600 B.C.) the Egyptians established a military occupation of northern Nubia and erected a series of forts, as at Semna and Buhen, to secure Egyptian control of trade and access to the area's gold deposits. This control extended into Upper Nubia, upstream of Wadi Halfa, into the area that became known as Kush, with its centre at Kerma near the Third Cataract.

For reasons that are not known to us, but which may be connected with political troubles in their homeland, the Egyptians retreated from Nubia under the Thirteenth Dynasty, late in the eighteenth century B.C. This period correlates with the rise of a rich culture at Kerma, located in the most fertile part of Sudanese Nubia at the northern end of the Nile's Dongola Reach. Kerma's powerful rulers were buried, accompanied by the bodies of numerous retainers, under large grave mounds up to 80 m in diameter (fig. 6.5). Great wealth was evidently accumulated through Kerma's control of wide-ranging trade and a remarkable level of craftsmanship was attained, particularly in pottery. Egyptian

6.5 The brick substructure of one of the royal burial mounds at Kerma

stylistic influences remained strong but many local features are apparent (Reisner, 1923; Adams, 1977).

Early in the Eighteenth Dynasty (c. 1500 B.C.) Nubia was re-occupied by the Egyptians, the old forts repaired, and Kush conquered. This time the Egyptianisation of Nubia was cultural as well as political, as is witnessed by the temple of Ramesses II at Abu Simbel, erected in the thirteenth century B.C. (fig. 6.6). Both the C-Group culture and its Kerma variant withered away. In about the ninth century B.C., the viceroys of Kush ceased to be Egyptian appointees and an independent kingdom of Kush came into existence. In the eighth century the king of Kush conquered Egypt and established the Twenty-fifth Dynasty.

The Egyptian Nile Valley

Probably owing to the abundance and reliability of wild food resources there, and despite much early experimentation, the beginning of food-production on a significant scale in the Egyptian Nile Valley seems to have been abrupt and late in comparison with its inception in the Western Desert (p. 131). In the delta and in the Fayum Depression small villages of farming people broadly resembling those from adjacent parts of south-west Asia were established from about 5000

6.6 The temples at Abu Simbel, before clearing and restoration (after Gau, 1822)

B.C. (fig. 6.7). That at Merimde on the western side of the Nile delta is an example (Baumgartel, 1955). It covered an area of some 18 ha and consisted of small oval dwellings measuring only about 2 m by 3 m, built of lumps of mud mixed with straw, sunk slightly into the ground and presumably originally roofed with reed thatch. These structures were set on either side of narrow lanes and interspersed with mud-lined storage pits, basket granaries and open shelters which appear to have been used as workshops. The dead were buried within the settlement in mat-lined graves. Bifacially flaked stone tools and undecorated pottery serve to link this settlement with its counterparts in the

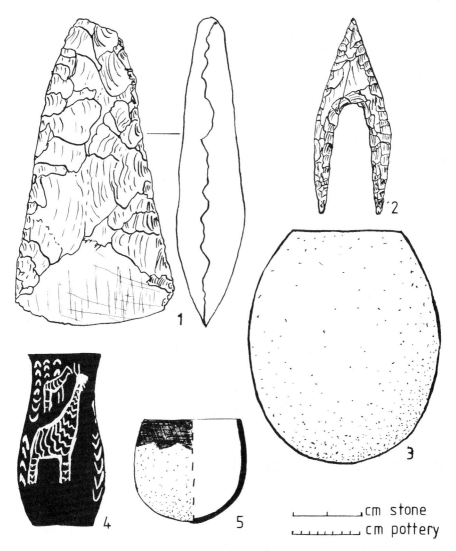

6.7 Pre-dynastic Egyptian artefacts (after Arkell, 1975): 1–3 – ground axe, arrow-head and pot from Fayum, 4 – Nakada I pot, 5 – Badarian bowl

Fayum Depression (Caton-Thompson and Gardner, 1934). The economic basis for these Lower Egyptian settlements was the cultivation of barley, emmer-wheat and flax. Cattle, sheep, goats and pigs were kept, as were dogs. The donkey, an indigenous African species, was first domesticated in the Nile Valley at about this time. Hunting and fishing continued to be practised. Although the Fayum settlements may have been of short duration, that at Merimde and allied sites such as those near Helwan were clearly occupied on a permanent basis, with food-production on a substantial scale supporting communities which probably numbered well over a thousand persons (Hoffman, 1980). In such circumstances specialist craftsmen were able to establish themselves, and non-utilitarian products such as stone vessels and objects for personal adorn-ment proliferated.

Subsequently there arose the Egyptian cultures conventionally known to archaeologists as pre-dynastic, because they were prior to the sequence of numbered dynasties that form the chronological framework for the literate civilisation of ancient Egypt. For many years the pre-dynastic cultures were known mainly from their graves, and their ordering and chronology were based upon detailed typological studies of their pottery. A succession of closely related industries was thus proposed, consisting of Badarian, Nakada I (Amratian), Nakada II (Gerzean) and Nakada III. The earlier phases occur in the 200 km stretch of the Nile Valley south of Asyut; their descendants spread rapidly both to the north and to the south. It is only in recent years that significant settlement sites of the pre-dynastic period have been investigated. Of prime importance is the town at Hierakonpolis, 100 km north of Aswan: estimates of its population vary greatly but it is likely to have held well over 5,000 people. Other settlements include those of Badari and Hamamiya. Both round and rectangular houses are attested. The food-producing economy followed the pattern of the earlier sites, with the cultivation of barley and emmer-wheat and the keeping of domestic cattle and small stock, supplemented with hunting, fishing and the gathering of wild plant foods.

Technological advances at this time included the development of methods of superb pressure-flaking to impart a regular rippled finish to stone tools. Fine stone vessels were now carved from basalt, alabaster and even porphyry. Occasional small copper objects appear early in the pre-dynastic period, mainly pins and beads; they seem to have been produced by hammering native (unsmelted) metal. In later pre-dynastic times, from Nakada II (c. 3600 B.C.) onwards, techniques of copper-smelting were introduced, presumably from western Asia where they had been known for many centuries, and flat axes, daggers and knives were cast. Fine basketry was made, linen was woven and the simple black-topped pottery was now supplemented by more elaborate wares with painted decoration (Hoffman, 1980; Hassan, 1980).

The general trend through much of the fourth millennium B.C. was one of steady development of centres such as Hierakonpolis, Nakada and This, with increasing evidence for craft specialisation and social stratification. It appears that these centres, and many others, each became the nucleus of a small state, with its own king and patron deity. By about 3100 B.C., or slightly before, the kings of This established themselves as rulers, or pharaohs, of the whole of the Egyptian Nile Valley north of Aswan, thus becoming the first of the thirty dynasties which provide the conventional framework for the history of ancient Egypt (James, 1979) (fig. 6.8). The unification of Egypt was not achieved without conflict, and the First Dynasty pharaohs are often depicted as conquerors or plunderers. Concurrently with these political developments there was a marked florescence in crafts and industries, which must have been connected with the start of extensive trade in raw materials. We now find for the first time evidence for contact with the older literate civilisations of Mesopotamia, and certain Egyptian innovations in art and technology – including methods of building with bricks – may owe much to the latter area. It was even formerly suggested that the Egyptian state system itself may have been of Mesopotamian inspiration, but it is important to emphasise its unique local character. The same is true of the Egyptian hieroglyphic script which developed under the First Dynasty (fig. 6.9).

A detailed description of ancient Egyptian civilisation lies beyond the scope of this book, but I will summarise some of its essential features (Aldred, 1961; James, 1979; J. D. Clark, 1982b). The first point which requires emphasis is the civilisation's remarkable continuity through three thousand years. The second is its great material wealth, based both upon the annual Nile flood laying down

Period	Dynasty	Date B.C.
Early Dynastic	I	*c.* 3100–2890
	II	*c.* 2890–2686
Old Kingdom	III	*c.* 2686–2613
	IV	*c.* 2613–2494
	V	*c.* 2494–2345
	VI	*c.* 2345–2181
First Intermediate	VII–XI	*c.* 2181–1991
Middle Kingdom	XII	1991–1786
	XIII	1786–1633
Second Intermediate	XIV–XVII	1633–1567
New Kingdom	XVIII	1567–1320
	XIX	1320–1200
	XX	1200–1085
Late Dynastic	XXI	1085–945
	XXII–XXIII	945–730
	XXIV–XXV	730–656
	XXVI–XXXI	664–332

6.8 The chronology of ancient Egypt

fertile silts which supported the agriculture needed to feed the population concentrated in the narrow valley, and upon large-scale external trade.

The head and epitome of the Egyptian state was the divine ruler, the pharaoh. The whole complex bureaucracy of the state was ultimately responsible to him and, particularly in the earlier periods, senior officials were often members of the royal family. The pharaoh was also the figurehead of the official religion, the personification of the sun-god Ra, counterpart of Osiris the god of the land of the dead. Preparation for life after death was of immense importance to the ancient Egyptians, as is shown by the complex efforts made to protect deceased bodies by mummification and to immure them with many belongings in elaborate tombs. As a result, archaeological research for many years tended to concentrate on the tombs of the dead rather than on the settlements of the living. The royal tombs in particular reflect the great wealth and concentration of resources, both human and material, at the pharaohs' disposal, whether they were buried in the mighty pyramids of the Old Kingdom or the hidden underground chambers of the New Kingdom (fig. 6.10).

In evaluating the structural achievements and technological skill of the ancient Egyptians it is necessary to remember the limitations under which they worked. The wheel was unknown before the New Kingdom, yet the pyramids, for example, were built of stone blocks weighing over 2.5 tonnes, presumably

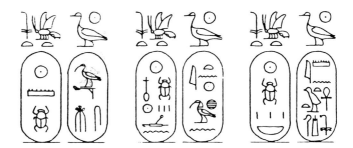

6.9 Ancient Egyptian hieroglyphic writing. Egyptian hieroglyphic writing was developed about 3100 B.C. and continued in use with remarkably little change until the end of the fourth century A.D. Its meaning seems to have been forgotten soon afterwards and it was not re-deciphered until the early nineteenth century.

It incorporates some seven hundred signs. Most of these are ideograms – simplified pictorial representations of the concepts to which they relate. Some of these ideograms also had a phonetic value representing one or more consonants. (Vowels were not indicated in ancient Egyptian writing, so it is often not possible to ascertain the original pronunciation.) Often ideograms and phonetic symbols were combined, for example *depet* – meaning 'boat' – could be written ⟨hand = d⟩ ☐ (stool = p) ⌒ (loaf = t) (boat). Reading is further complicated by the fact that words were not divided and that inscriptions could be written from left to right, right to left, or vertically.

Royal names may be recognised by their inclusion in an oval shape or cartouche, as in the examples above which give, from left to right, the names of the Eighteenth Dynasty pharaohs Tuthmosis III, Akhenaten and Tutankhamun.

moved and erected with the aid of rollers and levers. Copper, bronze and gold were effectively the only metals used, for iron did not come into regular use before the Twenty-sixth Dynasty in the eighth century B.C.

Much of our information about ancient Egyptian history comes from the records that were carefully maintained by the Egyptians themselves, notably by the priests who were regarded as the guardians of the state's accumulated wisdom. The value of this source of information was recognised in ancient times, as by the Greek historian Herodotus in the fifth century B.C. Scenes of everyday life, at least for the upper classes of society, were often depicted on the walls of tombs. Here we see representations of the ships which carried Egypt's trade along the Nile and further afield. We see the huge bands of labourers – enslaved foreign captives and peasants providing work as a tax-payment – on whom the state's public works depended. It is from this source also that we obtain our sole information about another little-understood aspect of Old Kingdom culture: the capture and taming of animals such as gazelle, oryx and even perhaps giraffe (J. D. Clark, 1971; see also fig. 6.11). Ancient Egypt was responsible for major advances in knowledge in such fields as literature, mathematics, medicine and law (J. R. Harris, 1971), discussion of which falls outside the scope of this book.

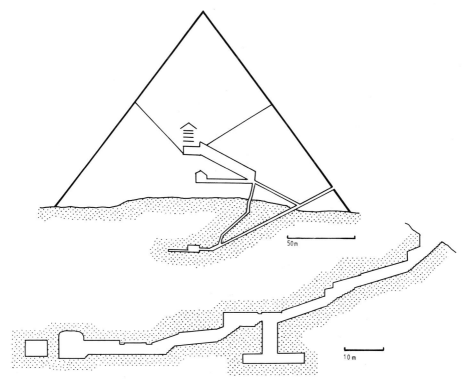

6.10 Egyptian royal graves (after James, 1979): top – pyramid of Khufu, Fourth Dynasty, below – rock-cut tomb of Seti I, Eighteenth Dynasty

The political history of ancient Egypt may be summarised briefly. Since much of our information comes from contemporary written sources our knowledge of this topic is of a different order of detail from that which is available for other parts of Africa at this time; the chronology is also known with far greater precision.

After the Early Dynastic period, during which the unification of the Egyptian state was consolidated, the accession of the Third Dynasty in about 2700 B.C. marks the start of the first great period of prosperity, the Old Kingdom. Through patronage and control of trade, power and wealth were effectively concentrated in the hands of the ruling dynasty. This is reflected first and foremost in the scale at which resources and manpower were devoted to state works, notably to the construction of pyramids for the burial of deceased pharaohs.

By later Old Kingdom times the pharaoh's control over the state bureaucracy seems to have weakened, and the proportion of Egypt's resources that was devoted to royal works was consequently diminished; for example, the Fifth Dynasty pyramids were smaller than those of the Fourth Dynasty. Shortly after 2000 B.C., following a period of contraction from the peak of Old Kingdom prosperity and wide-ranging trade, Egyptian political unity broke down during the First Intermediate period of some two centuries. Famine may have added to the general impoverishment of this time. Reunification under the Eleventh Dynasty heralded the Middle Kingdom, based at a new capital near Thebes. Egypt's authority in Nubia was further strengthened at this period, as shown by the erection of the forts which have been noted above.

The new-found stability was short-lived, however, and during the Thirteenth and Fourteenth Dynasties there was a rapid succession of pharaohs as different factions competed for supremacy. Early in the resultant Second Intermediate

50 cm

6.11 Relief carving at Kalabsha, Nubia (after Gau, 1822), showing the taming of wild animals including gazelle and other antelope, ostrich, monkeys and a big cat, perhaps a leopard

period a group of invaders from Palestine – the so-called Hyksos rulers – took advantage of Egypt's weakness and established themselves in Lower Egypt as the Fifteenth Dynasty in about 1670 B.C. The rise of independent Kerma, described above, may also be seen as a result of Egyptian weakness at this time. Increased frequency of trade-goods of Palestinian origin, particularly in the delta, indicates greater contact with south-west Asia during the period of Hyksos rule.

Eventually, a dynasty (the Seventeenth) from Thebes in Upper Egypt expelled the Hyksos rulers and re-established Egyptian unity and independence. The New Kingdom which followed marked the greatest florescence of ancient Egyptian power and prosperity. Egyptian control was re-established over Nubia as well as over substantial areas of the Near East, all governed by a complex imperial bureaucracy set up by the pharaoh Tuthmosis III (fig. 6.12). Egyptian trade ranged far and wide, even to the Land of Punt in eastern Africa (p. 140). During the Eighteenth Dynasty occurred the remarkable reign of the pharaoh Akhenaten, who attempted to impose monotheism in place of the traditional pantheistic religion. Akhenaten's successor was the young Tutankhamun, the only pharaoh whose grave has survived virtually undisturbed and unrobbed, to reveal the full richness and splendour which surrounded the New Kingdom rulers.

From the Twenty-first Dynasty onwards, Egypt's cohesion once again broke down, and from the eleventh to the seventh centuries B.C. Libyan, Asian and Nubian contenders vied with Egyptians for control of the state. The Twenty-fifth

6.12 The Eighteenth-Dynasty pharaoh Tuthmosis III

Dynasty originated in Kush and finally, as will be described in chapter 7, lost control of Egypt to an invasion from Assyria, after which ancient Egypt never regained its independence.

North Africa

On the North African coast, to the west of the Nile, the advent of food-production is best illustrated at Haua Fteah in Cyrenaica (McBurney, 1967). Here, by the early sixth millennium B.C. or shortly thereafter, the local Libyco-Capsian stone industry was followed by a period of occupation during which the economy of the site's inhabitants was based upon their herds of domestic sheep and/or goats. There is no evidence for the presence of domestic cattle at this time. The artefact assemblages show signs of continuity from the underlying Libyco-Capsian, with pottery in evidence from c. 5000 B.C., but it is clear that the domestic animals must have been introduced to the area from elsewhere – presumably from the Near East. Not only does Haua Fteah provide no evidence for the gradual development of pastoral techniques, but the sheep/goats that were herded there were clearly not descended from the wild Barbary sheep which is their only possible local progenitor, and which was in fact intensively hunted by the Libyco-Capsians. The evidence for the beginnings of food-production in Cyrenaica was thus at least as early as that for the Nile delta region. There is no evidence that cereal agriculture, which was practised in the delta, was known further to the west at this time.

In the Maghreb, pottery appeared in the context of the Capsian-related stone industries by the sixth millennium B.C. From this time onwards the somewhat diverse industries north of the Atlas Mountains and extending eastwards to Tunisia have generally been classed by archaeologists as 'Neolithic of Capsian tradition'. In fact, several distinct traditions may be discerned. In northernmost Morocco, adjacent to the Straits of Gibraltar, the earliest pottery, as at El Khril near Tangier, is decorated with impressions of cardium shells, in a manner widespread in the western Mediterranean coastland (Jodin, 1959). To the east in coastal Algeria the pottery at Oued Guettara is impressed at the rim with sticks or plant stems (Camps, 1974). Throughout this area it seems likely that the introduction of domestic small stock was broadly contemporary with the beginning of pottery manufacture: bones of small stock are present from the lowest levels of El Khril. At Capeletti Cave in the Aures Mountains of eastern Algeria, transhumant pastoralism was practised from the fifth millennium B.C. onwards by people who had as yet no knowledge of cereal agriculture (Roubet, 1979). The local species of cattle may also have been domesticated by the third millennium. The human remains found associated with these 'Neolithic' industries are predominantly of Mediterranean type, and it has been suggested that some of these people were directly ancestral to the more recent Berbers (McBurney, 1975; Camps, 1982).

The Sahara

The earliest food-producing communities in the Egyptian Western Desert appear to have been direct descendants of their late Pleistocene predecessors, described in chapters 4 and 5. The microlithic stone industries of the two phases are very similar and have more in common with contemporary assemblages to the north than with those of the Nile Valley to the east.

It is important not to overestimate the lushness of the environment which prevailed in the Western Desert, as elsewhere in the Sahara, when food-production began. There was undoubtedly more surface water than in earlier or more recent times, but this was concentrated in and around the highland areas, or in localised lakes or ponds. On the plains between these well-watered areas the vegetation remained very sparse, and the fauna consisted of such creatures as ostrich and gazelle, which can survive in arid conditions. More varied faunas, like the human population, were concentrated around the ponds and other better-watered places.

The first food-production in the Western Desert is best known from Nabta Playa, a pond-basin of 100 km² near the Egyptian–Sudanese border. The sites that were occupied around 7000 B.C. were more extensive than their predecessors of only a thousand years earlier and their distribution was more markedly restricted to the pond margin. The stone industry was essentially the same as it had been in earlier times, but with the addition of concave-based arrow-heads such as those from the Fayum. Pottery makes its appearance, bearing stamped decoration resembling in some respects that from Early Khartoum. Hunting of the wild fauna evidently continued, but cattle are now also represented and are believed to have been domestic. Plant remains, abundantly preserved in these lacustrine deposits, included two types of barley, one of which was domestic, as well as provisionally identified sorghum. Other plants were dom palm, date palm and several types of weed which are known to flourish in cultivated ground. The Nabta barley is the earliest confirmed occurrence of a domestic plant in the continent of Africa. It is evident that the sites' inhabitants were indigenous to the area rather than new arrivals from elsewhere, and that they continued the hunting-and-gathering economy of their predecessors. However, they had acquired by 7000 B.C. some domestic animals and plants; domestic sheep or goat are additionally attested at a broadly contemporary site at Kharga Oasis some 300 km north of Nabta (Wendorf and Hassan, 1980).

During Neolithic times in the eastern Sahara, as in the Nile Valley, people seem to have experimented with the control of wild animals, including ante-lopes and giraffes. The evidence for this comes from rock art, notably that at Jebel Uweinat in south-eastern Libya, which unfortunately cannot be dated (fig. 6.13). Giraffes are shown tethered and being led by halters (van Noten, 1978). With the concentrations of human and animal populations which are attested it is easy to see how such experimentation could have taken place. Animals thus controlled may have been taken to the Nile Valley, where they are known to have been in demand.

In most of the central Sahara there is less convincing evidence for continuity between the earliest food-producers and their predecessors – who in this case included harpoon-using fishers – than was the case in the Western Desert. Around 6000 B.C. a relatively brief period of desiccation may have resulted in the reduction of human populations or even the temporary abandonment of some areas. After this interval the inhabitants, who at several sites may now be shown to have been herdsmen, had significantly weaker connexions with their contemporaries in the Nile Valley than had been maintained in earlier times.

One of the earliest dated occurrences of domestic animals in the central Sahara is at Uan Muhuggiag in the Acacus, where the skull of a domestic shorthorn ox is dated to about 5000 B.C., although at a nearby site the same industry extends back some seven centuries further. Sheep/goat were also present at about the same period. At Uan Muhuggiag rock paintings of cattle, buried in the archaeological deposits, are demonstrably earlier than 3400 B.C. (Mori, 1965; Shaw, 1977). There were numerous grindstones but no positive evidence that cereals – or any other plants – were cultivated; intensive use of wild cereals

6.13 Rock engravings at Jebel Uweinat, showing tethered giraffes (after van Noten, 1978)

seems probable. The associated stone industry and pottery are characteristic of that found on sites of this time over an enormous area of the Sahara, although regional variants may readily be recognised.

One such variant is the Ténéréan, best known from Adrar Bous and Arlit in Air but extending eastwards to Borkou in Chad (fig. 6.14). The industry dates between 4500 and 3300 B.C., the earliest date relating to the skeleton of a domestic shorthorn ox from Adrar Bous (J. D. Clark *et al.*, 1973; Carter and Clark, 1976). Domestic small stock were also herded but the sole evidence for plant cultivation, other than the ubiquitous grindstones, consists of a single impression on a potsherd of a grain that is thought to be sorghum. Hunting was also important, and the prey included warthog, antelope, hippopotamus and rhinoceros. Pottery and ground stone axes show some resemblance to those from the Nile Valley sites of Esh Shaheinab and Kadero. Backed microliths were abundant. Projectile points and disc-shaped knives were bifacially flaked.

Our knowledge of the early Saharan pastoralists may be amplified by study of the rock paintings and petroglyphs which are widely distributed in the highlands. Only rarely has it proved possible to date individual paintings precisely, but several attempts have been made to distinguish stylistic sequences, notably in the Hoggar, Acacus and Tibesti highlands. These sequences may then tentatively be linked by their subject-matter with the archaeological succession to provide a provisional chronology. That most generally accepted suggests that line-engravings of exclusively wild animals comprise the oldest art, extending back at least as far as the eighth millennium B.C. The later paintings show human figures with characteristic round heads (perhaps seventh millennium) overlapping in time with the so-called bovidean paintings in which pastoral scenes are frequently shown and which are believed to date between the sixth/seventh and second millennia B.C. Later styles are marked by the successive appearance

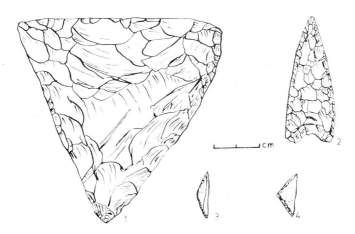

6.14 Artefacts from Adar Bous (after Camps, 1974): 1 – bifacial triangular knife, 2 – bifacial projectile point, 3,4 – backed microliths

of horses and camels (P. E. L. Smith, 1968; Willcox, 1984). The art shows many details of clothing and illustrates the domestic, social and ritual life of the Saharan pastoralists. Breeds of cattle may also be recognised, as may the practice of artificial deformation of the horns which has continued in the Sahara, as in parts of East Africa, into recent times. Milking and use of cattle for riding are also depicted (Muzzolini, 1986).

To the south-west the beginning of pastoralism seems to have taken place rather later, as shown in the Tilemsi Valley which enters the Niger from the north near Gao. In the upper part of the valley, cattle herders lived at Asselar in about 3300 B.C., but they probably did not penetrate the previously uninhabited flood plains to the south until early in the second millennium, when the Karkarichinkat sites were occupied. At these sites cattle were represented both by abundant bones and by clay figurines. Fishing, hunting and fowling were also attested, but there was no evidence for the cultivation of any vegetable foods (A. B. Smith, 1974). This movement down the Tilemsi Valley may be regarded as the first stage of the southward spread of cattle-herding into West Africa (see p. 139).

The late date of the first food-production in the western Sahara is well illustrated at Dhar Tichitt on the southern edge of the desert in south-central Mauritania. This is within the area of the natural distribution of wild sorghum and bulrush millet. Detailed research has distinguished eight successive phases of occupation preceding the appearance of iron. During the first phase, which probably extended back beyond 2500 B.C., the economy was based upon hunting, fishing and collecting beside then-extensive lakes. After a period of abandonment the area was re-occupied about 1800 B.C. by people who, to judge by the style of their pottery, were direct descendants of the earlier inhabitants. They were now herders of both cattle and goats. By the last quarter of the second millennium, desiccation led to shrinking of the lakes, and cereal collection is indicated at the extensive villages of the Naghez phase, where people made use of a variety of wild grasses of types that are still eaten today in times of famine. Grain-impressions preserved on potsherds have provided an excellent basis for the study of changing patterns of cereal collection and cultivation. In the succeeding Chebka phase, after 1200 B.C., bulrush millet suddenly became the most frequent cereal represented, and was clearly of a domestic type. The sites of this phase were both larger and more numerous than the earlier ones, and were located not on the lake-shores but high on the neighbouring escarpment, where each village was surrounded by a defensive stone wall. Competition among an increasing population for use of a restricted area of arable land may be the reason for this sudden and pronounced change. By about the fifth century B.C., bulrush millet accounted for over 90 per cent of the grain impressions, and at this point the Dhar Tichitt sequence came to an end, apparently as a result of an invasion by iron-using peoples from the north (Munson, 1976).

Although detailed conclusions should not be drawn from the very incomplete coverage of the research that has so far been undertaken, the radiocarbon dates so far available from the Sahara may indicate a gradual expansion of knowledge of food-production techniques from the north and east to the south and west. In the process domestic animals were introduced into areas where their species were previously unknown, and indigenous African plants were brought under cultivation.

West and Central Africa

It may be shown botanically that many of the food-crops traditionally cultivated in the western sudanic region are species that are indigenous to the sub-Saharan latitudes. Among the cereals the most important are bulrush millet, fonio and various types of sorghum. The homelands of these species extend in a broad belt from the Nile Valley to Senegal, as shown in fig. 6.1. Essentially different techniques are used for the cultivation of African rice in the valleys of the Niger and Benue. The propagation of yams, which is presumed to have originated near the northern fringes of the West African forests, involves distinct methods yet again. It is not necessary to postulate a common source for these varied types of indigenous African agriculture. Unfortunately, conclusive archaeological evidence for early cereal cultivation is scarce, for rice extremely rare and for yams non-existent. In the last case, physical traces of the crop itself are highly unlikely to survive in the archaeological record, and the traditionally used artefacts are almost all perishable.

In West Africa as a whole, predominantly mode 5 stone industries, such as were described in chapter 4, continued in use until the beginning of iron-working. However, an important change is attested from about 4000 B.C. onwards, when two previously unknown cultural items make their appearance. These are pottery and ground stone axe-like or hoe-like implements (Shaw, 1977). There is no evidence for the practice of any form of food-production before these items appeared and, in later times, they were certainly used in connexion with farming activities. It would be misleading, however, to assert that the presence of pottery and/or ground stone artefacts in an archaeological assemblage indicates that its makers were necessarily food-producers. The evidence from Ghana may be cited as an example.

At Bosumpra Cave near Abetifi a microlithic industry basically similar to that from earlier, pre-pottery, sites is associated with simple pottery and ground stone hoe-like or axe-like implements (Shaw, 1944; A. B. Smith, 1975). The occupation had begun by the end of the fifth millennium B.C. and lasted intermittently for over 3,500 years, with pottery and ground stone artefacts becoming progressively commoner with the passage of time. If they were not food-producers (and there is no firm archaeological evidence that they were), the inhabitants of Bosumpra were presumably able in some way to follow a reasonably settled life-style permitting the use of such a fragile, heavy type of equipment as pottery. Such conditions also prevailed by the mid-fifth millennium on the Ghana coast, on settlements where the economy was based on the exploitation of marine food-resources (Calvocoressi and David, 1979).

At Iwo Eleru rockshelter in south-western Nigeria (the lower levels of which were described in chapter 4), pottery and ground stone implements likewise first appear around the middle of the fifth millennium. At about the same level there is reported the earliest occurrence of implements bearing so-called sickle-sheen (see p. 99), but this does not necessarily mean that the inhabitants cultivated cereals (Shaw, 1969). A rockshelter at Afikpo in south-eastern Nigeria probably provides a counterpart sequence (Shaw, 1981a). Further to the east, at Shum Laka near Bamenda in Cameroon, stamp-decorated pottery seems to have been in use as early as about 5000 B.C., associated with chipped hoe-like stone artefacts (de Maret, 1982). Although as yet undated, ground stone implements are reported from many areas of Cameroon, from several sites in Gabon and as far south as the lower reaches of the Congo. In this area it seems that, at Gombe Point, Kinshasha, they may be as early as the mid-second millennium B.C. (de Maret *et al.*, 1977). Pottery was used in the lower Congo by the last few centuries B.C. and it is possible, though not proven, that some forms of food-production may have been practised by this time. Linguistic studies indicate that some of the inhabitants of the Cameroon/eastern Nigeria region during the last millennia B.C. were speakers of Bantu languages.

Archaeological evidence from more westerly regions is even less complete and precludes any assessment of early food-production practices. In the Ivory Coast pottery and ground stone artefacts are found in association with microlithic industries both on inland sites and in coastal shell mounds, but cannot yet be shown to be earlier than the late third millennium B.C. (Mauny, 1973). In Sierra Leone, however, similar associations at Kamabai and Yagala rockshelters extend back to around the end of the fourth millennium (Atherton, 1972). Throughout this region discoveries of ground stone artefacts need to be evaluated with care because they were extensively traded in ancient times from factory sites such as those near Cape Three Points in Ghana, on Bioko Island and in the Oueyanko Valley near Bamako in Mali. They have also been sought after and preserved until recent times in the belief that they possess magical properties, being preserved, for example, on altars at Benin (Connah, n.d.).

Reliable information concerning prehistoric industries in Guinea and Guinea-Bissau is almost totally lacking. In Senegal, however, extensive shell-middens attest coastal settlement, with pottery, beside the Casamance estuary and near Saint Louis; in the latter area the occupation dates back to the fourth or late fifth millennium (Linares de Sapir, 1971; Ravise, 1970).

Despite the incomplete and widely scattered nature of the evidence, the general picture that emerges is one of the broadly contemporaneous adoption by the inhabitants of West Africa of techniques for the manufacture of pottery and of ground stone artefacts in the mid-fifth millennium B.C., perhaps somewhat earlier in Cameroon. Both these technologies were known in the Sahara in earlier times and there is no evidence to suggest that they were independently rediscovered in West Africa rather than introduced from the north. In fact, in several areas, the pottery decoration strongly suggests a Saharan affinity. As noted elsewhere, it seems probable that yam cultivation near the forest/woodland savanna ecotone may have begun at approximately this time. However, it is not until significantly later times that there is clear primary evidence for the practice of any form of food-production.

In Ghana the earliest such evidence belongs, in about the eighteenth century B.C., with the Kintampo industry, sites of which appear to be restricted to the forest margin and the southern part of the woodland savanna to the west of the Volta. The Kintampo industry (Flight, 1976; see also Davies, 1973) presents a sharp discontinuity with its predecessor and may indicate influences from the north and west, apparent both in the pottery decoration and in the typology of the stone arrow-heads. At one site bones of small domestic cattle and goats have been identified: the cattle may be of a type ancestral to modern dwarf shorthorn breeds of West Africa. Wild species were also represented. Oil-palm nuts and cowpeas were preserved in the Kintampo deposits. A highly characteristic but enigmatic artefact which is frequently encountered on Kintampo sites is a soft stone slab with deeply scored surfaces (fig. 6.15). The purpose of such objects

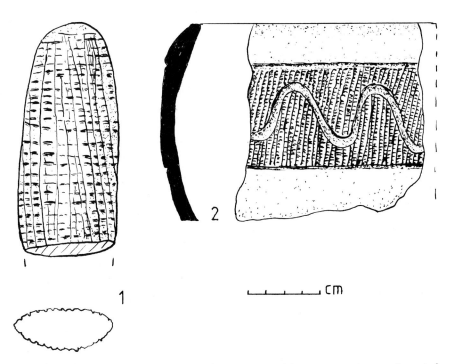

6.15 Artefacts from Kintampo sites (after Davies, 1967): 1 – stone rasp, 2 – decorated potsherd

remains completely unknown. Suggestions include use in pottery manufacture, or for grating yams, or for removing hard skin from the feet. The Kintampo people lived in villages with permanent rectangular wattle and daub structures incorporating carved wooden mouldings (Dombrowski, 1980); at Ntereso, overlooking the White Volta 50 km west of Tamale, the settlement covered an area of at least 750 square metres. The northern affinities of the Kintampo industry seem to be particularly strong with the Tilemsi Valley area north of the Niger bend in Mali (p. 134).

In the Bornu plains of the extreme north-east of Nigeria, bordering on Lake Chad, a composite sequence at Daima (fig. 6.16) and neighbouring sites extends back to late in the second millennium B.C. (Connah, 1976; 1981). From this early period the settlements were permanent, with wooden-walled, clay-floored houses. In the absence of local stone, many tools were made of bone. The

6.16 Excavation through the deep accumulation of occupation deposits at Daima

pottery shows little change during the sequence. Domestic cattle and goats were present throughout, although hunting and fishing were also important activities. Similar mound-sites are known from north and east of the lake in both Chad and Cameroon.

In conclusion, we may note that food-producing communities making pottery and ground stone artefacts are known to have been living in the Sahara for at least two thousand years before any of these traits is attested in West Africa. Their apparent southward dispersal into West Africa seems to have occurred at about the time of the major period of Saharan desiccation, when climatic and vegetational zones would have shifted to the south. The effect which these changes may have had on the distribution of tsetse flies probably allowed the eventual entry of domestic cattle into West Africa.

There is as yet no evidence to suggest that all food-production in West Africa began as a direct result of contact with more northerly areas. It appears certain, however, that domestic animals were so derived, and probably cereal agriculture also. Yam cultivation, however, although nowhere conclusively attested in the archaeological record, may well have been an indigenous development and perhaps one which pre-dated any other form of food-production in this region (cf. Coursey, 1976). The antiquity of West African rice cultivation also remains totally unknown. There are good botanical and environmental reasons for regarding the inland Niger delta as one of the centres for early domestication of this crop and, indeed, it is there, at Jenne-Jeno, that its earliest archaeological attestation occurs: in a context dated to the first century A.D. (R. and S. McIntosh, 1981).

Ethiopia and the Horn

For a long time it has been recognised that the highland areas of Ethiopia must have played an important part in the development of African food-production, particularly agriculture (Harlan, 1969). Not only has there been considerable diversity in recent Ethiopian agricultural practices, with wheat and barley being grown, for example, alongside indigenous African crops. But there are also several food-crops which are traditionally cultivated in Ethiopia and nowhere else, and which must presumably have been originally domesticated there; these include the tiny but highly nutritious grain teff, the banana-like plant ensete and the oil-yielding noog (Simoons, 1965). Botanical studies suggest that cultivated finger millet may also be of Ethiopian origin. Unfortunately, very little archaeological evidence has yet been recovered to illustrate the early development of Ethiopian food-production, so that many aspects, including its chronology, remain poorly understood.

Only two widely separated areas of Ethiopia have yielded archaeological sequences which span the period when food-production began. At Gobedra rockshelter near Axum, the earlier occupation of which was noted in chapter 4

(p. 82), pottery first appears in association with the backed-microlith industry at a level which probably dates to between the mid-fifth and the third millennium B.C. Seeds of cultivated finger millet were found at the same level, as was the tooth of a camel. If these objects are correctly associated, they are of major significance, for the finger millet would be the earliest actual remains of any of the putatively Ethiopian crops, and the camel would be shown to have a much greater antiquity in this part of Africa than had previously been believed. The presence of domestic cattle is indicated in a later level in the Gobedra sequence (D. W. Phillipson, 1977b).

The second Ethiopian sequence which is relevant to the present discussion comes from the area around Lake Besaka near the escarpment west of Harar. Here, the local backed-microlith industry was changed early in the second millennium B.C. by the presence of large numbers of scrapers. Domestic cattle make their appearance at the same time. There is also a fragment of a stone bowl akin to those found on early pastoralist sites in East Africa (J. D. Clark and Williams, 1978).

Away from these two areas the evidence for early Ethiopian food-production is indirect or circumstantial. The only other significant archaeological discoveries are of late date, such as those from Lalibela Cave, east of Lake Tana, which included remains of barley, chickpeas, cattle and small stock, dated to the middle of the last millennium B.C. (Dombrowski, 1970). It would be reasonable to propose that there were two main agricultural traditions in Ethiopia during the last three or four thousand years B.C., that in the north being based on cereal cultivation and that in the south-west on ensete. In the south-west large numbers of ground stone hoe-like tools were found many years ago in association with pottery and, only occasionally, with metal objects, but their age and significance remain completely unknown pending further research (Bailloud, 1959). The northern, cereal, zone is more likely to have had contact with the Nile Valley, but so far the only early sites which provide evidence for such connexions are at Agordat in Eritrea. The Agordat sites (Arkell, 1954) are undated and have not been excavated, but the surface finds of ground stone tools and ornaments, including an ox figurine, may possibly show some features in common with those of the Nubian C-Group of the late third millennium B.C. (p. 119).

Rock paintings provide another possible source of information concerning domestic animals, notably cattle which are frequently depicted (fig. 6.17). Unfortunately the paintings cannot be dated directly. Humpless longhorned cattle are shown in paintings in Eritrea and in Harar Province as well as in engravings at Chabbe in the south. Ancient Egyptian carvings of the Eighteenth Dynasty (middle second millennium B.C.) at Deir el Bahari depict the Land of Punt, which is generally believed to be the African coast near the southern end of the Red Sea (Naville, 1898). They indicate the presence at that time of domestic small stock, two breeds of cattle, and cultivated cereals (fig. 6.18).

Linguistic research is not able to add very much to the findings of archaeo-logy. Vocabulary relating to the cereal-plough agriculture complex in northern Ethiopia appears to be of Cushitic origin and to pre-date the arrival of Semitic-speakers during the earlier part of the last millennium B.C. Taking the story further back, intensive cereal use and the subsequent early stages of cultivation are, both in north-eastern Africa and in adjacent parts of the Near East, first encountered in areas occupied by speakers of Afroasiatic languages (see chapter 1, p. 5). This language family probably has a time-depth in the order of fifteen thousand years, which effectively covers the formative phases of incipient food-production as revealed by archaeology (Ehret, 1980). The most likely location of the homeland of the Afroasiatic languages, on the south-western side of the Red Sea in Ethiopia and easternmost Sudan, suggests that we may still have much to learn about the beginnings of Ethiopian food-production.

6.17 Rock paintings of domestic cattle at Genda Biftu, Ethiopia (after J. D. Clark, 1954)

East Africa

The earliest evidence for food-production in East Africa comes from the plains of northern Kenya. Domestic cattle and sheep/goat are represented at three sites in the Ileret area on the north-east shore of Lake Turkana, dated to the middle of the third millennium B.C. (Owen *et al.*, 1982). Associated artefacts are stone bowls and pottery, including vessels with jabbed decoration and internal scoring which resemble the Nderit ware (see p. 144) of southern Kenya. Similar pottery has also been reported from sites west of Lake Turkana, which appear long to pre-date the local beginning of pastoralism, but the age of this material cannot be regarded as certain. Fishing remained an important source of food for the early Ileret pastoralists. These people exploited a more extensive territory than their fishing and hunting predecessors, and they brought obsidian from a distant source to use in their microlithic stone industry.

Inland, east of Lake Turkana, an extensive and long-occupied settlement was established during the third millennium on the shores of the then shallow but

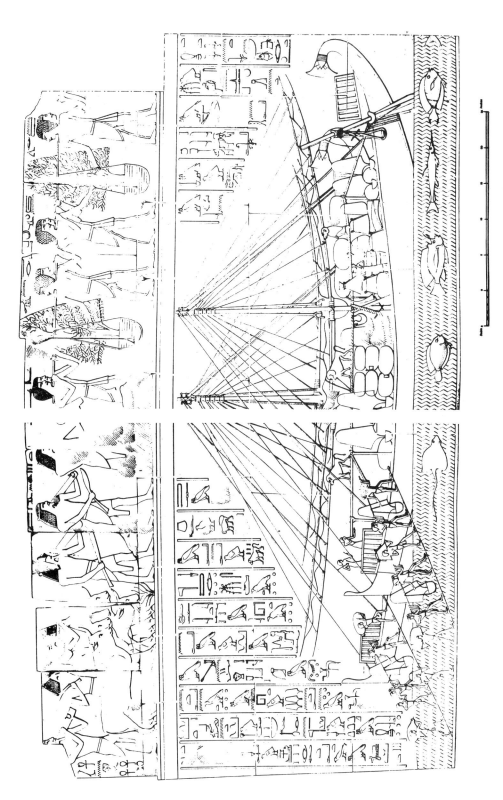

6.18 The Land of Punt, as illustrated in relief carvings on the mortuary temple of Queen Hatshepsut at Deir el Bahari (after Naville, 1898). The hieroglyphic inscription reads, in part: 'The loading of the cargo-boats with great marvels of the Land of Punt, with all the good woods of the divine land . . . with ebony, with pure ivory, with pure gold of the land of Amu . . . resin, antimony, with apes, monkeys, hounds, with skins of leopards of the south, with inhabitants of the country and their children. Never were brought such things to any king, since the world was.'

extensive Chalbi Lake at North Horr (D. W. Phillipson, 1977a), where the pottery, stone bowls and microliths may be compared with those from Ileret (fig. 6.19). Information about the economic developments which took place at this time in more arid areas has been obtained from a rockshelter at Ele Bor, near the modern border between Kenya and Ethiopia (D. W. Phillipson, in press). Here, meat was obtained mainly by hunting until very recent times but sheep/goat and, interestingly, camel were present in small numbers from about 3000 B.C., which is also the time of the first appearance of pottery. This incidence of camel may not be much later than that at Gobedra, (p. 140), and its presence here helps to substantiate its early date at the Ethiopian site also. Particularly important is the evidence at Ele Bor from seeds and numerous grindstones for the intensive exploitation of cereals, presumably wild, at this same period, which faunal evidence shows to have had a climate somewhat wetter than that of today. Subsequently, as the climate deteriorated, cereal use was abandoned but small stock continued to be herded in small numbers.

The available archaeological evidence from northern Kenya shows that in some areas a settled life-style based at least in part on the herding of domestic stock continued until early in the present millennium. Sites of this period as, for example, a second settlement at North Horr, contain abundant pottery. Even at this late date iron was evidently unknown or exceedingly rare and microlithic artefacts continued in use. Further climatic deterioration, leading to today's arid conditions, caused the people to adopt the present nomadic pastoral way of life within the last few centuries.

Further to the south, the highlands of southern Kenya and northern Tanzania were the scene of one of the best known complexes of food-producing industries which pre-date the beginning of iron-working. These first appear in the archaeological record late in the second millennium B.C. Recent claims (e.g. Bower and Nelson, 1978) that domestic animals were herded in this region in far earlier times should be discounted since they are, in the present writer's opinion, based upon inadequate evidence (see also Owen *et al.*, 1982; Robertshaw and Collett, 1983). These industries have been named collectively 'Pastoral

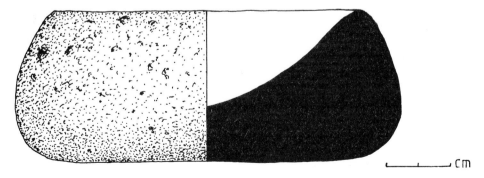

6.19 Stone bowl from North Horr (after D. W. Phillipson, 1977a)

Neolithic' after their most obvious mode of food-production, but it remains an open question whether any form of horticulture was also practised (Bower *et al.*, 1977). I have therefore not used the term in the discussion which follows.

The archaeological material relating to these early East African herdsmen most logically divides most of them into two groups. One industry, known as the Elmenteitan, has a very restricted distribution in the high-rainfall area on the west side of the Kenyan Rift Valley; its flaked stone artefacts are characterised by large double-edged obsidian blades and its pottery by plain, mostly bowl-shaped vessels. Shallow stone bowls, akin to those described above from earlier times in northern Kenya, are also present on Elmenteitan sites. An unusual feature was the practice of cremating the dead, as at Njoro River Cave where each burial was accompanied by a stone bowl, pestle and mortar. Charred remains of a gourd and of an elaborately carved wooden vessel were also recovered from this site, as were large numbers of stone beads (M. D. and L. S. B. Leakey, 1950). Dated to about the twelfth century B.C., Njoro River Cave may be one of the earliest Elmenteitan sites. The industry appears to have continued well into the first millennium A.D.

The second major grouping is less well defined. Both stone industries and pottery types are more varied (fig. 6.20). Several distinct pottery styles have been recognised and named after such sites as Nderit, Narosura, Akira and Maringishu (Bower *et al.*, 1977; Wandibba, 1980). The significance of this stylistic diversity is far from clear, for none of the so-called 'wares' has well-defined geographical or chronological parameters and frequently more than one 'ware' seems to have been in use in the same place at the same time. Nderit ware (formerly known as Gumban A), characterised by decoration produced by jabbing large areas of a pot's surface with a wedge-shaped object and often by scoring of the vessel's interior surface, is the only type which has clear affinities with material from other areas. As noted above, closely similar pottery occurs in early pastoral contexts of the early third millennium B.C. in northern Kenya, while west of Lake Turkana it may extend back into earlier, pre-pastoral times.

Since no clear subdivisions (other than Elmenteitan) are apparent, the material relating to the stone-tool-using herdsmen of southern Kenya and northern Tanzania during the last millennium B.C. must – if only provisionally – be discussed together. There are, in fact, many common features. The dead were buried, without cremation, under stone cairns or in crevices between rocks. Stone bowls occur in settlements as well as on burial sites. There is considerable variation in size of site and in the proportion of the faunal remains represented by domestic animals. It is tempting to suggest that there was some seasonally changing settlement pattern in which, at certain times of the year, the whole community was dependent upon the produce of the herds, while at others smaller groups obtained their livelihood by more varied means. This is the pattern with several recent pastoralist societies and there are indications, as noted above for the Khartoum area, that it is one of considerable antiquity, although the details for East Africa have yet to be worked out.

To the west, around the western, southern and eastern sides of Lake Victoria, a further type of pottery, called Kansyore ware, is found on sites apparently as early as the middle of the last millennium B.C. at Nyang'oma near Mwanza (Chapman, 1967; Soper and Golden, 1969). Its predominantly stamped decoration comprises a variety of motifs some of which may be derived from much earlier pottery styles further to the north. Particularly in view of the fragmentary nature of most of the finds, such conclusions must be regarded as highly tentative, as must claims for sherds of Kansyore ware from far to the east and south-east of Lake Victoria. So far, Kansyore ware has not been found with evidence for the working of iron, and the only indication that its makers may

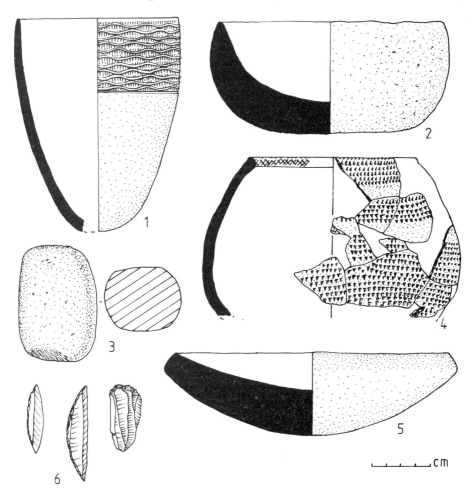

6.20 Artefacts from Hyrax Hill, Kenya (after M. D. Leakey, 1945): 1 – pottery of 'Maringishu ware', 2,5 – stone bowls, 3 – stone pestle, 4 – pottery of Nderit ware, 6 – backed microliths

have practised any form of food-production is its apparent association with remains of domestic cattle at Gogo Falls in south-western Kenya (Robertshaw and Collett, 1983).

It will be instructive now briefly to compare the archaeological evidence for the beginnings of food-production in East Africa with that which has been deduced from linguistic investigations. Study of modern linguistic distributions and loanwords indicates that much of highland southern Kenya and northern Tanzania now settled by Nilotic and Bantu-speakers was formerly occupied by people who spoke languages that may be classified as Southern Cushitic (Ehret, 1974). The vocabulary that has been reconstructed indicates that these Southern Cushitic-speakers were herders of domestic stock who milked their cattle and who seem also to have possessed some knowledge of agriculture. Two points require emphasis here. First, although purely linguistic considerations can provide only a very approximate estimate of the time-depth at which these Southern Cushitic languages were spoken, the indications that we possess are that their antiquity is broadly the same as that of the stone-tool-using herders. Secondly, the area where the former presence of the Southern Cushitic-speakers is attested is approximately the same as that covered by the distribution of sites which have yielded evidence for domestic animals at this time. It therefore seems reasonable to accept as a working hypothesis the view that most if not all the inhabitants of these sites were speakers of Southern Cushitic languages. The identity of the makers of Kansyore ware remains a matter for speculation pending further research.

This conclusion has in the past been used to support the view that early East African pastoralism was derived from Ethiopia. However, it is now known that northern Kenya was itself an important dispersal area for Cushitic speech being, for example, the region whence the Somali languages were derived (Heine, 1978). There is also evidently a very long history of Nilotic/Cushitic contact in the area around Lake Turkana. All this would be fully in keeping with the archaeological indications for the relatively high antiquity of food-production in northern Kenya. It suggests that a predominantly Ethiopian origin for East African food-production should not be accepted as proved, and that Sudanese connexions may eventually be shown to have been at least equally important.

The evidence of physical anthropology, although far from conclusive, is in keeping with these conclusions. Human skeletons from early pastoralist sites have been known for some decades; and early descriptions, which emphasised their caucasoid features, were misinterpreted as suggesting European affinities. More recent investigations have demonstrated that negroid features are in many cases dominant, and that such non-negroid characteristics as are present would be in keeping with north-east African caucasoid affinities (Rightmire, 1975).

Although the archaeology of central and southern Tanzania remains poorly investigated, there are no indications from sites of the first millennium B.C. that domestic animals were ever acquired by the stone-tool-using peoples to the south of the Serengeti Plain. In more southerly latitudes, indeed, it seems that food-production was not practised before the beginning of iron-working. For reasons that are imperfectly understood, the relatively rapid diffusion of food-production techniques through the stone-tool-using populations of the northern half of Africa seems here to have come to a temporary halt. Although there is little archaeological evidence from the forested regions of the Congo basin, it appears that the only parts of sub-equatorial Africa where food-production was known prior to the first millennium A.D. were in southern Kenya and northern Tanzania and, less certainly (p. 136) in a restricted area around the lower reaches of the Congo River. Possible factors which may have hindered the adoption of farming techniques further to the south at this time include rich and reliable food supplies from wild sources, coupled with very low human population densities. Also relevant are the traditionalism and well-adapted hunter–gatherer life-style of the Khoisan-speaking peoples who were probably the exclusive inhabitants of the more southerly latitudes. Later history, as will be described below, shows how reluctant these well-adapted and conservative people have often been to adopt alien life-styles and economic practices. Whatever the reasons, the beginning of food-production in the southern half of Africa had to await the large-scale population movements which there accompanied the beginning of iron-working.

CHAPTER 7

IRON-USING PEOPLES BEFORE A.D. 1000

Iron

The greater part of Africa differs from most other regions of the Old World in that there was (except in Egypt and some other areas of northern Africa) no distinct 'Bronze Age' or 'Copper Age' during which softer metals, often including gold, were utilised but when techniques of smelting iron had not yet been mastered. Especially in the sub-Saharan latitudes, iron was the first metal to be brought into use; the working of copper and gold began at the same time or somewhat later (van der Merwe, 1980); and in most of Africa south of the equator, the beginnings of food-production and of iron-working took place at the same time. There was thus a pronounced contrast between metal-using farming people and their immediate stone-tool-using hunter-gatherer neighbours and predecessors.

At least in Africa, the beginnings of metallurgy cannot be said to have made such a great impact on prehistoric life-styles as did the advent of food-production. The civilisation of ancient Egypt provides a vivid example of the technological achievements that could be attained with virtually no use of iron. Basically, the advantages of iron are ones of increased efficiency. The clearance of forest, the working of wood, the cultivation of ground and the slaughter of enemies may all be accomplished more effectively and with less effort by people who are equipped with iron tools and weapons. These advantages may serve to explain why the knowledge of iron-working techniques spread so rapidly through Africa – as this chapter will demonstrate – in comparison with the slow and often hesitant processes by which food-production was adopted. They also help to account for the great prestige which, in many African societies, is traditionally associated with the knowledge and ownership of iron. The word which the early Bantu-speaking people applied to signify iron seems originally to have meant 'a thing of value'.

The technology required to smelt iron – to produce workable metal from the naturally occurring ore – is complex (Wertime, 1980). The ore, having been extracted from the ground and broken up, must be heated to a temperature of at least 1,100° centigrade under carefully controlled conditions. To achieve such temperatures, aided only by the natural draft of a clay-built furnace and, usually, by hand-operated bellows, is a major task in itself (fig. 7.1). Once smelted, the usable metal has to be separated from the waste-products – the slag

– and brought to its desired shape by repeated heating and hammering. This last process is known as forging. African iron-working technology did not include the melting and casting of iron although copper and its alloys, with their much lower melting temperatures, were successfully cast.

Knowledge of how to smelt iron on any significant scale seems first to have been discovered in western Asia early in the second millennium B.C. (Wertime and Muhly, 1980). Iron-working was probably brought to North Africa, west of Egypt, by Phoenician colonists in about the eighth century B.C. (van der Merwe, 1980). At about the same time iron objects first came into common use in Egypt. One theory is that iron technology spread, with great rapidity, from these two sources through the rest of the continent. Because the associated technology is so complex, and in earlier African societies no other process involved heating materials to such high temperatures, we have to consider the possibility of a northerly source of sub-Saharan iron-working knowledge rather than duplicate independent discovery. The radiocarbon dates that are now available for early iron-working in Africa lend some support to the view that iron was introduced from the north and spread southwards. We will examine the archaeological and other evidence for these processes, and follow the history of the early iron-using societies up to about the year A.D. 1000.

7.1 Traditional African iron-smelting: a re-enactment in Ghana

North Africa

During the last millennium B.C., the indigenous inhabitants of North Africa west of Egypt were essentially pastoralists, probably often transhumant. They also practised agriculture on the plains of what is now Tunisia and in the better-watered river valleys of the Maghreb. There can be little doubt that in these people may already be recognised the ancestors of the modern Berbers (Camps, 1974; 1982). Remarkably little archaeological work has been done on Berber sites of this period, attention having been concentrated almost exclusively on the colonies that were established on the North African coast by a succession of trading peoples from the north and east. A certain amount of information about the early Berbers may, however, be gleaned from the writings of Greek authors, notably Herodotus, whose work dates from the fifth century B.C. As traders, the Berbers penetrated throughout the Sahara; they used mules as beasts of burden and their horses drew wheeled vehicles along well-established routes, which may today be traced by studying the distribution of rock paintings (Mauny, 1978) in which these journeys are depicted (fig. 7.2). There is no evidence for camels before the last two centuries B.C.

Through most of the last millennium B.C. metal was a very scarce commodity among the indigenous peoples of North Africa. Knowledge of the working of copper is likely to have reached a limited area of north-western Africa from Spain during the second millennium B.C. Elsewhere, although copper and bronze ornaments were occasionally obtained by trade, metal objects generally were very rare; North African warriors of this period were famous for their use of fire-hardened wooden spears without metal points.

Such were the indigenous peoples amongst whom successive colonists settled. The first to arrive were the Phoenicians who, from their homeland in the

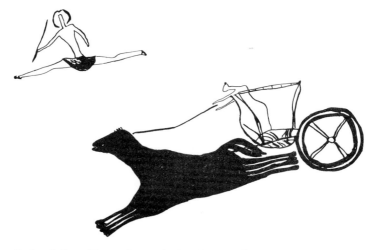

7.2 Rock painting of horse-drawn chariot, Acacus (after Mori, 1978)

Levantine coastlands of the eastern Mediterranean, penetrated by sea as far to the west as Mogador in southern Morocco (Law, 1978a). Phoenician expansion into the western Mediterranean may have begun as early as the end of the second millennium B.C., but was placed on a firm footing late in the ninth century with the foundation of Carthage near the modern Tunis. The map (fig. 7.3) shows the location of the principal Phoenician settlements on the African coast. The type of square-rigged ship used by the Phoenicians, which could not sail close into the wind, makes it highly unlikely that any of their vessels would ever have been able to return from a voyage which penetrated further down the coast of north-western Africa than southernmost Morocco, and this is in fact the limit of well-documented archaeological evidence for a Phoenician presence. The claim mentioned by Herodotus (who himself disbelieved it) for a Phoenician circumnavigation of Africa from the Indian Ocean to the Atlantic should not be dismissed out of hand but is incapable of proof or disproof, although the objections about the difficulty of a northward voyage along the north-western coast still apply.

The Phoenicians were great traders and their colonies provided a stimulus and end-point for the Berbers' trans-Saharan trade with the central Saharan highlands and, perhaps, West Africa. Salt, ivory, animal skins and slaves were the major items that found their way northwards; manufactured goods, including pottery, glass and metalwork, probably went south in exchange. The Phoenician colonies prospered on the profits of this trade, aided by cereal agriculture on the

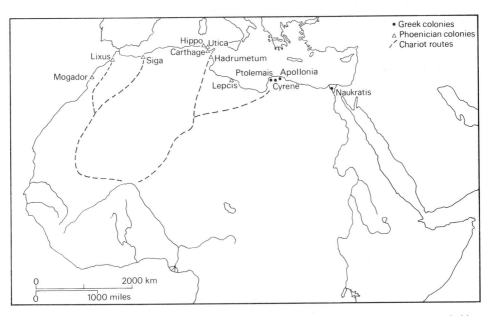

7.3 Greek and Phoenician colonies in North Africa, together with the most probable lines of trans-Saharan routes as indicated by the distribution of rock paintings of horse-drawn chariots

Tunisian plains, most of which was controlled by Carthage from the fifth century B.C. onwards. As a result, the settled Berbers of the coastal regions were drawn into the Phoenician cultural and technological sphere; there came into existence Berber kingdoms, nominally independent but often Phoenician clients.

There can be little doubt that both bronze and iron were introduced to much of North Africa by the Phoenicians, but conclusive archaeological evidence for this is so far lacking. It is particularly unfortunate that we have no details of the type of iron-smelting furnace that was in use in Punic North Africa, since without this information it is difficult to evaluate whether iron-working technology could have spread from here to more southerly parts of Africa.

While the Phoenicians controlled the maritime trade of the western Mediterranean, including the African coast west of Tripolitania, Greek colonies were established from the late seventh century B.C. onwards on the coast of Cyrenaica. The region takes its name from that of the principal Greek colony, Cyrene. The southernmost point of the Gulf of Sirte was eventually accepted as the boundary between the Greek and Phoenician spheres of influence. The prosperity of Greek Cyrenaica was based upon agriculture, the surplus of which was exported.

7.4 Ruins of the Roman city of Timgad in eastern Algeria. Note the regular street grid centered on forum and theatre

By the third century B.C., Rome was challenging Carthaginian supremacy in the western Mediterranean. Several of the Berber kingdoms were won over as allies of Rome, the most notable being that ruled by Massinissa (201–148 B.C) in what is now eastern Algeria (Law, 1978b). Following the final and absolute defeat of Carthage by the Romans in 146 B.C., these allies were rewarded with tracts of formerly Carthaginian territory. Rome now became the main external power and trading partner in the area; but political annexation followed slowly, and it was some two and a half centuries after the sack of Carthage before Rome established herself as mistress of all the Maghreb north of the Atlas and of the coastal strip further to the east.

The heyday of Roman North Africa was in the second century A.D., when major cities were built, public works including roads, aqueducts and irrigation schemes undertaken, and agriculture developed to such an extent that the area became a major economic force in the Roman empire (fig. 7.4). The colonists often regarded Africa as their permanent home and their society fused with that of the Berber elite (Law, 1978b). In the third century more than one emperor of Rome was descended from North African stock (fig. 7.5). Christianity gained many adherents both in the cities and in rural areas during the second and third centuries. North Africa at this time was a Roman province as effectively colonised as at any subsequent period of the region's history: its economy and industries were essentially those of the empire of which it formed an integral part. However, by the late third century and throughout the fourth, Berber uprisings led to a reduction in Roman influence. North Africa did not escape the collapse of Roman power in the west which came early in the fifth century. In A.D. 429 Vandals, raiders from the Baltic area, crossed from Spain; Carthage fell to them six years later and they took control of what was left of the urban settlements, while the more distant Roman estates were once again taken over by the Berbers.

7.5 The Roman emperor Septimius Severus (A.D. 193–211) was of North African descent

Egypt and the Arab invasion

To the east, the coming of iron meant that Egypt also lost her independence, though in a significantly different manner. The pharaohs of the Twenty-fifth Dynasty were the Nubian kings of Kush; they were driven back upstream to their homeland by an invasion of Assyrians in 671 B.C. Despite the country's tributary status to a foreign power, the traditional culture of ancient Egypt survived with few important modifications for over six centuries. The developing Greek-dominated trade networks of the eastern Mediterranean brought Egypt, through her entrepôt at Naukratis in the Nile Delta, into closer contact with Europe. The Greek historian Herodotus, who visited Egypt in the fifth century B.C., has left us (in his Book 2) a detailed and informative account both of what he saw and of what he learned about the Egypt of earlier times.

Late in the fourth century B.C. the Macedonians from northern Greece under their king, Alexander the Great, destroyed Persian power in the eastern Mediterranean. They conquered Egypt in 332 B.C. The succession of pharaohs, after almost three thousand years, was now brought to an end; and one of Alexander's generals was appointed ruler of Egypt as Ptolemy I. He and his descendants controlled Egypt until 30 B.C., severing the formal link with Macedon and building the country to a pre-eminent commercial and cultural position in the Greek-speaking world. The Ptolemaic capital at Alexandria became not only a great centre of learning but also a port from which traders sailed throughout the Mediterranean as well as through the Red Sea to India and far down the East African coast.

The Roman conquest of Egypt came in 30 B.C. The country's wealth was partly drained in tribute and through taxation, but this did little to shake Alexandria from its position of influence throughout the eastern, Greek-speaking, part of the Roman empire. After the Jewish revolt late in the first century A.D., many refugees settled in Egypt. Among these people and others Christianity rapidly took root. It was by way of Egypt that Christianity was passed southwards to Nubia and, less directly although at an earlier date, to Ethiopia. Following the division of the Roman empire in the fourth century, Egypt was included in the eastern (Byzantine) hegemony, where it remained until the Arab invasion of the seventh century.

Byzantine-ruled Egypt was so weakened by religious differences that it offered little resistance to the invading Arabs in 639. Conversions to Islam proceeded steadily; and Arabic replaced Greek as the language of government. The Arab invasion did not stop in Egypt, but extended rapidly westwards through North Africa (Brett, 1978). By 647 the Arabs had reached Tunisia and defeated the Byzantine forces, who themselves had ousted the Vandals early in the sixth century. Later in the seventh century the Arab conquest of the area was consolidated, and a local headquarters established at Kairouan (fig. 7.6). In the eighth century the front was pushed further west to Morocco and northwards into Spain. Islam spread more rapidly in North Africa than in Egypt, but some Christian communities survived for several hundreds of years. Technologically, this period saw the end of Roman skills, and the resurgence of native North African ones. Many aspects of Arab culture were introduced and flourished, advances in architecture, science and literature being particularly noteworthy. As in the days of the Phoenicians, Tunis again became an entrepôt for trade with the south: goods from West Africa and from Europe were to be found in the markets of the North African coast. This trade was now in the hands of nomadic Arabs as well as Berbers, and was institutionalised by the establishment of regular journeys by large camel caravans. Through these, Islam was introduced to the areas south of the desert, as will be described below; and these same areas came into the knowledge of Arab geographers (Levtzion, 1978).

7.6 The mosque of Sidi Okba at Kairouan, founded A.D. 670, rebuilt and enlarged in the ninth century

The Sudan

Following the expulsion from Egypt of the kings of Kush after the Assyrian invasion of 671 B.C., the Kushites retreated to their former homeland. Their rule in the Sudan continued for another thousand years with the capital initially at Napata near the Fourth Cataract, moving about 600 B.C. upstream to Meroe, beyond the Nile–Atbara confluence (Shinnie, 1967; 1978).

Meroe lies to the south of the most arid stretch of the Nile Valley, in an area that appears to have been well wooded during the last millennium B.C. The move of the state capital to Meroe was thus of threefold importance. It marked an effective break from dependence upon Egypt, it brought the capital within reach of the fuel that was needed to maintain the iron-smelting industry which soon arose, and it provided the town with surroundings that enabled crops and herds to be raised on a scale sufficient to feed its growing population. Millet and sorghum were cultivated; herds consisted of cattle (humpless shorthorns being depicted on painted pottery), with some small stock. Horses were in use, but camels are not attested before late Meroitic times. Meroe could also take advantage of new trade routes that more than replaced the old Nile Valley route downstream into Egypt. To the east was the way to the Red Sea, while the valley of the Atbara led south-eastwards to the highlands of Ethiopia where a distinct urban civilisation was arising during the last few centuries B.C. (see below). To the south the Nile flowed through fertile plains where the mixed farming life-style of earlier times continued, and supported substantial settlements such as those at Jebel et Tomat and Jebel Moya (Addison, 1949; J. D. Clark and Stemler, 1975). Westwards the dry plains stretched away to Darfur and, beyond, to Lake Chad. Its Egyptian connexions were still emphasised in its monumental architecture (fig. 7.7), but Meroe was now able to strengthen its links with peoples to the south of the Sahara and to import luxuries from the north and east via the Red Sea ports.

Gradually Meroitic replaced Egyptian as the language of monumental inscriptions. By the last two centuries B.C. Egyptian hieroglyphs had been replaced by a local cursive script. The meaning of these Meroitic inscriptions cannot yet be fully understood.

Archaeologists have attached great importance to the evidence for Meroitic iron-working which, to judge from the size of the slag heaps that are to be seen on the site, was at some period carried out on a very substantial scale. Recent research (Shinnie and Bradley, 1980) has shown that although some smelting may date back close to the seventh or sixth centuries B.C. – about the time of the establishment of the royal capital – the industry did not reach a massive scale until the last centuries B.C. or the beginning of the Christian era. The furnaces that have been excavated were of this late period and were cylindrical structures rather over one metre high, fired with the aid of bellows. It appears that much of the iron produced at Meroe was dispersed through trade, since relatively few iron objects – hoes, axes, arrow-heads and the like – have been found on the site itself.

In the second century A.D. the prosperity of Meroe began to decline rapidly. Environmental deterioration, perhaps partly brought about by over-grazing and deforestation, may have been a contributing cause; another was the rise to trade-based prosperity of the kingdom of Axum in northern Ethiopia, discussed below. It may have been King Ezana of Axum who finally destroyed Meroe in about A.D. 350 (Kirwan, 1960).

The immediately post-Meroitic centuries in the northern Sudan are marked by sites attributed to the poorly understood X-Group – possibly Nubians whom the Romans used as a buffer to protect their southern Egyptian frontier (Kirwan, 1974). Early in the sixth century Christianity was introduced, and soon afterwards Arab expansion cut the Nubians off from their co-religionists in Egypt. Remarkably, the Nubians were able to maintain their Christian culture for some seven hundred years; their artistic accomplishments are best illustrated in the frescoes (fig. 7.8) recovered from the cathedral at Faras near Wadi Halfa (Michalowski, 1964). Village life in Christian Nubia, as illustrated by excavations at Debeira West, followed a pattern of irrigation agriculture which has continued into recent times (P. L. and M. Shinnie, 1978).

7.7 Meroitic temple at Naqa

7.8 Saint Anna depicted in a painting of the eighth century A.D. at Faras

Ethiopia and adjacent regions

Highland Ethiopia during the last millennium B.C. saw a gradual influx of Semitic-speaking peoples across the Red Sea from southern Arabia. The new arrivals may be assumed to have encountered a settled, agricultural, Cushitic-speaking population who had perhaps, although this cannot yet be proven, already learned techniques of copper-working through contacts with the Nile Valley. By the fifth century B.C., the South Arabians established in Tigre a literate urban culture which retained many features – artistic, architectural and technological – derived from their homeland (de Contenson, 1981). Iron-working was introduced into Ethiopia at this time, as were the worship of the South Arabian moon-god, symbolised by the crescent and disc, and also writing, in the form of the Himyaritic script (fig. 7.10). It seems likely that this so-called pre-Axumite culture was originally restricted to a relatively small number of

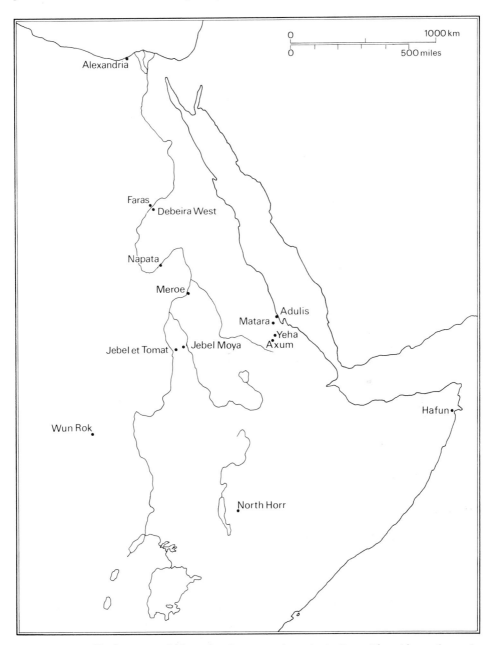

7.9 North-eastern Africa, showing some important sites with evidence for early metal-working

settlements, most notably Yeha near Adua (Anfray, 1963), and that it only slowly influenced the lives of the indigenous Cushitic-speaking population.

By the first century A.D. Axum, some 50 km south-west of Yeha, developed as the capital of an extensive state in which there was a fusion of indigenous Ethiopian and South Arabian cultural elements. Through its port of Adulis on the Red Sea coast, Axum was in trade contact with the Roman empire, exporting ivory and skins in exchange for imported manufactured luxury goods. Ge'ez – basically Semitic but with a strong Cushitic element – seems to have been the general language of Axum, but Greek was also in use for commercial purposes. Coins were struck at Axum; and on the earlier issues the king's name and titles were given in Greek (fig. 7.11). In the fourth century Axumite power seems to have reached its peak. It was at this time that King Ezana is believed to have conquered Meroe. It was also in Ezana's reign that Christianity became the state religion of Axum: on his later coins the crescent and disc of the moon-god are replaced by the cross (Anfray, 1981).

The monumental architecture and tombs of Axum are relatively well known, but very little research has yet been devoted to domestic sites or to investigating

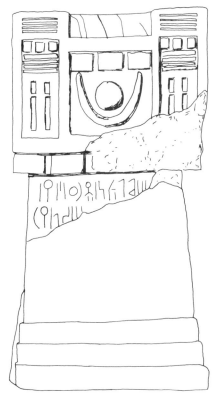

7.10 A pre-Axumite altar showing the crescent and disc symbol of the moon-god, and part of a Himyaritic inscription (after Sergew, 1972)

the life-style of the state's rural population (Littmann, 1913; Chittick, 1974a).
Great stelae – pillars hewn from a single piece of rock – up to 33 m high and
carved as stylised representations of multi-storey buildings were erected in a
burial area on the edge of the town (fig. 7.12). At Axum and other sites, notably
Matara, large rectangular buildings, interpreted as palaces, reached heights of
several storeys. The architecture of these buildings, like that represented on the
stelae, shows several features which may be paralleled in southern Arabia and
which have also continued into more recent times in Ethiopian ecclesiastical
buildings (Buxton, 1970).

Axum in its heyday was a major trading and imperial power. With the eclipse
of Meroe it effectively controlled the trade between the Red Sea and the rich
hunting grounds of the Sudanese Nile Valley, whence came the ivory which was
one of Axum's major exports. In the third century, and again in the sixth, the
kings of Axum held sway also over parts of southern Arabia. When, in the
seventh century, Arabs gained control over the Red Sea ports, Axum was cut off
from much of the trade on which its prosperity had depended, and the kingdom
then declined into obscurity (Sergew, 1972).

The Red Sea trade of the first few centuries A.D. was not restricted to Axumite
commerce. Most of our information comes from a Greek work, *The Periplus of the
Erythraean Sea*, which describes trade, originating in Alexandria, extending into
the Indian Ocean (Huntingford, 1980). There, contact was made with sailors
from Yemen who penetrated down the East African coast as far as a port called

7.11 Axumite coins (After Littmann, 1913): 1 – pre-Christian King Aphilas, late third
century A.D. (gold, Greek inscription), 2 – Christian King Armah, seventh century
A.D. (bronze, Ethiopic inscription)

Rhapta. The exact location of this place is unknown, but it is generally believed to have been somewhere on the coast of modern Tanzania. The traders brought metal and glass objects which they exchanged for gums, spices, ivory and rhinoceros horn. Excavations at Hafun on the coast of Somalia some 150 km south of Cape Guardafui have revealed traces of a trading settlement which probably dates back to this period (Chittick, 1976). To the south, however, no coastal settlements in East Africa that may have been visited by these early seafarers have yet been discovered.

The later archaeology of southern Ethiopia remains almost completely unknown; and research in the southern Sudan is at such a preliminary stage that few firm conclusions can yet be drawn. It appears that iron tools remained extremely scarce until relatively recent times and that in some areas backed-microlith stone industries continued well into the second millennium A.D. At Jebel et Tomat, between the Blue and White Niles not far south of Khartoum, an

7.12 Stela at Axum, 23 m high

extensive settlement was occupied through the first five centuries A.D. Cattle, sheep and goats were herded, sorghum was cultivated, and food was also obtained through hunting, fowling and fishing. The pottery tradition at this site appears to have been a continuation of that practised in far earlier times in the Sudanese Nile Valley, and also shows connexions with contemporary Meroitic wares. Iron tools were rare, and backed microliths were in use throughout the occupation (J. D. Clark and Stemler, 1975). In the absence of evidence to the contrary, it is tempting to suggest that Jebel et Tomat represents a type of rural settlement that was widespread at this time both in the central Sudan and further to the west and south-west.

In the southern Sudan, the Wun Rok mounds 150 km north of Wau provide a view of the iron-using communities who inhabited the plains of the Bahr el Ghazal during the first millennium A.D. They herded humpless cattle, hunted and fished. Iron was used primarily for personal adornment and many tools were made of bone. Throughout the second half of the first millennium A.D. these people produced roulette-decorated pottery similar to that made in more recent times by Nilotic-speakers (David *et al.*, 1981).

In northern Kenya, pastoral peoples, probably speaking languages of both the Nilotic and Cushitic types, using stone tools and evidently still ignorant of iron-working technology, continued the life-style of their predecessors throughout the first millennium A.D. Extensive settlements existed beside permanent sources of water, as at North Horr. In more arid areas, nomadic pastoralism was now the only effective means of subsistence. To the south, in the highlands west of the Rift Valley, it seems likely that iron-users of southern Sudanese affinities, speaking Nilotic languages, were established by early in the first millennium A.D. The evidence for this is primarily linguistic; and archaeological confirmation is not yet forthcoming (Ehret, 1974). In the Rift Valley itself, the herders described in chapter 6 appear to have continued in occupation until late in the first millennium A.D., perhaps obtaining some knowledge of iron – which, however, remained very rare – towards the end of that period. The coming of iron to the Bantu-speaking parts of East Africa is discussed below; elsewhere, informative evidence for use of metal prior to A.D. 1000 remains extremely scanty.

West Africa

Two areas of sub-Saharan West Africa are of particular interest as they are the only parts of the sub-continent that have yielded evidence for the working of copper before iron. Near Akjoujt in south-western Mauritania, copper ore was mined and smelted by the fifth century B.C. Around Agadez in Niger, furnaces of elongated plan were used for smelting copper at a similar period. At an even earlier time, during the early second millennium B.C., simple pit furnaces were used for melting native copper (Tylecote, 1982). The implications of these early dates are discussed below. The advent of iron in this area, subsequent to that of copper, is not yet dated. However, elsewhere in Niger, in southern Air, iron is known to have been in use by the last three centuries B.C. Other evidence for early iron-working in the immediately sub-Saharan latitudes comes from Rim, in Upper Volta, in a context of the first centuries A.D. showing continuity from earlier times. The earliest occupation of the large settlement at Jenne-Jeno, near the upper Niger in Mali, dates from the last two centuries B.C. The clear implications of these data are that use of iron in the southernmost Sahara and adjacent northern savanna of West Africa dates back to the last few centuries B.C., and was widespread (Posnansky and McIntosh, 1976; Calvocoressi and David, 1979). There is no evidence to suggest that any major replacement of population accompanied the beginning of iron-working.

In more southerly parts of West Africa, the earliest evidence for iron so far known is that associated with the Nok 'culture' found in a restricted area on the southern and western slopes of the Jos Plateau in Nigeria (Shaw, 1978; 1981b). Nok artefacts were originally discovered during mining operations of river gravels which, as noted in chapter 4, have also yielded abundant remains from earlier periods. The most striking discoveries were of pottery figures, mostly of humans, some of which are life-size (B. Fagg, 1979). These terracottas show great technical competence and an artistically accomplished, though

7.13 Nok terracotta heads

idiosyncratic, style of modelling. Examples are shown in fig. 7.13. Particularly characteristic are the elaborate hairstyles and the treatment of eyes, which are shown as sub-triangular areas delineated by grooves, with a deep circular hole for the pupil. The faces are unmistakably negroid. The presence of parts of limbs and torsos as well as heads suggests that some specimens were fragments of complete figures, although none of these has survived intact. Particular attention was paid to reproducing physical peculiarities and deformities.

The attributes of some of the figures provide information about their makers' material culture: one man carries a hafted axe, others sit on stools or wear beads and pendants; a fluted pumpkin is represented. Because they came from disturbed contexts, which also yielded archaeological material of several distinct periods, there was initially considerable controversy about the date of the Nok terracottas, or even as to whether they were earlier or later than the local beginning of iron-working.

The situation has now been clarified, because Nok settlement sites at Taruga and Samun Dukiya have been found and investigated. These have yielded radiocarbon dates between the fifth and the third centuries B.C., associated with fragments of typical Nok terracottas, domestic pottery and the remains of furnaces which conclusively demonstrate that iron was worked by the Nok people (A. Fagg, 1972; Tylecote, 1975). The shallow pit furnaces with cylindrical clay walls are of particular interest for comparison with later examples from other parts of sub-Saharan Africa (fig. 7.14). Knives and points for arrows and spears were the principal types of iron artefact produced, together with occasional bangles. The Nok 'culture' continued to flourish into about the second quarter of the first millennium A.D.

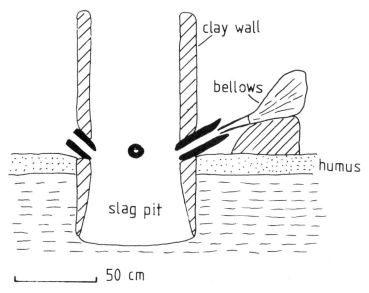

7.14 Reconstruction of iron-smelting furnace at Taruga (after Tylecote, 1975)

Unfortunately we know nothing about the local predecessors of the Nok people, and we cannot evaluate the impact which the start of iron-working made on their life-style. In fact, the only excavated site in West Africa where the beginning of iron-working may be pinpointed in a continuous sequence is the Daima mound in the extreme north-east of Nigeria, the lower levels of which were discussed in chapter 6. Here, only 800 km from the Nok area and a similar distance from Air, iron seems not to have been known before the first millennium A.D. – perhaps as much as eight hundred years later than at Taruga. At Daima, the economy of the early iron-workers, like that of their predecessors, was based on their herds of domestic cattle. Sorghum was cultivated, as it may have been in earlier times. There was no significant change in the associated pottery, but more substantial houses were now built of mud rather than of wood and grass. Some time after the initial appearance of iron a new population arrived at Daima and the site became part of a more extended trade system (Connah, 1976; 1981). The poorly documented Sao sites (Lebeuf, 1962) of southern Chad are probably similar to, and broadly contemporary with, Daima although there are indications that the advent of iron may in this more easterly area have been somewhat earlier. In the Koro Toro area of north-central Chad extensive iron-working is attested from the fifth century A.D.

In Ghana, iron-working near Begho, as at Atwetwebooso, extends back to around the second century A.D., but there is a dearth of other excavated sites that have been dated to the first millennium. In the same general area, sites which are traditionally associated with the origins of Akan groups are dated from the fifth century A.D. onwards and show a pottery style which developed into those produced by Akan in later times. Rockshelter sites in Ghana, notably Akyekyema Buor, show that microlithic industries and ground stone artefacts continued in use through the first millennium A.D. (Calvocoressi and David, 1979; Posnansky and McIntosh, 1976).

In more westerly regions only isolated discoveries have so far been reported, and no comprehensive account can be presented. It appears, however, that iron-working was not widely adopted prior to the middle centuries of the first millennium A.D., this being the range of the earliest relevant radiocarbon dates from Liberia, Sierra Leone and Senegal. The majority of these dates come from rockshelters or coastal shell-middens where there is evidence for continuous occupation from earlier times. A remarkable series of megalithic monuments (fig. 7.15) – settings of large, erect stones – in the Gambia and adjacent parts of Senegal have burials within them that date from the second half of the first millennium A.D. (Thilmans et al., 1980).

The Nok sites do not represent the only iron-using communities in Nigeria at the beginning of the Christian era, as is shown at several settlement sites that were investigated in the area now flooded by the waters of the Kainji Dam on the Niger. Near Yelwa, for instance, a small village probably of some eighty inhabitants seems to have been occupied through most of the first seven centuries A.D. by people who herded domestic animals and made stone beads as well as pottery vessels in two successive styles. They also made clay figurines which, in comparison with those of the Nok 'culture', are small and lack refinement. Stone tools had almost completely fallen out of use, while those of iron – notably axes, knives, fish-hooks and heads for spears and arrows – were abundant (Breternitz, 1975). In view of the major developments in art, technology and the socio-political fields which, to judge from the evidence of later times, must have taken place during the first millennium A.D., it is unfortunate that the archaeology of this period in Nigeria remains so little known.

In eastern Nigeria, south of the Benue, there is no evidence that iron was known before the early centuries A.D. However, the discoveries from an apparently ninth-century context at Igbo Ukwu near Onitsha show that, by the end of the first millennium, a great concentration of wealth was in the hands (or at the disposal) of a minority who held considerable religious power and perhaps, to judge from later parallels, political authority also. The Igbo Ukwu site was a grave where a person of great importance had been buried in an elaborate manner and accompanied by rich belongings. Meticulous excavation has enabled the burial to be reconstructed in considerable detail. The corpse, sitting on a stool, dressed in and surrounded by his regalia of office, was placed with three ivory tusks in a deep earth-dug, wood-lined burial chamber which was then roofed over. In the upper chamber thus created were placed the remains of at least five attendants, and the whole grave was filled in with earth. Nearby, two further caches of artefacts were discovered; in one case the objects appeared to have been laid out in a relic house; in the other they had been

7.15 Megalithic stone circle at Sine Saloum, Senegal

unceremoniously buried in a pit. There could be little doubt that the whole site represented a single burial complex; radiocarbon dates provide good evidence that it belongs to the ninth century A.D., although some archaeologists continue to argue for a later date. The excavator has suggested that the person buried at Igbo Ukwu may have held a position analogous to that of the Eze Nri of the recent Igbo peoples (Shaw, 1970).

Without doubt the most remarkable feature of the Igbo Ukwu discoveries was the superb bronze castings that were found in all three parts of the site (fig. 7.16). They had been produced by the 'lost wax' method, in which a wax model is encased in clay to produce a mould, the wax then being replaced by molten metal. The bronzes include a series of elaborate vases with delicate surface decoration, bowls, and models of shells, as well as a breast-ornament, fly-whisk handle and other regalia which accompanied the main burial. Their style and the nature of their elaborate decoration are unlike those of other West African bronze-casting traditions. Comparison with the domestic pottery at Igbo Ukwu indicates that the bronzes were of local manufacture, although the metal from which they were made may have been obtained by long-distance trade, as were the glass beads, of which over 150,000 were found at the site. To evaluate the nature of this trade it will be necessary to discuss contemporary events in the savanna regions to the north.

The Igbo Ukwu discoveries indicate that craft specialisation and the concentra-

7.16 Bronzes from Igbo Ukwu: left – stand for an altar, right – land-snail shell

tion of wealth which are seen in later times, in the Ife and Benin kingdoms for example (see chapter 8), were already taking place by the end of the first millennium A.D. It is logical to conclude that state-formation processes were also taking place, at least in some parts of West Africa, during the late first millennium, and this is rendered more probable by evidence from further to the north. By the eighth century A.D., when Muslim traders first reached the south-western Sahara, they found that the gold trade with the north was controlled by the powerful kingdom of Ghana, centred between the upper reaches of the Niger and Senegal Rivers in the borderlands of the modern southern Mauritania and south-western Mali (fig. 7.17). Ancient Ghana was thus far removed from the modern state which has taken its name. The principal goldfield exploited at this time was located to the south, around Bambuk in the Senegal headwaters, but the kingdom of Ghana controlled its access to the trading centre of Awdaghast, at the southern end of the main caravan route from the north. The capital of the kingdom of Ghana is thought to have been at Kumbi Saleh, where the remains of an extensive stone-built town have been discovered and partially excavated (Thomassey and Mauny, 1951; 1956). The date of the establishment of this state remains uncertain, but must have been well before the eighth century, when Muslim visitors from the north were impressed by the power and wealth of its ruler (Levtzion, 1973).

Further states arose to the east of ancient Ghana before the close of the first millennium A.D. Among these, adjacent to Lake Chad, was Kanem which grew rich through trade with the north, primarily to Tunis. Traditions suggest that the Zaghawa rulers of Kanem originated in the southern Sahara. Their penetration

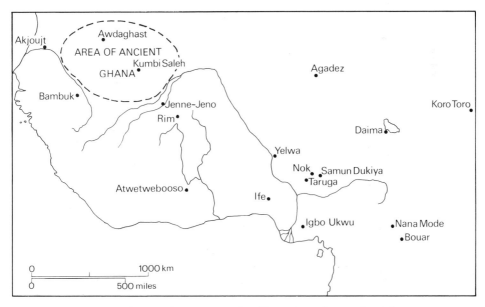

7.17 Principal West African sites with evidence for early use of metal

southwards to establish themselves as overlords of the settled farming people to the south may have been stimulated by continuing desiccation of the desert and also by desire to control the source of the slaves and ivory on which their prosperity depended (H. F. C. Smith, 1971). It is tempting to link this process with the change in artefact types at Daima which, as noted above on p. 166, accompanied evidence for an expansion and intensification of trade late in the first millennium A.D. The later history of these sudanic states is described in chapter 8.

The more easterly regions of the northern savanna, stretching from Cameroon into the Central African Republic, remain very poorly known archaeologically. It was shown in chapter 6 how some of the stone-tool-using farming peoples of the Cameroon/eastern Nigeria area are assumed to have been Bantu-speakers. Probably before the coming of iron, some of these people had begun to expand southwards, into the forest, and probably also eastwards along its northern margin. To the north, at Nana Mode in the Central African Republic, an iron-using settlement in the savanna is dated to about the seventh century A.D.; the pottery from this site was decorated by means of a carved wooden roulette. It has been suggested that the inhabitants of this site were speakers of an Ubangian language (David and Vidal, 1977).

In conclusion, it is appropriate to attempt a generalised overall picture of cultural development in West Africa around the beginning of the Christian era. It is essential to bear in mind that the very incomplete coverage of the research which has so far been undertaken makes any such attempt tentative. An understanding, however provisional, of the West African sequence is particularly important in view of the indications, to be cited below, that this area played a very important part in the transmission of iron technology and associated culture to more southerly parts of Africa.

The first point is that knowledge of iron-working can no longer be assumed to have been brought to West Africa from the north. The restricted areas where copper was known and used before iron are not yet adequately investigated or understood. It is possible to envisage that people living in southern Mauritania obtained their knowledge of copper-working from a Phoenician source or even an Iberian one. However, in Niger, it now appears that native copper was melted in bellows-assisted furnaces as early as 2000 B.C. Some authorities have suggested that Nubian contacts early in the last millennium B.C. were responsible for the beginning of copper-smelting there; but it would be premature to regard the case as proven, and the presence in the same area over one thousand years earlier of an appropriate high-temperature technology makes it at least equally probable that smelting techniques were independently discovered south of the Sahara. The most plausible explanations for the initial development of West African iron-working are either that it was a local invention based upon earlier copper-smelting technology, or that the relevant knowledge was transmitted south of the Sahara from North Africa. Elaboration of these hypotheses, which are not mutually exclusive, will have to await the recovery of detailed evidence as to the smelting methods that were practised in these two areas.

There can be little doubt that iron was adopted in the West African savanna by peoples who had been settled there for many centuries previously. The beginning of iron-working in parts of the forest was, on the other hand, probably at least partly due to eastward penetration by immigrant groups. Some forest-dwellers initially retained their stone-tool technology, but these late survivals have so far been only cursorily investigated.

Archaeological research in West Africa has been concentrated on sites which illustrate the history of the known states, especially on those which have also yielded art objects. This has tended to obscure the fact that the earliest iron-using communities were composed essentially of peasant farmers, and that such people probably formed the majority of the West African population throughout the last two thousand years. Inter-regional exchange of commodities has also been seen as a major factor during this period and one that acted as a significant stimulus to the processes of urbanisation and state-formation, long before the development of formal trans-Saharan trade.

The last millennium B.C. saw the establishment of substantial villages in southern Cameroon, an area where pottery-making agriculturalists appear to have been settled for several thousands of years previously. At Obobogo, near Yaounde, such a site covered about 2 hectares: iron seems to have been in use here from about the fourth century B.C. (de Maret, 1985). In Gabon and Congo preliminary reconnaissance has revealed evidence for settlements of iron-using peoples from the end of the first millennium B.C. (Peyrot and Oslisly, 1986). To the east and south-east, current research (Eggert, 1984) is beginning to illustrate a long archaeological sequence beside the major rivers of the Zaire rainforest, where iron-using peoples made elaborately decorated pottery in which stylistic affinities may be discerned with ceramic traditions of both the Ubangi and Lower Zaire regions. In the latter area iron working is clearly demonstrated on the Kay Ladio sites from the second century A.D. (de Maret, 1986). It is noteworthy that, throughout this vast region of west-central Africa, there are signs of continuity between the material culture of the earliest iron workers and that of their predecessors. The picture that emerges from the very preliminary archaeological research that has so far been undertaken is thus one of the gradual adoption of pottery and ground-stone tools in the western Congo basin by people who may have cultivated yams and other non-cereal crops. Later, following the inception of iron-working techniques, these innovations may be recognised in the more densely forested regions further to the east.

Bantu-speaking Africa

The earliest iron-using communities over an enormous area of eastern and southern Africa show a very remarkable degree of homogeneity, to the extent

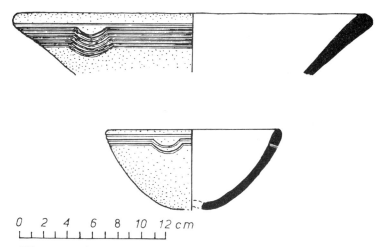

7.18 Urewe ware from sites in south-western Kenya (after M. D. Leakey *et al.*, 1948)

that archaeologists generally attribute them to a single complex, here named the Chifumbaze complex.* Radiocarbon dates indicate that the complex first appeared in the area around Lake Victoria during the last few centuries B.C., and that in the first three hundred years of the Christian era it expanded south-wards as far as Natal (D. W. Phillipson, 1975). The archaeological sites and artefacts of the Chifumbaze complex make a marked contrast with those that had gone before, and contain the first evidence in these southerly latitudes for food-production, for settled village life, for metallurgy and, south of Tanzania, for the manufacture of pottery. In each case, these are cultural features for which there is archaeological evidence in more northerly regions of Africa in earlier times. The fact that so many important aspects of culture were introduced together over such a wide area and so rapidly makes it highly probable that the beginnings of iron-using in sub-equatorial Africa were brought about as a result of the physical movement of substantial numbers of people. As will be shown below, it is likely that these people were speakers of Bantu languages.

The first use of iron in the Lake Victoria area is attributed to the Urewe group, named after a site in south-western Kenya. Its characteristic pottery (fig. 7.18), in which several local sub-styles may be recognised, is found in Rwanda and adjacent parts of Zaire, in southern Uganda, north-western Tanzania and around the Winam Gulf in south-western Kenya (van Noten, 1979). In Buhaya on the south-western shore of the lake, extensive settlements and iron-smelting sites, such as Katuruka, date at least to the very beginning of the Christian era and may be several centuries older (Schmidt, 1978).

* Following my earlier proposal (1968a), the interim term 'Early Iron Age' has been applied to this complex. However, now that its parameters are relatively well known, and to avoid confusion with contemporary early iron-using societies in other parts of Africa, it appears preferable to use a more distinctive name. The name 'Chifumbaze' has been chosen from the rockshelter in Mozambique where pottery of this complex was first excavated (D. W. Phillipson, 1976).

There is only indirect evidence that the makers of Urewe ware practised any form of food-production. Bones of domestic animals recovered from rockshelter sites near the Winam Gulf may be associated with an Urewe presence, but this attribution cannot be demonstrated with certainty. Sediments on the bed of Lake Victoria contain dateable pollen which suggests that there was a significant reduction in forest vegetation around the lake about the middle of the last millennium B.C. (Kendall and Livingstone, 1972). This could, of course, have been brought about by climatic causes or by charcoal-burning for iron-smelting, rather than by ground-clearance for agriculture.

Much more research needs to be done before we shall be able to understand the antecedents of the Urewe group. Their predecessors in the Lake Victoria area appear to have been the makers of Kansyore ware, described in chapter 6, and the relationship, if any, between the two populations remains unknown. No close parallels are known for Urewe ware, but there are similarities with pottery from far to the north-west, in Chad (Soper, 1971), and also with certain West African wares. It is in these northerly and westerly areas, also, that we must presumably look for the origins of the Urewe group's iron-working technology. Linguistic studies throw further light on this problem, and will be discussed below.

Studies of pottery typology suggest that the earliest iron-using communities of more southerly latitudes may have been descended from those of the Urewe group, and a large number of radiocarbon dates confirm that this is probable on chronological grounds. Although points of controversy remain, there is broad agreement among many archaeologists that the Chifumbaze complex to the south of the Urewe area may best be considered as representing two or three separate facies, of which the easterly probably derived directly from the Urewe group (D. W. Phillipson, 1977a). The ancestry of the western facies also may have had Urewe connexions, but its origins remain less well understood: it probably incorporated local elements from the western Zaire/northern Angola region. The distributions of these facies and of their constituent groups are shown in fig. 7.19.

The easternmost facies extended by about the second century A.D. to the coastal regions of south-eastern Kenya and the adjacent parts of north-eastern Tanzania, where it is represented by sites yielding the characteristic type of pottery named Kwale ware, after a site south-west of Mombasa. Settlement seems here to have been restricted to the relatively well-watered hilly country where the villages of the region's present Bantu-speaking farming communities are still concentrated (Soper, 1967a; 1967b). It may be noted that in the Rift Valley territory of the stone-tool-using herders no contemporary traces of iron or of Kwale-related pottery have been discovered. Presumably either this comparatively arid country was unsuited to settlement by the Chifumbaze people, or the herders were able to prevent penetration by the newcomers. Whatever the reason, it is probable that the Kwale industry was introduced to the East African coast by a southerly

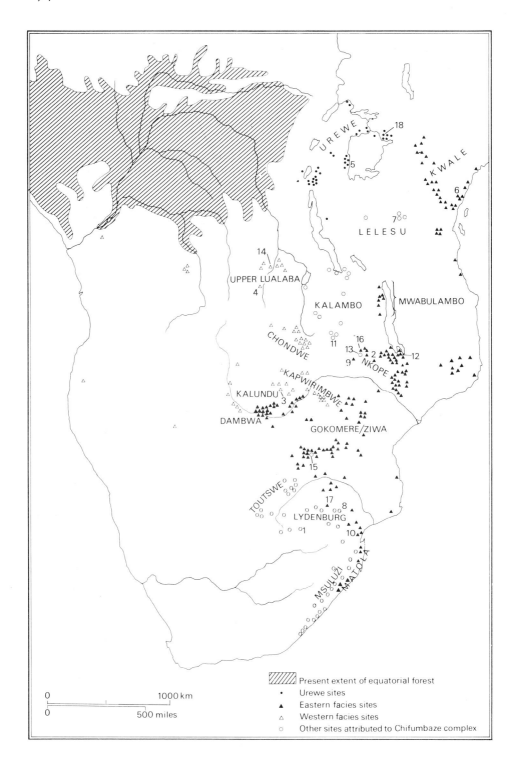

Present extent of equatorial forest
- •   Urewe sites
- ▲   Eastern facies sites
- △   Western facies sites
- ○   Other sites attributed to Chifumbaze complex

0   1000 km

0   500 miles

route through what is now central Tanzania, where Chifumbaze sites such as Lelesu have been reported (Smolla, 1956; Sutton, 1968).

Between the second and fourth centuries A.D. there took place an extremely rapid dispersal of iron-using farmers of the Chifumbaze complex through a wide area extending southwards through Mozambique, Malawi, eastern Zambia and Zimbabwe into the Transvaal, Swaziland and Natal. The easternmost manifestation was largely restricted to the coastal lowlands and clearly sprang from the Kwale group settlements of East Africa. More than 2,000 km appear to have been covered in less than two centuries. The characteristic Matola tradition pottery by which this coastal dispersal may readily be recognised has been identified in Mozambique both in the Nampula region and at Matola near Maputo (Cruz e Silva, 1980; Morais, 1984). South of the Zambezi it is now represented at more than 40 sites in the coastal regions of southern Mozambique, in the eastern Transvaal lowlands, and in Natal as far as latitude 30° south (Maggs, 1984). Villages, up to 2 hectares in extent, were generally sited a few kilometres inland of the Indian Ocean shore, in locations suited to the cultivation of cereals. Further inland, in Malawi, eastern Zambia and much of Zimbabwe, the Chifumbaze complex is represented both by substantial villages and by pottery occurrences in rockshelters that apparently continued to be frequented by stone-tool-using hunter-gatherers throughout the first millennium A.D., making only occasional contact with the immigrant farmers (D. W. Phillipson, 1976; 1977a; Crader, 1984). These inland manifestations are attributed to the Nkope and Gokomere/Ziwa traditions. Their relationship with the Matola tradition remains unclear and it is uncertain whether they should be regarded as representing coastal and inland manifestations of an eastern facies of the Chifumbaze complex, or as two distinct facies (cf. Huffman, 1982).

The archaeology of the more westerly regions has so far been much less intensively investigated, being well known only in the Shaba Province of Zaire and in central Zambia, where iron-working is known as early as the second century A.D. In the former area, furthermore, our knowledge is virtually restricted to cemetery sites of late date, such as Sanga and Katoto in the valley of the upper Lualaba River (Nenquin, 1963; Hiernaux *et al.*, 1972; de Maret, 1977). Despite the apparently late arrival of the Chifumbaze complex in central Zambia, there are some indications both from northern Angola and from the valley of the upper Zambezi River that this material belongs to a relatively late phase in the

7.19 Sites of the Chifumbaze complex in East and southern Africa

1 Broederstroóm	7 Lelesu	13 Sakwe
2 Chifumbaze	8 Lydenburg	14 Sanga
3 Kalundu	9 Makwe	15 Silozwane
4 Katoto	10 Matola	16 Thandwe
5 Katuruka	11 Nakapapula	17 Tzaneen
6 Kwale	12 Nkope	18 Urewe

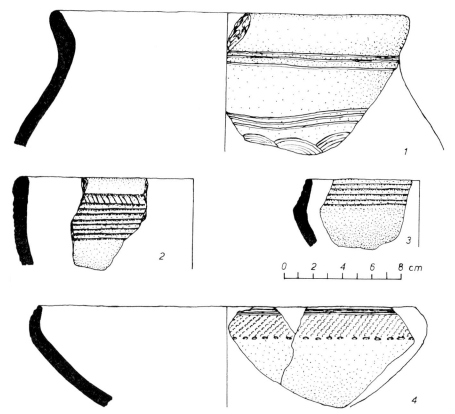

7.20 Pottery of the eastern facies of the Chifumbaze complex, from Malawi (after Robinson and Sandelowsky, 1968; Robinson, 1973)

development of the western facies. An early date – perhaps in the last century B.C. or thereabouts – for the initial southward spread of the western facies would, as will be shown below, provide an excellent fit with what is currently known about the earliest beginning of pastoralism in south-westernmost Africa, and with certain linguistic evidence.

Particularly significant are the manifestations of the Chifumbaze complex in eastern Botswana and adjacent parts of the Limpopo Valley. In the former area developments from around the seventh century are attributed to the Toutswe tradition, marked by a hierarchical settlement system with a small number of large easily defended sites surrounded by more numerous smaller settlements (Denbow, 1984; 1986). Cattle provided the mainstay of the system's economy and there are good reasons for tracing back to this period the important role played by cattle in the culture of southern Bantu-speaking people. The large central Toutswe sites, with evidence for the herding of very large numbers of cattle, suggest the rise of an elite such as may be recognised also in rather later times at the Limpopo Valley sites of Schroda, Bambandyanalo and Mapungubwe, where it was supported by the development of long-distance trade in ivory and, from the eleventh century, in gold (Huffman, 1982; Maggs, 1984).

The sites of the first millennium A.D. in the southern Transvaal and parts of Natal are for the most part attributed to the Msuluzi/Lydenburg tradition of the Chifumbaze complex. Opinion is divided as to whether this tradition arose, around the fourth century, from the earlier Matola tradition of the Mozambique and Natal coastlands, or whether its connexions lay further inland, perhaps with the western facies of the Chifumbaze complex (Huffman, 1982; Maggs, 1984). In Natal, evidence for early farming settlement is restricted to the lower reaches of the river valleys where fertile soils are available together with vegetation which provides year-round grazing (Maggs, 1980). Two sites in the Transvaal deserve special mention. An extensive site at Broederstroom, west of Pretoria, has provided a particularly complete picture of village life at this time (Mason, 1981). At Lydenburg in the eastern Transvaal a remarkable series of elaborate pottery human heads was recovered (fig. 7.21), some of them life-sized, apparently dating to the fifth century A.D. Fragments of similar objects have been found on other Transvaal sites, but the heads are without parallel elsewhere (Inskeep and Maggs, 1975; Evers, 1982).

Throughout the area inhabited by the Chifumbaze people, iron-working was practised on a scale adequate to ensure that they only rarely, if ever, used stone

7.21 Terracotta head from Lydenburg

tools. In regions where the appropriate mineral deposits occur, copper and gold were also worked. Mining appears to have been restricted to small-scale operations during the first millennium A.D.; and we have as yet little reliable information concerning the types of smelting-furnaces that were used, except in the interlacustrine region. Iron artefacts were mainly utilitarian: axes, hoes, arrow-heads and the like. Copper was used for bangles and items of personal adornment; by A.D. 1300 in Shaba it was being cast into small cross-shaped ingots which may have served as a form of currency (Bisson, 1975). Gold-working, effectively restricted to Zimbabwe, is attested only from the end of the first millennium A.D. and seems largely to have been geared to an export trade through the ports of the Indian Ocean coast, from which imported glass beads and, perhaps, other more perishable items found their way inland (Summers, 1969).

Detailed evidence concerning the food-producing economies of the Chifumbaze communities and the plant and animal species on which they were based has only rarely been recovered. A settlement pattern based on large semi-permanent villages of up to several hectares' extent in areas which lack concentrated non-seasonal potential food resources such as fish, of course strongly suggests an economy based largely on some sort of food-production. While the presence of iron hoes and of numerous grindstones may indicate agriculture, conclusive proof of this in the form of specifically identifiable remains of the domestic animals and plants that were exploited has been recovered from disappointingly few sites.

Virtually all the detailed information so far available concerning the food-producing economy of the Chifumbaze complex comes from Zambia, Zimbabwe and South Africa. The cultivated crops for which there is evidence include sorghum, cowpeas and unidentified varieties of squash and beans. It is unfortunate that more detailed botanical descriptions of this material are not yet available as, until they are, meaningful comparisons cannot be made with the crops that were grown in more northerly regions. Such comparisons might throw light on the manner in which their cultivation was begun in south-central Africa.

The evidence for domestic livestock is somewhat more comprehensive. Cattle appear to have been relatively rare in most areas until around the seventh or eighth century A.D. Sheep and/or goats are, in contrast, attested on sites which cover the whole time-span of the Chifumbaze complex.

Throughout this period, the hunting of wild animals retained considerable economic importance. Iron arrow-heads and spear-points (which need not, of course, have been used exclusively for hunting) have been recovered from many sites, and those from which bones of wild animals have been excavated are appreciably more numerous than those that have yielded remains of domestic stock. At Kalundu, in southern Zambia, the faunal remains from successive layers show the gradual replacement of wild by domestic species (Fagan, 1967).

The wild animals represented include wildebeest and buffalo, as well as many of the lesser antelope. Fish bones are rarely preserved, but are recorded in Malawi, notably at Nkope.

In order that maximum use may be made of the evidence afforded by linguistic studies, we must consider the possibility of a correlation between the archaeological picture described above and the processes of the dispersal of the Bantu languages. The geographical distribution of the Chifumbaze complex is almost identical with the area occupied in more recent times by peoples speaking languages of the closely inter-related Bantu type. This observation lends support to the widely held belief that this complex represents the archaeological manifestation of the initial southward spread of the Bantu-speakers. The Bantu languages, which are today spoken by upwards of 130 million people spread over an area of nearly 9 million square kilometres, show a remarkable degree of inter-comprehensibility; and there can be no reasonable doubt that they have attained their present wide distribution as a result of dispersal from a common localised ancestral language within the comparatively recent past – certainly within the last 3,000 or 4,000 years. Linguists are virtually unanimous in the belief that this ancestral Bantu language was spoken close to the north-western border of the present Bantu-speaking area – in what is now Cameroon and eastern Nigeria (cf. Dalby, 1975).

To the south and east of the equatorial forest, in the areas where the Chifumbaze complex is attested in the archaeological record, the modern Bantu languages fall into two major groups. These have been designated the Western Highland group, which is centred in Angola and northern Namibia, and the Eastern Highland group, which is of far greater extent and covers all the eastern half of the sub-continent. Of these two groups, the Western Highland languages show appreciably more internal diversity than do their eastern counterparts, and the dispersal of the Eastern Highland group may thus be assumed to have been significantly later in date than that of the Western Highland group. The boundary between these two language groups does not, it must be emphasised, coincide with that between the eastern and western facies of the Chifumbaze complex; but the general picture that emerges from linguistic studies is nevertheless strikingly similar in several ways to that deduced from the archaeological evidence.

The consensus of linguistic opinion suggests that the dispersal of the Bantu languages from their north-western homeland took roughly the following course. From the Cameroon area expansion initially took place either through or along the fringes of the equatorial forest, eventually leading both to the interlacustrine region and to the country around the mouth of the Congo River. In this area a second dispersal took place that gave rise to the Western Highland languages. Subsequently the Eastern Highland languages were dispersed, most probably from somewhere in the vicinity of the Zambia/Shaba Copperbelt (Heine *et al.*, 1977; Dalby, 1975).

It appears reasonable to suggest that the lower Congo branch of Bantu was spoken by the inhabitants of that area during the last few centuries B.C., and that the Western Highland languages may be derived from those spoken by the bearers of the Chifumbaze complex's western facies. It is tempting also to propose that the languages spoken by the people responsible for the eastern facies were derived from the early Bantu of the interlacustrine region, or were a form of Eastern Highland Bantu. The alternative attribution of the Eastern Highland languages to a later dispersal, although archaeologically plausible (D. W. Phillipson, 1977a), has been criticised on linguistic grounds (Ehret, 1973). There is thus an acceptably close fit between the archaeological picture of the spread of the Chifumbaze complex and that independently derived from linguistic data for the dispersal of the Bantu languages.

Despite the novelty of the metal-using farmers' life-style, economy and technology, it is clear that these were not rapidly or totally accepted by the indigenous populations. In several areas, indeed, there is plentiful evidence both from archaeology and from oral tradition for the survival of a microlithic technology long after the appearance of metallurgy. In some parts of south-central Africa this continued until only two or three centuries ago, although the degree of this survival obviously varied according to the intensity of farming settlement in the various areas. The best studied of these very late microlithic industries are those of northern and eastern Zambia. Here, detailed analyses of industrial successions covering the last three millennia, such as those from Nakapapula, Thandwe and Makwe, indicate no significant discernible typological changes such as might be expected had there been any major change in the hunter-gatherer economy and life-style of the stone-tool-makers as a result of cultural contact with their farming contemporaries (D. W. Phillipson, 1976; 1977a). That some form of contact did in fact take place between the indigenes and the immigrant food-producers is indicated by the presence in nearly all the microlithic assemblages of this period of varying numbers of sherds of characteristic Chifumbaze pottery. The persistence of the microlithic industries, showing only gradual typological development following trends that were already apparent before any contact was established with the farmers, suggests that such contact between the two groups was usually minimal. By contrast, in areas where farming settlement at an early date was relatively dense, there seems to have been fairly rapid displacement of the hunter-gatherer populations as, for example, in much of southern Zambia. A plausible reconstruction of the interactions which must have taken place between the hunter-gatherers and the food-producers is that of a temporary client relationship, such as has been recorded in recent times both in southern Africa and further to the north (Silberbauer, 1965). This analogy also suggests that, in some areas, relations between these two population groups were characterised by aloofness or mutual avoidance. It must be remembered that virtually all our evidence for interaction comes from the territory of the Chifumbaze complex's eastern facies. We have as yet no reliable means of knowing whether the processes were similar in more westerly areas.

The final absorbtion, conquest or displacement of the stone-tool-using hunting peoples in south-central Africa may be attributed to the expanding population of the early second millennium, which was marked by increased emphasis on the herding of domestic animals, notably cattle. With the passage of time, continued expansion would have brought the cattle-keeping farmers and the hunters into intensified competition. Except where stable symbiosis was established, the ultimate result was apparently the disappearance of the stone-tool-making traditions in all but the few areas which were unsuitable for farming settlement.

An example of the former situation is provided by the pygmies of the eastern equatorial forest (d'Hertefelt, 1965; Turnbull, 1961; 1965). The early history of these small-statured hunting people is completely unknown, as is the language or languages which they originally spoke. Today, most pygmy groups are involved in a client relationship with their agricultural neighbours whose language, whether Bantu, Sudanic or Ubangian, they have adopted.

The arrival of the farming peoples in the territories of the indigenous hunter-gatherers of southern Africa also appears to be recorded by the latter in rock paintings. In chapter 4 we saw that six successive styles could be recognised in the rock art of Zimbabwe; and it was in the third of these that the painters began to depict scenes and objects that indicated their acquaintance with the farmers. A painting of a group of people on the walls of Silozwane Cave in the Matopo Hills is believed to show grain-grinding and other activities of agriculturalists; the people themselves are quite different in appearance from the hunters represented in the earlier paintings (fig. 7.22). Elsewhere, fat-tailed sheep are clearly recognisable (Summers, 1959). Later paintings and occasional engravings, consisting mainly of geometric and schematic designs (fig. 7.23), are best attributed to the farmers themselves. In some areas, notably Malawi and eastern Zambia, they may be linked with art forms associated with religious practices that have continued into recent times (D. W. Phillipson, 1972; 1976).

From the data which have been summarised above, there can be little doubt that the Chifumbaze complex was introduced into sub-equatorial Africa as a result of a substantial and rapid movement of population. The entire culture represented on sites of this complex can be shown to be foreign to the areas in which it occurs; and most of its constituent features may be traced to a source or sources in the northern savanna. The large number of available radiocarbon dates accords with this view; and linguistic evidence also lends it a considerable degree of support.

It is much more difficult to suggest what may have been the causes and motivation of this population movement. While the number of people involved at any one time may not have been very large, it was evidently sufficient to sustain the migrants' distinctive life-style and customs. It is most probable that entire family groups were involved in the movements. While population pressure in the original Bantu homeland in what is now Cameroon and eastern Nigeria may have been one of several causal factors, it would not explain why they moved over such a vast and sparsely inhabited area so rapidly – the eastern facies appears to have expanded southward at an average rate of some 10 km a year. The advantages conferred by the knowledge of metallurgy, stock rearing and, probably to a lesser extent, agriculture would greatly have facilitated this expansion, but there are likely to have been other factors also of which we are as yet unaware.

It is useful to speculate on the reasons why the first millennium A.D. expansion of the Chifumbaze complex, which proceeded with such remarkable rapidity as far to the south as the Transvaal and Natal, was there arrested so abruptly. Although the site distribution remains very imperfectly known, especially in the west, it is nevertheless reasonably clear that its southern limit broadly coincides with the northern edge of the south-west African zone of desert vegetation and that of the long-grass veld of the Orange Free State. On the eastern side of the continent the southernmost extent of the Chifumbaze complex is restricted to the west by the Drakensberg and to the south by the Cape winter-rainfall zone. Recent societies have demonstrated that this frontier presents no barrier to pastoralist communities; but it is an effective southern limit for the cultivation of traditional African cereals and other food crops. It seems reasonable to suppose, therefore, that agricultural potential limited the

7.22 Rock painting at Silozwane Cave, Zimbabwe

initial expansion of farming people into southern Africa. It was not until the development of the more pastorally oriented societies of the early second millennium A.D. that further southward expansion took place, resulting in the settlement by Bantu-speaking peoples of such marginal lands as those of the Orange Free State and parts of Namibia.

7.23 Schematic rock painting at Sakwe, Zambia. The scale is in feet

Stone-tool-using pastoralists of south-western Africa

Beyond the area that was settled by the farmers of the Chifumbaze complex, in Namibia and the Cape Province of South Africa, the stone-tool technology of earlier times continued throughout the first millennium A.D. and even into more recent times. There can be little doubt that the people responsible for these stone

industries were Khoisan-speakers, ancestors of the more recent Khoi ('Hottentots') and San ('Bushmen') of southern and south-western Africa. At an early
date these stone-tool-using people obtained domestic sheep and – although this
is less certain – cattle (fig. 7.24). Domestic animal bones make their appearance
on sites in the south-western Cape that are dated to around the second century
A.D. (Schweitzer, 1974; Sandelowsky *et al.*, 1979; H. J. Deacon *et al.*, 1978).
Pottery first occurs in the local archaeological sequence at about the same time.

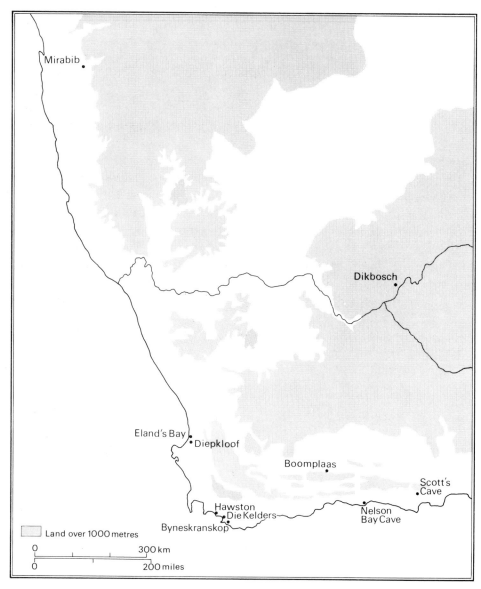

7.24 Sites in south-western Africa which have yielded remains of domestic sheep in
contexts dating to the first millennium A.D

This characteristic Cape coastal pottery, typified by pointed-based jars and beakers (fig. 7.25), shows no particular similarity to any other wares in adjacent regions from which it could have been derived (Rudner, 1968). It seems also to have been produced, or at least used, by communities who did not have access to domestic stock and who continued their traditional reliance on gathering wild vegetable foods, collecting shellfish, hunting and fishing.

Recent archaeological research in the south-western Cape has revealed a complicated pattern of local seasonal resource-exploitation. At least in some areas, such as the west coast north of the Cape of Good Hope, this seems to have involved movement of population between, on the one hand, the inland regions where wild vegetable foods were plentiful during the summer and where the diet could then readily be supplemented by the meat of small animals and, on the other hand, the caves and open sites near the coast where shellfish were exploited during the winter (Parkington, 1972). This appears to have been the main regimen of life during the centuries which preceded the advent of food-production, and a life-style which has continued into relatively recent centuries without significant discernible modification.

The extent to which sheep-herding was adopted by these seasonally migrating groups cannot yet be ascertained. It is possible that the herders formed a distinct population element, whose sites have not yet been located or differentiated in the archaeological record. Archaeologists cannot yet determine with any confidence whether the sheep bones which have been recovered represent animals that were herded by the inhabitants of the sites on which the bones were found, or ones that were obtained by exchange or raiding from elsewhere.

There is no local wild ancestor to domestic cattle in the relatively well studied South African faunal assemblages of the last millennia B.C., so there can be no reasonable doubt that the first domestic animals in southernmost Africa were introduced into the region from more northerly latitudes. The present archaeological picture reveals no potential source for these animals other than the

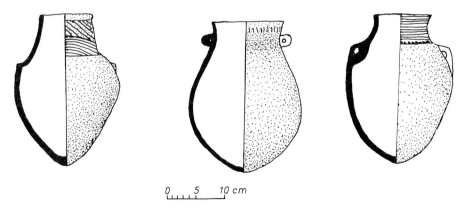

0   5   10 cm

7.25 Cape coastal pottery (after Rudner, 1968)

Chifumbaze complex. It has been pointed out that the first appearance of domestic stock in the south-western Cape preceded by two centuries or so the earliest manifestations of the Chifumbaze complex yet known in South Africa – those of the Transvaal and Natal. However, it must be emphasised that, while virtually nothing is definitely known concerning the chronology of the western facies in southern Angola and northern Namibia, there are grounds – as has been indicated above – for supposing that the Chifumbaze complex was introduced there significantly earlier than it was further to the east. Its western facies thus stands as the most likely source of the domestic stock adopted by the stone-tool-using inhabitants of the Cape during the first centuries of the Christian era (D. W. Phillipson, 1977a). There is, however, little evidence as to where this contact may have taken place. One possibility is northern Botswana and adjacent parts of eastern Zimbabwe. In the latter area, as noted above, sheep and pottery (the latter probably related in some way to the wares of the Chifumbaze complex) are represented in the Matopo Hills around the last century B.C. (Walker, 1983); and similar pottery is now known from northern Botswana. Linguistic evidence also points to this area as that where the Khoisan languages of the later southern African herders were initially differentiated (Ehret, 1982). It is possible that knowledge of pottery-making techniques also reached southernmost Africa from the same source and that the Cape coastal wares represent a local adaptation of this technology; alternatively, it may have been an independent local invention.

CHAPTER 8

THE SECOND MILLENNIUM A.D. IN SUB-SAHARAN AFRICA

The last 1,000 years

In many parts of Africa the last 1,000 years comprise a period for which archaeology, although still of considerable importance, is by no means our only source of information. Linguistic reconstructions which, when taken together with the results of archaeology, have been valuable for finding out about earlier periods, now become less speculative. For the more recent periods the oral historical traditions of many African societies preserve a great deal of valuable information. In some areas of the continent, written records are also available. For much of northern Africa, indeed, the last 1,000 years fall fully within the period of written history, and for that reason this chapter is concerned only with the sub-continent lying to the south of the Sahara. Here, some areas, such as those of the sudanic kingdoms and parts of the East African coast, were in more or less regular contact with people of literate communities, in whose records has been preserved much useful historical detail. These records may be used in conjunction with information from other sources in the building up of a composite picture of the period's events and developments. Elsewhere, we have no significant written records pre-dating contact with the European traders and colonisers who gradually established control over Africa between the fifteenth and the nineteenth centuries. With this process the subject-matter of this book comes to an ill-defined end; and the study of the African past enters the field of conventional history.

To a large extent recent interest in the history of sub-Saharan Africa after A.D. 1000 has focussed on the development of long-distance trade and on the formation of states (cf. Garlake, 1978a). In many areas the two processes may have been to some extent concurrent and dependent on one another. Trade provided both a stimulus and a mechanism for state-formation through the opportunities it gave for individuals or groups to monopolise or control the distribution of wealth. However, as will be shown below, it is in several areas becoming increasingly apparent that purely local exchange systems often provided the necessary basis. Political centralisation made it possible for the products of a region to be gathered together for organised re-distribution. These factors have had a significant effect on our sources of historical information. State centres or capitals provide many opportunities for the archaeologist; such sites, because of their size, wealth or monumental architecture, may be readily discovered, leading to a tendency to ignore less conspicuous sites that were inhabited by peasants or subject communities. Thus trade and political power may be over-emphasised in archaeological studies. Likewise, as was shown in chapter 1, oral traditions often serve to record and to support the position of ruling groups or dynasties, and here, too, this aspect of history may be studied at the expense of others. A result of this bias in our available sources is that we tend to know far more about the history of those peoples who developed centralised state-systems than of those who did not, and more about activities relating to long-distance trade than about those connected with domestic economy. One of the strengths of archaeology as a data-source for African history and later prehistory is its ability to throw light on aspects of past societies which are not stressed by studies rooted in other disciplines. Archaeology is of particular relevance also to the study of the historical development of acephalous societies.

West Africa

Some account was given in chapter 7 of the early stages of state formation in the savanna country of West Africa before A.D. 1000, with particular reference to the kingdoms of Ghana and Kanem. Later centuries saw the further development and proliferation of such kingdoms as well as the establishment of comparable institutions further to the south. For the sudanic kingdoms, much of our information now comes from written Arabic sources, which are in some areas beginning to be supplemented by the testimony of archaeology (Levtzion, 1973; 1977).

To the second half of the eleventh century belongs al-Bakri's description of Ghana. He commented on the near-divine status of the ruler, who was succeeded, not by his son, but by his sister's son; on his death he was buried beneath a large earth mound, accompanied by the bodies of his retainers. A large armed force enabled the king to maintain control over many tributary chiefdoms. The capital of ancient Ghana was divided into two areas. One, surrounding the royal residence, was built in the local African style with predominantly round houses of mud; while the other, inhabited mainly by Muslim traders and other immigrants from the north, was built of stone and included several mosques. The site of the capital of ancient Ghana may be represented by the ruins at Kumbi Saleh in southern Mauritania (fig. 8.1), which cover more than 2 sq. km, the adjacent cemeteries being even more extensive (Robert, 1970; Mauny, 1978). Here, a wide central avenue and market area are lined by the remains of two-storey stone buildings. The artefacts indicate the North African connexions and long-distance trade of the site's inhabitants. The trade on which the prosperity of ancient Ghana largely depended was conducted chiefly in gold from the south, in salt from the Sahara, and in copper and a variety of manufactured goods imported from the north. Trade in these commodities was controlled and taxed by the rulers of Ghana, although none was actually produced within the territory that was subject to their jurisdiction, the source of gold being around Bambuk on the upper Senegal far to the south-west. Ancient Ghana was in a strong position to exploit its intermediary position between the suppliers and the trans-Saharan traders. The majority of the people of the kingdom of Ghana were probably of northern Mande stock. Oral traditions recorded in Timbuktu during the sixteenth century suggest that its founding rulers may have been of Saharan Berber Sanhaja (ancestral Tuareg) origin, although by the time of al-Bakri's account in the mid-eleventh century this dynasty had apparently been replaced by a negroid one.

During the eleventh century several of the Berber peoples of the western Sahara were converted to Islam. They then united as the Almoravids, a militant group which expanded rapidly both to the north and to the south. Late in the eleventh century they conquered ancient Ghana and imposed their Islamic faith upon its rulers and traders. The stability of the kingdom was severely weakened and, although the Mande rulers soon regained control, it never fully returned to its former prosperity. More southerly Mande groups now rose to prominence; and by early in the thirteenth century the empire of Mali came into being as the effective successor to ancient Ghana. Mali had a richer agricultural base than its predecessor, and more direct control of the goldfields. By the fourteenth century its rulers held sway, from their capital on the upper Niger, over an extensive territory (fig. 8.2), stretching from the southern Sahara to the northern edge of the forest.

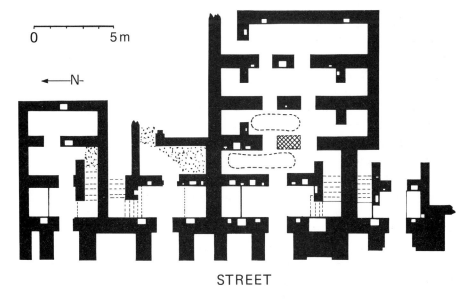

STREET

8.1 The ruins at Kumbi Saleh

Downstream along the Niger the Songhai had, by the end of the first millennium A.D., formed their own riverine kingdom, with its capital at Gao. Before the end of the thirteenth century the Mande had established their control over the Songhai kingdom, greatly increasing the power and prosperity of Mali. Not long afterwards, Musa, ruler of Mali, went on a pilgrimage to Mecca; the wealth and size of his entourage created a lasting impression and served to consolidate Mali's position in the Islamic world. The works of North African writers now become major sources for our knowledge of the sudanic kingdoms.

The power of Mali was broken in the late fifteenth century by the Songhai sultan, Ali, who extended his rule eastwards through Hausaland and northwards to Aïr. Mali was now restricted to a small area west of the upper Niger. The enlarged Songhai empire of Gao was short-lived, being destroyed at the end of the sixteenth century by a force from Morocco.

To the east, the rulers of Kanem were converted to Islam late in the eleventh century. For some hundreds of years, Kanem did not receive the attentions of trans-Saharan contacts on the same scale as did Ghana and Mali; its exports, although valuable, lacked the lure of the gold of Bambuk. Eventually, after a long period of internecine strife among the rulers, the former Bornu province south-west of Lake Chad became the centre of a new empire, with Kanem reduced to tributary status. Troops of cavalry were important in maintaining the power of the state. By the sixteenth century the main trans-Saharan trade had shifted eastwards: the Hausa states and Bornu were established as major markets where the products both of the sudan and the more southerly regions

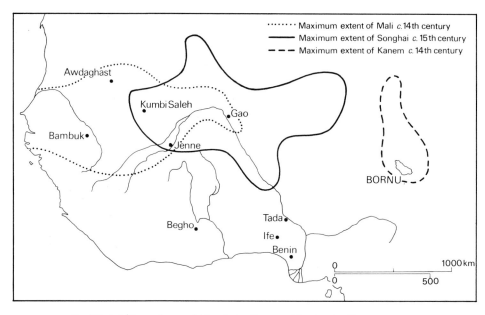

8.2 West African sites and kingdoms discussed in chapter 8

were exchanged for goods from North Africa and beyond. The direct successors to these states have played an important part in the more recent history of the area, into the present century. Future archaeological research may be expected to throw much light on their chronology and on the economic processes which underlay their development.

To the south, in the West African forests and on their northern fringes, a contrasting situation prevailed, for here the events of the period between A.D. 1000 and the arrival of the first European voyagers at the end of the fifteenth century are known only from archaeology, supplemented to some extent with the oral traditions preserved by more recent peoples. Only very indirectly are events of these southerly regions recorded in the Arabic writings which have proved such useful sources for the history of the sudanic kingdoms. Unfortunately, archaeological investigation of the second millennium A.D. in the West African forest regions is still in its infancy, and has so far been largely restricted to parts of modern Ghana and Nigeria.

In Ghana, a series of small states arose by the fourteenth century among the Mossi, adjacent to the trade route that ran from Jenne near the Niger bend southward into the forest, to the Akan goldfield (Posnansky, 1973; S. and R. McIntosh, 1980). The best known of these Mossi states was that centred on Begho near the Volta River, just north of the forest margin. Excavations at Begho have demonstrated both the relevance of recent oral traditions concerning the early history of the town, and also the cultural continuity which has prevailed between the first inhabitants and the modern Brong (fig. 8.3). The separate quarters of Begho that were inhabited by artisans and by visiting traders may still be identified (Posnansky, 1973; 1976). Imported materials confirm the close connexions with Jenne. Begho was finally eclipsed by the rise of the Asante kingdom, probably at the beginning of the eighteenth century (Anquandah, 1982); but before this the flow of gold northwards had been significantly reduced, because the European traders who had arrived on the coast were also trading in gold. Knowledge of the subsequent history of the Ghanaian forest areas is, for the most part, derived from the oral traditions of the Asante and their neighbours and from the records of European visitors to the coast.

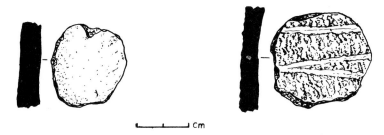

8.3 Pottery discs from Begho. These appear to be of standardised weight and may have been used for weighing gold (after Posnansky, 1976)

In southern Nigeria, the most significant archaeological discoveries of early second-millennium sites have been made at Ife (Willett, 1967; Garlake, 1974, 1977; Eyo, 1974). The site had evidently been occupied in earlier times, but little is known about its initial phases. By about the eleventh century more intensive settlement is indicated, marked archaeologically by pavements made of large numbers of pieces of broken pottery set on edge. These pavements evidently belonged in open-air courtyards that were used for domestic purposes, although in one case there were also the remains of an altar, likewise decorated with potsherds. Of the associated buildings, which were made of sun-dried mud, little has survived. The greatest attention in archaeological work at Ife has been devoted to a remarkable series of highly realistic figures in bronze or terracotta, which are thought by most art historians to represent a tradition derived – albeit perhaps indirectly – from that of the much earlier Nok 'culture' described in chapter 7 (fig. 8.4). These figures apparently had a religious significance and were on occasion kept in shrines or on altars, which formed part of domestic houses. They occur in several different areas of Ife, away from the royal palace quarter, so they were not a prerogative of the ruler. Although the archaeological arguments are tenuous, they suggest that the Ife terracottas and bronzes were created for a variety of ritual situations, which may be paralleled in the more recent traditional beliefs of the Yoruba.

 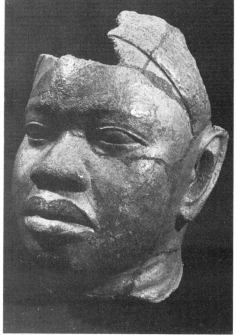

8.4 Terracotta heads from Ife

Ife may have been heir to an ancient artistic tradition, but it probably owed much of its prosperity to long-distance trade. The metal used in its bronze-work was almost certainly imported; and connexions with the Niger Valley to the north are attested by the presence there, at Tada, of bronzes in the Ife style (Eyo and Willett, 1980). Glass beads were imported in large numbers and were then melted down and re-worked. Ife's central position in Yoruba tradition indicates its past importance, which may have been supported by trade through which the products of the forest were exchanged for imported luxury goods. Virtually no information has survived concerning the domestic economy of early Ife, but it is reasonable to assume that yam cultivation, then as now, provided its main food supply.

The 'lost-wax' bronzes – they are actually made of brass – of Ife are few in number in comparison with the terracottas. Bronze-working was carried out on a far greater scale at Benin, where archaeological excavation shows that there was a town from at least the thirteenth century. At this site extensive linear earthworks surrounding the city and its suburbs show clearly the prolonged processes of expansion and incorporation which accompanied Benin's urban development. Comparable earthworks and/or walls are known from other areas of Nigeria but have not been so intensively investigated. The earliest Benin bronzes, which probably date to the fifteenth century, show some stylistic connexions with those of Ife (fig. 8.5). At Benin, bronze-working was carried out

8.5 Bronze head in early style from Benin

for the ruler, the Oba; and it is relevant to note that the Obas of Benin originally had strong ties with Ife. The history of Benin is fairly well known both from oral traditions and from written sources, for the city was in contact with Portuguese traders from the sixteenth century (Dark, 1973; Connah, 1975; see also Willett, 1967). Although most of the recorded history of Benin falls outside the period of time covered by this book, it shows how, as in the earlier states, political power was supported by the control of trade.

Further to the east, in the equatorial forests of the Congo basin and in the savanna country to their north, the recent archaeology remains almost completely unknown. The information about past events that we can derive from other sources suggests that in the first half of the second millennium A.D. there continued to be small-scale settlement of Bantu-speaking peasant communities in the forest and of Ubangian-speakers on its northern fringes, some of the latter still expanding eastwards, following the pattern that had been established in earlier times (David, 1980). The end result of this process was the establishment in what is now the extreme south-eastern Sudan and adjacent parts of Zaire and the Central African Republic of the Ubangian-speaking Zande as rulers of a cluster of peoples of varied Bantu, Sudanic and Nilotic antecedents.

Ethiopia, the southern Sudan and adjacent regions

Elsewhere in the southern Sudan, in the Bahr el Ghazal territory of the Nilotic-speakers, the most significant development of this time, as we see from the Wun Rok mound-sites early in the second millennium A.D., was the replacement of the earlier humpless cattle by humped ones, which may have been obtained from Arabic-speaking peoples further to the north (David et al., 1981). The pottery, decorated with twisted-cord roulettes as in earlier times, continued with no significant change. Indeed, the general picture which emerges from the rather little research so far undertaken is one of basic continuity from the first millennium A.D. into recent times. The first half of the second millennium was, however, a period of major southward expansion by Nilotic-speakers into East Africa, as will be further discussed below. In parts of the south-eastern Sudan, as in much of northern Kenya and, probably, Uganda, iron remained extremely rare, and use of stone tools continued into the last few centuries (fig. 8.6).

In highland Ethiopia, the history of this period is marked by the southward shift in the centre of Christian culture from Axum into the Lasta and Shoa regions, the spread of Islamic culture in the east and south-east, and the continued obscurity of events in the south. At the end of the first millennium A.D. the kingdom of Axum was overthrown by a revolt of the Cushitic-speaking Agau. By this time, the inhabitants of the mountainous Lasta area east of Lake Tana had adopted much of the earlier Christian culture. Here, around the beginning of the twelfth century, the Zagwe dynasty arose and established its

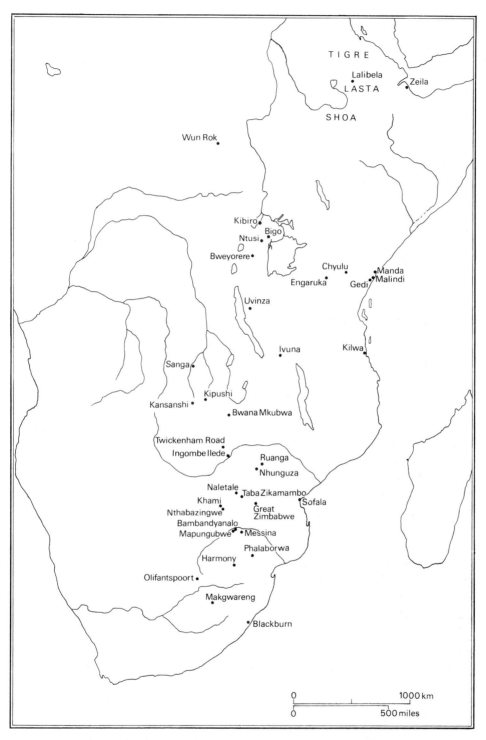

8.6 Principal archaeological sites of the second millennium A.D. in eastern and southern Africa

political authority over the area. Like the written records, the surviving sites of this period are exclusively ecclesiastical. Pride of place goes to the rock-cut churches at Lalibela, the Zagwe capital (fig. 8.7). Hewn on both the exterior and the interior from solid rock, these churches show several architectural features that may be traced back to Axumite buildings (Gerster, 1970). Similar, though less elaborate, rock-cut churches are also known in Tigre. Towards the end of the thirteenth century the Semitic-speaking Amhara of Shoa, south of the Blue Nile, replaced the Zagwe ruling dynasty and the centre of political power shifted southwards (Sergew, 1972); and their pattern of authority survived, albeit in modified form, into the twentieth century.

Christian Ethiopia at this time was almost entirely cut off from the outside world. Islamic culture, by the beginning of the second millennium A.D., was reaching large areas of eastern Ethiopia from the port of Zeila near the mouth of the Red Sea. So far, our knowledge comes primarily from written records, but there are also extensive sites of ruined towns which await archaeological investigation. To the south, the later archaeology of southern Ethiopia remains almost totally unknown apart from the presence of varied megalithic monuments, some at least of which date within the last one thousand years (Azais and Chambard, 1931). In northern Kenya and much of Somalia stone tools probably continued in use until the last few centuries: archaeological traces of nomadic pastoralist populations such as the present Eastern Cushitic-speaking peoples of this area are notoriously sparse and difficult to interpret. The surviving oral

8.7 The rock-cut church of Abba Libanos, Lalibela

traditions (Lewis, 1966; Turton, 1975) mostly relate to a southward expansion of the Galla at the expense of the Rendille and Somali, a process which has continued into recent times.

In the better-watered areas of Kenya's western highlands and parts of Uganda, settled cattle-pastoralists are attested from the beginning of the second millennium. They built stone-walled semi-subterranean stock enclosures and, at least in later times, practised irrigation agriculture (Sutton, 1973). There are good reasons for believing that these people were Nilotic-speakers ancestral to the modern Kalenjin. Several later penetrations of Nilotic-speakers southwards into East Africa are attested (Oliver, 1977b). One incursion brought the Maasai into the Rift Valley territory, which had been occupied by the stone-tool-using herdsmen during the last millennium B.C. Another introduced the Luo to their present territory on the north-eastern shore of Lake Victoria. The extensive stone-built terraces and irrigation works at Engaruka in northern Tanzania may also be attributed, albeit tentatively, to an early Nilotic-speaking population (Sutton, 1978). To the south lay the territory of the Bantu-speaking people, discussed below.

The east coast of Africa

Mention was made in chapter 7 of the written evidence, contained in the *Periplus of the Erythraean Sea*, for trading voyages along the East African coast as early as the first centuries of the Christian era. No convincing archaeological evidence for such trade has yet been found. Indeed, it is not until the ninth century A.D. that we have clear traces of the coastal settlements that were established by the Indian Ocean traders, who penetrated as far to the south as the Maputo area of Mozambique (Sinclair, 1982). The two principal sites are on off-shore islands: Manda in the Lamu Archipelago of Kenya and Kilwa in Tanzania, some 350 km to the south of Dar-es-Salaam (Chittick, 1967; 1974b). At the more northerly settlement, Manda, a massive sea-wall protected stone-built houses with plastered walls. Imported pottery and glass were in frequent use, and much of it apparently came from the eastern shore of the Arabian Gulf, where the port of Siraf is known to have flourished at this time. The contemporary occupation of Kilwa shows weaker foreign influences: most of the houses were of local wood-and-mud construction and imported goods were less numerous. It may be concluded that overseas trading contact with the East African coast was re-established or intensified shortly before the close of the first millenium A.D. Settlements of foreigners were few, and the majority of the inhabitants of the coast were of indigenous African stock. In later centuries these elements were to fuse to form the urban Swahili culture which has survived into recent times, fed by the monsoon winds which carry the trading vessels on their annual circuit.

The chief items of export trade from eastern Africa were ivory, horn and skins. Slaves must also have been carried away, but probably not in large numbers. In the south, as will be shown below, gold from the Zimbabwe mines was of paramount importance. Beads, pottery, glass, cloth and other luxury manufactures were the principal imports, together with much of the skills and learning which contributed to the coastal culture at this time. Iron, which the *Periplus* states had been imported in earlier times, was now produced locally, as is shown both by archaeological discoveries at Manda and by contemporary Arabic writings. From the tenth-century record of al-Mas'udi we get further information. He refers to the indigenous coastal people as 'Zenj' and implies that, even in the towns, few of them were yet Muslims. They used domestic cattle as beasts of burden, and cultivated millet and bananas (the latter introduced from Indonesia). Ivory, obtained inland by Zenj hunters and collectors, was brought by them to the ports and then shipped to Oman and on to India and China. It was by similar means that the coastal traders obtained gold from what they called 'the land of Sofala and the Waqwaq'.

During the eleventh and twelfth centuries the coastal settlements increased in prosperity. This was particularly true in the case of towns on the Benadir coast of the modern Somalia, notably Mogadishu, and also in the south, as at Kilwa. In Kilwa the so-called Shirazi dynasty of rulers was established, and the town's importance increased rapidly. They erected elaborate stone buildings, imported pottery and glass, and issued coins. The greatest prosperity of the East African coast came in the late thirteenth and the fourteenth centuries, which saw the foundation of many new towns, such as Gedi and Malindi in Kenya, and the erection of the finest stone buildings at Kilwa (fig. 8.8). In 1331 the coast was

8.8 Ruins at Gedi

visited by ibn Battuta, who has left a vivid eye-witness description. By this time the rulers of Kilwa controlled the coast as far to the south as Sofala, near the modern Beira on the coast of Mozambique. As will be shown below, the export of Zimbabwean gold reached its peak in the period around A.D. 1400, and Sofala was its main point of export (Chittick, 1977).

Europe knew little about the civilisation of the East African coastal towns until the Portuguese rounded the Cape of Good Hope, reaching Sofala in 1497. To guard their sea-route to India, they rapidly established forts at both Sofala and Kilwa. The gold-rich interior then attracted their attention; and control of the coastal trade, with many of the settlements on which that trade depended, passed into European hands. Both the trade and the urban settlements of the East African coast have survived into the present day.

Bantu-speakers north of the Zambezi

In the interior of East Africa, the areas that had been settled by the people responsible for the Chifumbaze complex, described in chapter 7, saw more rapid cultural change around 1,000 years ago. In some more southerly Bantu-speaking regions, this development is fairly securely dated to about the eleventh century; but in East Africa neither the archaeological sequence nor the chronology is properly understood. It is commonly believed that in much of Bantu Africa the second millennium A.D. was marked by increased cattle-herding (Oliver, 1982), and the contribution of Nilotic-speaking peoples in East Africa has been emphasised. At the same time, it is important not to underestimate the very real cultural unity of the last two thousand years in the Bantu-speaking regions of Africa and the many lines of continuity which extend from early in the first millennium A.D. into recent times.

In much of southern Uganda, the archaeological occurrences of the second millennium A.D. are characterised by pottery decorated by means of a roulette made of cord. The affinities of this pottery are with more northerly areas, where it is particularly associated with speakers of Nilotic languages. It is attested in Rwanda from about the ninth century but its period of manufacture in Uganda cannot yet be shown to have begun until some 400 years later. This dating is in general agreement with that indicated by oral tradition for the establishment of the major kingdoms of the interlacustrine region, including those of Buganda, Bunyoro and Ankole. Although Bantu-speaking, at least in more recent times, these kingdoms preserve traditions which attribute their foundation to a group called the Bachwezi, who appear to have been cattle-herders, perhaps from Nilotic-speaking areas to the north.

There is much controversy concerning the date, identity and activities of the Bachwezi, but the most likely interpretation of the available evidence is that they were the alien founders of ruling dynasties who dominated sections of a pre-existing Bantu-speaking population. It should be noted that control of long-distance trade was apparently not the major stimulus for the formation of the interlacustrine states (Oliver, 1977b). If the origin of roulette-decorated pottery in this region is linked with the coming of the Bachwezi, its adoption by the indigenous population is not surprising in view of the speed with which such pottery has been copied by Bantu-speaking peoples in other parts of East Africa. Although this process is still continuing today, it is one for which the reasons are not at all clear; and it provides an excellent example of a major change in artefact style that is not accompanied by any significant shift in population or, indeed, by any apparent economic or practical advantage.

The archaeology of the interlacustrine kingdoms has been investigated at the capital sites of Bigo, Bweyorere and Ntusi (Posnansky, 1968; 1969). Extensive dams and earthworks – those at Bigo total more than 10 km in length – indicate the scale of organisation that was achieved. Remains of large circular houses resemble the royal residences of more recent times. Salt was evidently an important commodity at this time in East Africa, as elsewhere, and major workings have been investigated at Kibiro on Lake Albert and Uvinza in western Tanzania, as well as at Ivuna further south (Hiernaux and Maquet, 1968; Sutton and Roberts, 1968; Fagan and Yellen, 1968).

Elsewhere in East Africa our knowledge of this period is even less comprehensive. In parts of the eastern Kenya highlands pottery derived from the Kwale tradition may have continued to be made as late as the thirteenth or fourteenth centuries, before being replaced by one, still practised by the modern Kamba and Gikuyu, which may have originated in the Chyulu area of southern Kenya. In both Kenya and Tanzania there is evidence, early in the present millennium, for peasant farmers owning domestic cattle and sheep/goats and cultivating sorghum. Except in the immediate hinterland, glass beads and other items imported from the coast were effectively unknown until recent times (Odner, 1971; Soper, 1976; 1979).

A similar situation appears to have prevailed in most areas of the modern Zambia and Malawi. Here, however, (as in a wide area further to the south) there was a pronounced and apparently sudden change in pottery styles dated to around the eleventh century A.D. The main exception to this is in the Upper Zambezi region of western Zambia, which seems to belong to a western culture area, extending into Angola, where there is evidence for greater continuity in pottery style from the first millennium A.D. into more recent times.

In eastern and much of northern and central Zambia the main pottery style of the second millennium A.D. has been called the Luangwa tradition (fig. 8.9). Its appearance around the eleventh century represents a sharp break with its predecessors of both the eastern and the western facies of the Chifumbaze complex; and it has continued with relatively little modification ever since. The contrast is well seen at the site known as Twickenham Road in Lusaka (D. W. Phillipson, 1970).

The antecedents of the Luangwa-tradition pottery remain unknown but may lie in the direction of Shaba in south-eastern Zaire. Today, Luangwa-tradition pottery is traditionally made by women. In more westerly areas, vessels of the Lungwebungu tradition, apparently derived from the Chifumbaze complex, are made by men. This suggests that the contrast between the pottery of the Chifumbaze complex and that of the Lungwebungu tradition may have been due to the establishment of communities amongst whom potting was undertaken by women. Luangwa-tradition pottery is today made by people of many different societies, including the Bemba, Chewa and Nsenga. It was clearly established long before these societies became differentiated from each other through the arrival of chiefly dynasties (which claim a Zairean origin) in about the fifteenth and sixteenth centuries (D. W. Phillipson, 1974).

By the fourteenth/fifteenth century copper mining, which had begun on a small scale about one thousand years earlier, became much intensified, resulting in enormous workings such as those at Kipushi, Bwana Mkubwa and Kansanshi in the Zambia/Shaba Copperbelt area. Cross-shaped ingots were cast in closely standardised sizes and widely traded; they probably served as a form of currency (Bisson, 1975; de Maret, 1981). It is surely not coincidence that the development of copper mining and trading is indicated at the same general time as the local rise of centralised states, and that the chiefly dynasties of surrounding areas trace their origin to south-eastern Zaire, which saw the greatest development of the copper trade. A further feature of later metal-working in this

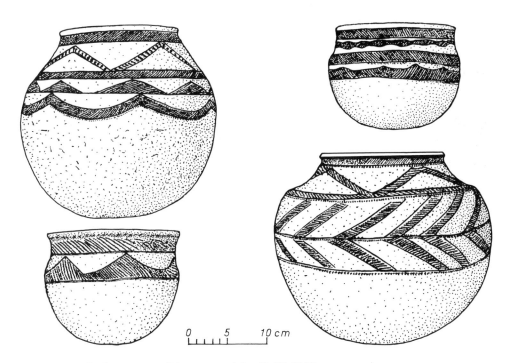

8.9 Luangwa-tradition pottery (after D. W. Phillipson, 1977a)

area was the tall natural draught iron-smelting furnace fired without the use of bellows (D. W. Phillipson, 1968b; van der Merwe, 1980).

The Zaire/Angola region appears to have contributed significantly to the cultural development of a very large part of central Africa during the second millennium A.D. It is thus particularly unfortunate that its archaeology for this period remains virtually unknown. A considerable amount of research has been undertaken on the oral traditions relating to the kingdoms which flourished in this area, especially along the southern and eastern margins of the forest, but we do not know when these kingdoms arose (Vansina, 1966).

Archaeologically, the only well-documented late sequence in the whole of this vast area is that based on excavations around Lake Kisale near the south-eastern corner of the forest (de Maret, 1977). The great cemetery of Sanga was noted in chapter 7 and attributed to a final stage of the Chifumbaze complex. Its main period of use is dated by radiocarbon to the eleventh and twelfth centuries. Already by this Classic Kisalian period considerable wealth had been accumulated; and flange-welded iron gongs, of a type which – at least in later times – served as symbols of kingship, were found in some of the richer graves (fig. 8.10). Later use of the cemetery, attributed to the Kabambian phase, continued at least into the sixteenth century. There is no good reason for regarding the Kabambian as other than a descendant of the Kisalian, although there are important differences between them, most pertinently in the much greater frequency of copper cross-ingots in the Kabambian graves. The most

8.10 A Kisalian grave at Sanga

recent graves at Sanga are attributed to the Luba and probably date within the last two centuries.

Two important points emerge from this discussion. One is that, as suggested above, there was a greater degree of continuity from the Chifumbaze complex into later times in some western areas than there was in the east. The second is that certain cultural items which became prevalent in eastern areas during the second millennium A.D. may have had a greater antiquity in the west. This view is supported by oral traditions which, as we have seen, derive the ruling dynasties of many states in Zambia, Malawi and adjacent regions from a Zairean origin. The most recent interpretation of these oral traditions places the origin of the Zairean savanna kingdoms at least as far back as the thirteenth century, and this is in accord with the scanty archaeological evidence (J. C. Miller, 1972; 1976). There can be no doubt that trade developed concurrently with these kingdoms; but at this early date it must have been an essentially local African trade in commodities such as metals and salt. In this western part of the sub-continent overseas contacts did not develop on any scale before the arrival of the Portuguese in Angola late in the fifteenth century. More precise information about these processes must await further archaeological research in Angola and Zaire.

Zimbabwe

To the south of the Zambezi, in Zimbabwe, the pottery industries from the eleventh century onwards show many features in common with that of the Luangwa tradition; and it looks at first sight as if they shared a common origin with the contemporary Zambian industries.

In south-eastern Zimbabwe, the Leopard's Kopje industry was established in about A.D. 1000. At the site of Nthabazingwe (Leopard's Kopje) itself, near Bulawayo, the people lived in circular pole-and-clay houses some 3 m in diameter. There were rare domestic tools of iron, and copper was used for personal adornment. Some contact with the coastal trade is indicated by the presence of occasional glass beads. Large numbers of cattle were herded, with some sheep/goats. Clay figurines of cattle show that these animals were of a humped, longhorned variety. Cultivated crops included sorghum, finger millet, ground beans and cowpeas (Huffman, 1974). In a second phase of the Leopard's Kopje industry, dated to the thirteenth/fourteenth century, cotton cloth began to be made and there is evidence for the construction of dry-stone walling. The Leopard's Kopje people were by this time engaged in the mining and working of gold, for pieces of their characteristic pottery have been re-covered from several ancient workings, and a crucible from a site of this period at Taba Zikamambo was found to contain traces of gold (Robinson, 1966).

A parallel process of development is revealed by excavations in the Limpopo Valley. At Bambandyanalo, a substantial village was established in about A.D.

1000. Its cattle-herding inhabitants worked extensively in ivory, which was evidently exchanged for large quantities of imported glass beads, presumably obtained through the trading settlements which are attested from this time on the coast of southern Mozambique (Eloff and Meyer, 1981; Sinclair, 1982). From the late eleventh century at nearby Mapungubwe, iron tools were more common and, as in the Bulawayo region, cotton cloth was produced (Davison and Harries, 1980). At both sites numerous graves have been investigated; the skeletons are indistinguishable from those of modern South African negroid people (Rightmire, 1970). At Mapungubwe the twelfth-century burials were more richly decorated, with glass beads and copper and gold ornaments. Gold foil was laid over carved wooden figurines of animals, bowls and staffs; there is also, as in earlier times, evidence for the working of ivory (Fagan, 1964; Hall and Vogel, 1980). As at contemporary sites further to the north, there can be little doubt that wealth, and presumably influence and political power, were becoming concentrated through trade in the hands of a minority (Huffman, 1982).

This process reached its greatest extent in the central regions of Zimbabwe at the site near Fort Victoria which has become known as Great Zimbabwe (Garlake, 1973a). (The word *zimbabwe*, in the language of the Shona, means either 'stone houses' or 'venerated houses'.) The site is renowned as the place where the indigenous southern African tradition of dry-stone architecture reached its most impressive achievement (fig. 8.11). After an initial Chifumbaze-complex occupation, during which there is no evidence for building in stone, the

8.11 Inside the great enclosure, with the conical tower, Great Zimbabwe

main sequence at Great Zimbabwe started with the Gumanye phase in about the eleventh century. At that time the economy of the site's inhabitants was probably similar to that described above from the Bulawayo region. By about A.D. 1250, simple stone walling began to be erected to form enclosures and platforms which supported pole-and-mud houses. All the finest and most elaborate stonework at Great Zimbabwe is now known to have been erected within a relatively brief period in the fourteenth and fifteenth centuries. These buildings fall into two groups. Those on a steep-sided rocky hill consist of lengths of well-coursed walling linking the natural boulders of the hill-top to form a series of easily defended enclosures. In the adjacent valley is a series of larger, free-standing walled enclosures in some of which stood circular pole-and-mud houses joined together by short lengths of similar walling. One enclosure stands out through its size and complexity: its perimeter wall reaches a height of over 10 m, as does a solid stone tower which stands within. Despite its massive scale and excellence of execution, the stone architecture at Great Zimbabwe is basically simple. There were no domes or arches; doorways were narrow and roofed with simple stone lintels over which the upper courses of stonework were laid without interruption. Internal structures were of puddled mud, sun-baked to great hardness and durability, in which material also the builders were masters of their techniques.

The architectural florescence of Great Zimbabwe clearly coincided with the site's greatest period of prosperity. The site must have been a centre of political authority, and the presence of large numbers of imported items indicates that this authority was linked with the control of trade. Imported objects – glass beads, Persian and Chinese pottery, Near Eastern glass, even a coin minted in the name of the ruler of Kilwa – are far more common here than on contemporary sites elsewhere in Zimbabwe. Gold and copper objects from other parts of the interior have also been found at Great Zimbabwe, so we may conclude that the products of outlying regions were collected there either through patronage, or as gifts or tribute; and from here trade for coastal imports was organised. Indeed, it may be shown archaeologically that Great Zimbabwe was the centre of a widespread network of related sites, for near-identical pottery is found in stone buildings of comparable style as far afield as Manekweni on the coastal plain of southern Mozambique and at Ruanga and Nhunguza in northern Zimbabwe (Garlake, 1973b; 1976). In the latter area the Great Zimbabwe people apparently settled in control over a peasant community with a distinct pottery tradition. One house within the Nhunguza stone enclosure seems to have served as an audience chamber (fig. 8.12). The importance of cattle-herding at Great Zimbabwe-related settlements has recently been emphasised (Garlake, 1978b).

Oral traditions of the Shona link Great Zimbabwe with the worship of their supreme god, Mwari. The most convincing interpretation of these traditions attributes to the earliest Shona an antiquity which matches the archaeological date for the start of the Gumanye phase (Abraham, 1962). It is thus reasonable to conclude that Great Zimbabwe was the centre of an empire ruled by the Shona group remembered in oral tradition as Mbire (Beach, 1980). Significantly, the site's greatest prosperity coincided with the peak in the export trade in gold, as attested on the Indian Ocean coast.

The decline of Great Zimbabwe in the fifteenth century came at a time when political power was transferred to a more northerly site, near the Zambezi Valley, which was then replacing the Sabi as the major trade route to the coast. This development may have been linked with an increase in the importance of copper from the northern mines as a valuable trade item (fig. 8.13). A trading site of this period has been excavated at Ingombe Ilede, on the bank of the Zambezi near Kariba (Fagan et al., 1969; D. W. Phillipson and Fagan, 1969). By the middle of the sixteenth century the Portuguese had penetrated the Zambezi Valley route to the interior. To the south-west, sites such as Naletale and Khami (K. R. Robinson, 1959), where elaborately decorated stone walling faced massive terraces, belong to this late period and may be attributed to the kingdom of

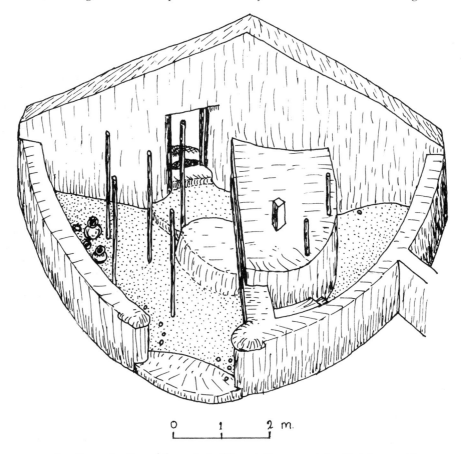

0   1   2 m.

8.12 Reconstruction of the main building at Nhunguza (after Garlake, 1973b)

Guruhuswa, which traded with the Portuguese during the seventeenth and eighteenth centuries (fig. 8.14). Archaeology thus serves to confirm the evidence of oral tradition for the essential continuity between the inhabitants of Great Zimbabwe and related sites and the modern Shona-speaking peoples.

8.13 Copper cross-ingot from Ingombe Ilede

8.14 Elaborate stone walling at Naletale

South of the Limpopo

Only a part of this southernmost region of Africa, as noted in chapter 7, was inhabited by the people of the Chifumbaze complex attributed to the Bantu-speakers. Later, early in the second millennium, there was some expansion. Most of Natal and the north-eastern Orange Free State was now settled by iron-using peoples. By the seventeenth century, when written records for this part of the continent effectively begin, it appears that Bantu-speakers occupied most of the territory lying north-east of a line extending roughly from the Windhoek area of Namibia to Port Alfred on the south-east coast of the Cape Province. Beyond this line, the indigenous populations were Khoisan-speaking, using stone and bone tools together with metal items which they obtained by trade with their northern and eastern neighbours or with European colonists. Some of these Khoisan-speakers were hunter-gatherers, others pastoralists (Wilson, 1969).

The available radiocarbon dates suggest that the post-Chifumbaze complex developments in the Bantu-speaking regions south of the Limpopo began in about the eleventh century – that is, at about the same time as the corresponding event further to the north. The typological contrast between the pottery of the Chifumbaze complex and later wares in South Africa, particularly in the Transvaal, is less pronounced than it is in Zimbabwe and Zambia. This has led at least one archaeologist to propose that the Leopard's Kopje and related industries of Zimbabwe were of southerly origin (Huffman, 1978). A major objection to such a view is that it does not account for the marked similarities of development at this time north and south of the Zambezi. A more probable explanation is that the Chifumbaze complex in the Transvaal, belonging to the western facies, showed less contrast with its succeeding industries (also ultimately of western origin) than did the predominantly eastern facies material of Zimbabwe (cf. Huffman, 1982). The clearest picture of a village site of the first half of the present millennium in the Transvaal comes from Olifantspoort in the south-west. Here, about twenty circular pole-and-mud houses were set around an open area where cattle were kept (Mason, 1974). Such a site plan may be seen as a characteristic feature of many southern African societies, and one which may be traced tentatively back into the first millennium A.D. (Huffman, 1982).

Ancient mines for iron, copper, tin and gold are reported from several areas of the Transvaal, but most were destroyed by modern mining operations before archaeological investigations could be undertaken. Fortunately this does not apply to the copper workings around Messina in the Limpopo Valley and those for both iron and copper in the Phalaborwa area of the eastern Transvaal. At Phalaborwa both shafts and horizontal passages were excavated for the recovery of copper ore, but iron ore was collected or quarried from the surface. The pottery sequence at Phalaborwa is continuous from the eleventh century and leads up to wares of the type made by north-eastern Sotho peoples (van der Merwe and Scully, 1971). At Harmony, in the Transvaal Lowveld, soapstone bowls were used for evaporating brine. Cattle, goats and chickens are attested at several sites.

Archaeological survey, much of it carried out by aerial photography, has revealed the presence in much of the Transvaal and Orange Free State Highveld of numerous enclosures of dry-stone walling incorporating circular structures, many of which were evidently houses or stock pens (fig. 8.15). The majority of these sites probably date to the period between the fifteenth and the very beginning of the nineteenth centuries. In the northern Transvaal, the stone structures tend to be smaller and resemble those erected by the Venda in recent times. This phase seems to have seen the first settlement by iron-using peoples south of the Vaal, where there are traces of several distinct types of stone enclosures which may be attributed to populations ancestral to certain Tswana and Sotho groups (Maggs, 1976), providing links between peoples recognised in the archaeological record and those whose history has been investigated from oral and written sources.

In Natal, which marks the most southerly extension of the pre-colonial iron-using peoples, the structures that were in use were far less substantial and may have been of dome-shaped grass-covered type, as at Blackburn near Durban (Davies, 1971). Evidently, between the eleventh and the sixteenth centuries, iron-using peoples dispersed southwards through Natal as far as the Kei River (Maggs, 1980). Cattle and sorghum appear to have been the bases of their food-producing economy. These archaeological reconstructions are in keeping with oral traditions preserved among the Xhosa.

Before concluding this survey of the second millennium A.D. in the Bantu-speaking regions, certain points require emphasis. They relate to most of the eastern half of the continent from Zambia southwards. In contrast with the previous Chifumbaze complex, cattle were of major importance. Population densities seem rapidly to have increased, to judge from the number of visible sites, many of which extend over a wide area into less favourable regions, and

8.15 Stone-walled enclosure at Makgwareng, Orange Free State

the remnant populations from earlier times seem to have finally disappeared. In many areas there are strong indications of cultural continuity into recent times. Lastly, the transition from the Chifumbaze complex to its successors cannot be seen as a clear break: there are many indications of continuity in culture and population. It follows, therefore, that many of the peoples who inhabit this part of Africa can regard themselves as having roots which extend back to the early centuries A.D. (cf. Garlake, 1982).

Beyond the Bantu-speaking zone, in the territory of the Khoisan-speakers, the varied life-styles noted for first-millennium times in chapter 7 continued, at first with little perceptible change. The first European colonists at the Cape of Good Hope divided the indigenous inhabitants into three categories. There were the 'strandlopers', who were gatherers of shellfish and wild vegetable foods, there were herders of cattle and sheep, and there were fishermen who also owned herds of cattle. It is not clear whether these groups represented three separate populations or representatives of a single society following different economic patterns at different seasons. Archaeology in this instance provides no clear means of distinguishing between separate populations, and the latter interpretation is perhaps the more likely. This picture probably holds good for much of the coastal region from Namibia to the south-eastern Cape (Wilson, 1969).

The aspect of the culture of the second-millennium Khoisan-speakers of southern Africa which has been studied in greatest detail by prehistorians is the rock art. In the south-western Cape several representations of fat-tailed sheep have been discovered but, interestingly, paintings of cattle only occur in the latest stylised series. Paintings of European-style ships must be later than the end of the fifteenth century. Human figures are shown in dress akin to that of the eighteenth and nineteenth century settlers, as are horse-drawn waggons. The finest and most abundant paintings occur in the Drakensberg. Most are apparently of late date, but domestic animals are not shown except in the most recent series which broadly correlates with the advent of European settlement (Vinnicombe, 1976). In this region the representations of wild animals, using a skilled blend of colours and showing an excellent understanding of perspective and shading, are probably the finest achievements of African rock artists (fig. 8.16).

In the drier interior regions of South Africa, backed microliths continued to be made well into the second millennium A.D., perhaps as late as the seventeenth century. The presence at sites of this period of glass beads, pottery and occasional metal objects probably indicates some degree of contact with iron-using peoples further to the north. From about the sixteenth century, peoples of the south-western Orange Free State and adjacent areas of the Cape began to adopt a more settled pastoralist life-style, erecting stone-walled enclosures apparently inspired by those of their Bantu-speaking neighbours (Maggs, 1971). The characteristic stone tools were now varied types of scraper, in place of backed microliths. It is not surprising that rivalry eventually developed between the two groups. Along much of the 'frontier' raiding, stock theft and open hostility became the order of the day. In Lesotho, Natal and the Orange Free State the process is vividly recorded in a number of rock paintings. Nor were the European colonists excluded from these events. Their herds likewise received the attentions of the raiders. As a result of European counter-measures and aggression the Khoisan-speaking population of much of South Africa was, by the early nineteenth century, destroyed or reduced to serfdom.

I have attempted in this chapter to outline the many connexions which may be made in sub-Saharan Africa between the evidence of archaeology and that of other historical sources for the events and processes which have taken place during the second millennium A.D. As archaeological and other research in these regions passes increasingly into the hands of indigenous scholars, whose own cultural roots are in the societies under study, such links can only be strengthened, to the benefit of mankind's understanding and appreciation of the African past and its heritage.

8.16 Rock painting at Mpongweni, Natal

REFERENCES

Abbreviations

I.F.A.N.	Institut Fondamental de l'Afrique Noire
J.A.H.	*Journal of African History*
J.R.A.I.	*Journal of the Royal Anthropological Institute*
P.P.S.	*Proceedings of the Prehistoric Society*
S.A.A.B.	*South African Archaeological Bulletin*
S.A.J.S.	*South African Journal of Science*
U.I.S.P.P.	Union Internationale des Sciences Pré- et Proto-historiques
W.A.J.A.	*West African Journal of Archaeology*

Abraham, D. P. 1962, 'The early political history of the empire of Mwene Mutapa', *Historians in Tropical Africa*, Salisbury: 61–91.

Adams, W. 1977, *Nubia: Corridor to Africa*, London.

Adamson, D. *et al.*, 1974, 'Barbed bone points from central Sudan and the age of the Early Khartoum tradition', *Nature*, 249: 120–3.

Addison, F. 1949, *Jebel Moya*, London.

Ajayi, J. F. A. and Crowder, M. (eds.), 1971, *History of West Africa – I*, London.

Aldred, C. 1961, *The Egyptians*, London.

Ambrose S. H. *et al.*, 1980, 'The taxonomic status of the Kenya Capsian', in R. E. Leakey and Ogot, 1980: 248–52.

Anfray, F. 1963, 'Une compagne de fouilles à Yeha', *Annales d'Ethiopie*, 5: 171–232.
  1981, 'The civilization of Aksum from the first to the seventh century', in Mokhtar, 1981: 362–80.

Anquandah, J. 1982, *Rediscovering Ghana's Past*, Accra.

Anthony, B. 1972, 'The Stillbay question', in Hugot, 1972: 80–2.

Arambourg, C. and Balout, L. 1952, 'Du nouveau à l'Ain Hanech', *Bull. Soc. d'Hist. Nat. Afrique du Nord*, 43: 152–9.
  1955, 'L'ancien lac de Tihodaine et ses gisements préhistoriques', in Balout, 1955: 281–92.

Arkell, A. J. 1949, *Early Khartoum*, Oxford.
  1953, *Esh Shaheinab*, Oxford.
  1954, 'Four occupation sites at Agordat', *Kush*, 2: 33–62.
  1964, *Wanyanga*, Oxford.
  1975, *The Prehistory of the Nile Valley*, Leiden.

Atherton, J. H. 1972, 'Excavations at Kamabai and Yagala rockshelters, Sierra Leone', *W.A.J.A.*, 2: 39–74.

Azais, R. P. and Chambard, R. 1931, *Cinq Années de Recherches Archéologiques en Ethiopie*, Paris.

Bailloud, G. 1959, 'La préhistoire de l'Ethiopie', *Cahiers de l'Afrique et de l'Asie*, 5: 15–43.

Balout, L. (ed.), 1955, *Actes du 2e Congrès Panafricain de Préhistoire*, Paris.

Balout, L. *et al.*, 1967, 'L'Acheuléen de Ternifine (Algérie): gisement de l'Atlanthrope', *L'Anthropologie*, 71: 217–38.

Barthelme, J. 1977, 'Holocene sites north-east of Lake Turkana: a preliminary report', *Azania*, 12: 33–41.

Baumgartel, E. J. 1955, *The Cultures of Prehistoric Egypt*, Oxford.

Beach, D. N. 1980, *The Shona and Zimbabwe 900–1850*, London.

Beaumont, P. B. 1973, 'Border Cave – a progress report', *S.A.J.S.*, 69: 41–6.

Beaumont, P. B. and Vogel, J. C. 1972, 'On a new radiocarbon chronology for Africa south of the equator', *African Studies*, 31: 67–89, 155–82.

Beaumont, P. B. *et al.*, 1978, 'Modern man in sub-Saharan Africa prior to 49,000 years B.P.', *S.A.J.S.*, 74: 409–19.

Behrensmeyer, K. 1976, 'Fossil assemblages in relation to sedimentary environments in the East Rudolf succession', in Coppens *et al.*, 1976: 388–401.

Berhanou Abebe *et al.* (eds.), 1976, *Proceedings 7th Panafrican Congress on Prehistory*, Addis Ababa.

Biberson, P. 1961, *Le Paléolithique Inférieur du Maroc Atlantique*, Rabat.

  1967, 'Some aspects of the Lower Palaeolithic of North-West Africa', in Bishop and Clark, 1967: 447–75.

Bilsborough, A. 1972, 'Anagenesis in hominid evolution', *Man (N.S.)*, 7: 481–3.

Bishop, W. W. (ed.), 1978, *Geological Background to Fossil Man*, Edinburgh.

Bishop, W. W. and Clark, J. D. (eds.), 1967, *Background to Evolution in Africa*, Chicago.

Bishop, W. W. and Miller, J. A. (eds.), 1972, *Calibration of Hominoid Evolution*, Edinburgh.

Bisson, M. S. 1975, 'Copper currency in central Africa: the archaeological evidence', *World Archaeology*, 6: 272–92.

Bouquiaux, L. (ed.), 1980, *L'Expansion Bantoue*, Paris.

Bower, J. R. F. and Nelson, C. M. 1978, 'Early pottery and pastoral cultures of the Central Rift Valley, Kenya', *Man (N.S.)*, 13: 554–66.

Bower, J. R. F. *et al.*, 1977, 'The University of Massachusetts Later Stone Age/Pastoral Neolithic comparative study in central Kenya', *Azania*, 12: 119–46.

Brain, C. K. 1958, *The Transvaal Ape-Man-Bearing Cave Deposits*, Pretoria.

  1967, 'Hottentot food remains and their bearing on the interpretation of fossil bone assemblages', *Scientific Papers Namib Desert Research Station*, 32: 1–11.

  1969a, 'The probable role of leopards as predators of the Swartkrans australopithecines', *S.A.A.B.*, 24: 170–1.

  1969b, 'New evidence for climatic change during Middle and Late Stone Age times in Rhodesia', *S.A.A.B.*, 24: 127–43.

  1976, 'A re-interpretation of the Swartkrans site and its remains', *S.A.J.S.*, 72: 141–6.

  1978, 'Some aspects of the South African australopithecine sites and their bone accumulations', in Jolly, 1978: 131–64.

  1981, *The Hunters or the Hunted?*, Chicago.

Brauer, G. 1978, 'The morphological differentiation of anatomically modern man in Africa', *Z. Morph. Anthrop.* 63: 266–92.

Breasted, J. 1962, *Ancient Records of Egypt – I*, New York.

Breternitz, D. A. 1975, 'Rescue archaeology in the Kainji Reservoir area, 1968', *W.A.J.A.*, 5: 91–151.

Brett, M. 1978, 'The Arab conquest and the rise of Islam in North Africa', in Fage, 1978: 490–555.

Brothwell, D. R. and Shaw, T. 1971, 'A late Upper Pleistocene proto-West African Negro from Nigeria', *Man (N.S.)*, 6: 221–7.

Brown, F. H. 1975, 'Barbed bone points from the lower Omo Valley, Ethiopia', *Azania*, 10: 144–8.

Bunn, H. *et al.*, 1980, 'FxJj50: an early Pleistocene site in northern Kenya', *World Archaeology*, 12: 109–36.

Butzer, K. W. 1971, *Recent History of an Ethiopian Delta*, Chicago.

   1974a, 'Geo-archaeological interpretation of two Acheulian calc-pan sites', *J. Arch. Sci.*, 1: 1–25.

   1974b, 'Paleoecology of South African australopithecines: Taung revisited', *Curr. Anthrop.*, 15: 367–82, 413–6.

   1980, 'The Holocene lake plain of North Rudolf, East Africa', *Phys. Geog.*, 1: 42–58.

Butzer, K. W. and Isaac, G. L. (eds.), 1975, *After the Australopithecines*, The Hague.

Butzer, K. W. *et al.*, 1973, 'Alluvial terraces of the lower Vaal river, South Africa', *J. Geol.*, 81: 321–62.

   1978, 'Lithostratigraphy of Border Cave, KwaZulu, South Africa', *J. Arch. Sci.*, 5: 317–41.

Buxton, D. 1970, *The Abyssinians*, London.

Bynon, J. and T. (eds.), 1975, *Hamito-Semitica.*

Cadenat, P. and Tixier, J. 1960, 'Une faucille préhistorique à Columnata', *Libyca*, 8: 239–58.

Cahen, D. 1978, 'Vers une revision de la nomenclature des industries préhistoriques de l'Afrique centrale', *L'Anthropologie*, 82: 5–36.

Calvocoressi, D. and David, N. 1979, 'A new survey of radiocarbon and thermoluminescence dates for West Africa', *J.A.H.*, 20: 1–29.

Campbell, B. G. 1978, 'Some problems in hominid classification and nomenclature', in Jolly, 1978: 567–82.

van Campo, M. 1975, 'Pollen analyses in the Sahara', in Wendorf and Marks, 1975: 45–64.

Camps, G. 1969, *Amekni, Néolithique Ancien du Hoggar*, Paris.

   1974, *Les Civilizations Préhistoriques de l'Afrique du Nord et du Sahara*, Paris.

   1975, 'The prehistoric cultures of North Africa: radiocarbon chronology', in Wendorf and Marks, 1975: 182–92.

   1982, 'Beginnings of pastoralism and cultivation in north-west Africa and the Sahara: origins of the Berbers', in J. D. Clark, 1982b: 548–623.

Carter, P. L. and Clark, J. D. 1976, 'Adrar Bous and African cattle', in Berhanou *et al.*, 1976: 487–93.

Carter, P. L. and Vogel, J. C. 1974, 'The dating of industrial assemblages from stratified sites in eastern Lesotho', *Man (N.S.)*, 9: 557–70.

Caton-Thompson, G. and Gardner, E. W. 1934, *The Desert Fayum*, London.

Chamla, M. C. 1968, *Les Populations Anciennes du Sahara et des Régions Limitrophes*, Paris.

   1970, *Les Hommes Epipaléolithiques de Columnata, Algérie Occidentale*, Paris.

   1978, 'Le peuplement de l'Afrique du Nord de l'épipaléolithique à l'époque actuelle', *L'Anthropologie*, 82: 385–430.

Chapman, S. 1967, 'Kantsyore Island', *Azania*, 2: 165–91.

Chavaillon, J. 1976, 'Mission archéologique Franco-Ethiopienne de Melka-Kontouré', *L'Ethiopie avant l'Histoire*, 1: 1–11.

Chittick, H. N. 1967, 'Discoveries in the Lamu archipelago', *Azania*, 2: 37–67.

   1974a, 'Excavations at Aksum: a preliminary report', *Azania*, 9: 159–205.

   1974b, *Kilwa: an Islamic Trading City on the East African Coast*, Nairobi.

   1976, 'An archaeological reconnaissance in the Horn: the British–Somali expedition, 1975', *Azania*, 11: 117–33.

   1977, 'The East coast, Madagascar and the Indian Ocean', in Oliver, 1977a: 183–231.

Chivers, D. J. and Joysey, K. (eds.), 1978, *Recent Advances in Primatology – III*, London.

Chmielewski, W. 1968, 'Early and Middle Palaeolithic sites near Arkin, Sudan', in Wendorf, 1968: 110–93.

Clark, J. D. 1942, 'Further excavations (1939) at the Mumbwa Caves, Northern Rhodesia', *Trans. Roy. Soc. S. Afr.*, 29: 133–201.

1950, *The Stone Age Cultures of Northern Rhodesia*, Cape Town.

1954, *Prehistoric Cultures of the Horn of Africa*, Cambridge.

1958, 'Some Stone Age woodworking tools in southern Africa', *S.A.A.B.*, 13: 144–52.

1959, 'Further excavations at Broken Hill, Northern Rhodesia', *J.R.A.I.*, 89: 201–32.

1962, 'The Kalambo Falls prehistoric site – a preliminary report', in Mortelmans, 1962b: 195–202.

1963, *Prehistoric Cultures of Northeast Angola and their Significance in Tropical Africa*, Lisbon.

1964, 'The influence of environment in inducing culture change at the Kalambo Falls prehistoric site', *S.A.A.B.*, 20: 93–101.

1967, *Atlas of African Prehistory*, Chicago.

1969, *Kalambo Falls Prehistoric Site – I*, Cambridge.

1971, 'A re-examination of the evidence for agricultural origins in the Nile Valley', *P.P.S.*, 37(2): 34–79.

1974, *Kalambo Falls Prehistoric Site – II*, Cambridge.

1976, 'African origins of man the toolmaker', in Isaac and McCown, 1976: 1–53.

1980, 'Human populations and cultural adaptations in the Sahara and Nile during prehistoric times', in Williams and Faure, 1980: 527–82.

1982a, 'The cultures of the Middle Palaeolithic/Middle Stone Age', in J. D. Clark, 1982b: 248–341.

(ed.) 1982b, *Cambridge History of Africa – I*, Cambridge.

Clark, J. D. and Haynes, C. V. 1970, 'An elephant butchery site at Mwanganda's village, Karonga, Malawi', *World Archaeology*, 1: 390–411.

Clark, J. D. and Stemler, A. 1975, 'Early domesticated sorghum from central Sudan', *Nature*, 254: 588–91.

Clark, J. D. and Williams, M. A. J. 1978, 'Recent archaeological research in southeastern Ethiopia, 1974–5', *Annales d'Ethiopie*, 11: 19–42.

Clark, J. D. *et al.*, 1950, 'New studies on Rhodesian Man', *J.R.A.I.*, 77: 7–32.

1973, 'The geomorphology and archaeology of Adrar Bous, Central Sahara: a preliminary report', *Quaternaria*, 17: 245–98.

1974, 'Interpretations of prehistoric technology from Ancient Egyptian and other sources: I – Ancient Egyptian bows and arrows and their relevance for African prehistory', *Paléorient*, 2: 323–88.

Clark, J. G. D. 1969, *World Prehistory: a new outline*, Cambridge.

1977, *World Prehistory in New Perspective*, Cambridge.

Clarke, R. J. 1976, 'New cranium of *Homo erectus* from Lake Ndutu, Tanzania', *Nature*, 262: 485–7.

Cole, S. 1964, *The Prehistory of East Africa*, London.

Connah, G. 1975, *The Archaeology of Benin*, Oxford.

1976, 'The Daima sequence and the prehistoric chronology of the Lake Chad region of Nigeria', *J.A.H.*, 17: 321–52.

1981, *Three Thousand Years in Africa*, Cambridge.

n.d., *Polished Stone Axes in Benin*, Lagos.

de Contenson, H. 1981, 'Pre-Aksumite culture', in Mokhtar, 1981: 341–61.

Cooke, C. K. 1963, 'Report on excavations at Pomongwe and Tshangula Caves, Matopo Hills, Southern Rhodesia', *S.A.A.B.*, 18: 73–151.

1969, 'A re-examination of the "Middle Stone Age" industries of Rhodesia,' *Arnoldia*, 4: no. 7.

1971, 'Excavation in Zombepata Cave, Sipolilo District, Mashonaland, Rhodesia', *S.A.A.B.*, 25: 104–27.

1973, 'The Middle Stone Age in Rhodesia and South Africa', *Arnoldia*, 6: no. 20.

1978, 'The Redcliff Stone Age site, Rhodesia', *Occ. Pap. Nat. Mus. Rhod.*, 4a(2): 45–73.

Coon, C. S. 1968, *Yengema Cave Report*, Philadelphia.

Coppens, Y. 1965, 'An early hominid from Chad', *Curr. Anthrop.*, 7: 584–5.

Coppens, Y. *et al.*, (eds.), 1976, *Earliest Man and Environments in the Lake Rudolf Basin*, Chicago.

Coursey, D. G. 1976, 'The origins and domestication of yams in Africa', in Harlan *et al.*, 1976: 383–408.

Cruz e Silva, T. 1980, 'First indications of Early Iron Age in southern Mozambique: Matola IV 1/68', in R. E. Leakey and Ogot, 1980: 349–50.

Dagan, T. 1956, 'Le site préhistorique de Tiémassas', *Bull. I.F.A.N.*, 18B: 432–61.

1972, 'Les gisements préhistoriques de Tiémassas et de Pointe Sarène, Sénégal', in Hugot, 1972: 92–4.

Dalby, D. 1975, 'The prehistorical implications of Guthrie's *Comparative Bantu*: problems of internal relationship', *J.A.H.*, 16: 481–501.

Dark, P. J. C. 1973, *An Introduction to Benin Art and Technology*, Oxford.

Dart, R. A. 1925, '*Australopithecus africanus*: the ape-man of South Africa', *Nature*, 115: 195–9.

1957, *The Osteodontokeratic Culture of Australopithecus prometheus*, Pretoria.

Dart, R. A. and Beaumont, P. B. 1968, 'Ratification and retrocession of earlier Swaziland iron ore mining radiocarbon datings', *S.A.J.S.*, 64: 241–6.

David, N. 1980, 'Early Bantu expansion in the context of central African prehistory', in Bouquiaux, 1980: 609–44.

David, N. and Vidal, P. 1977, 'The Nana-Mode village site and the prehistory of the Ubangian-speaking peoples', *W.A.J.A.*, 7: 17–56.

David, N. *et al.*, 1981, 'Excavations in the southern Sudan, 1979', *Azania*, 16: 7–54.

Davies, O. 1964, *The Quaternary of the Coastlands of Guinea*, Glasgow.

1967, *West Africa before the Europeans*, London.

1971, 'Excavations at Blackburn', *S.A.A.B.*, 26: 165–78.

1973, *Excavations at Ntereso*, Pietermaritzburg (cyclostyled).

Davison, P. and Harries, P. 1980, 'Cotton weaving in south-east Africa: its history and technology', *Textile History*, 11: 175–92.

Day, M. H. *et al.*, 1980, 'On the status of *Australopithecus afarensis*', *Science*, 207: 1102–5.

Deacon, H. J. 1966, 'Note on the x-ray of two mounted implements from South Africa', *Man (N.S.)*, 1: 87–90.

1970, 'The Acheulian occupation at Amanzi Springs, Uitenhage District, Cape Province', *Annals Cape Provincial Museums*, 8: 89–189.

1976, *Where Hunters Gathered*, Cape Town.

1979, 'Excavations at Boomplaas Cave – a sequence through the Upper Pleistocene and Holocene in South Africa', *World Archaeology*, 10: 241–57.

Deacon, H. J. *et al.*, 1978, 'The evidence for herding at Boomplaas Cave in the southern Cape', *S.A.A.B.*, 33: 39–59.

Deacon, J. 1972, 'Wilton – a re-assessment after fifty years', *S.A.A.B.*, 27: 10–48.

1974, 'Patterning in the radiocarbon dates for the Wilson/Smithfield complex in southern Africa', *S.A.A.B.*, 29: 3–18.

1978, 'Changing patterns in the Late Pleistocene/Early Holocene prehistory of southern Africa as seen from the Nelson Bay Cave stone artifact sequence', *Quat. Research*, 10: 84–111.

Dole, G. E. and Carnero R. L. (eds), 1960, *Essays in the Science of Culture*, New York.

Dombrowski, J. 1970, 'Preliminary report on excavations in Lalibela and Natchabiet Caves, Begemeder', *Annales d'Ethiopie*, 8: 21–9.

    1980, 'Earliest settlements in Ghana: the Kintampo industry', in R. E. Leakey and Ogot, 1980: 261–2.

Ehret, C. 1973, 'Patterns of Bantu and Central Sudanic settlement in central and southern Africa', *Transafr. J. Hist.*, 3: 1–71.

    1974, *Ethiopians and East Africans*, Nairobi.

    1976, 'Linguistic evidence and its correlation with archaeology', *World Archaeology*, 8: 5–18.

    1980, 'On the antiquity of agriculture in Ethiopia', *J.A.H.*, 20: 161–77.

Eloff, J F. and Meyer, A. 1981, 'The Greefswald sites', in Voigt, 1981: 7–22.

Ennouchi, E. 1962, 'Un néanderthalien: l'homme du Jebel Irhoud (Maroc)', *L'Anthropologie*, 66: 279–99.

    1972, 'Nouvelle découverte d'un archantropien au Maroc', *C.R. Acad. Sci. Paris*, 274D: 3088–90.

Epstein, H. 1971, *The Origin of the Domestic Animals of Africa*, New York.

Evernden, J. F. and Curtis, G. H. 1965, 'The potassium-argon dating of late Caenozoic rocks in East Africa and Italy', *Curr. Anthrop.*, 6: 343–64.

Evers, T. M. 1982, 'Excavations at the Lydenburg Heads site, eastern Transvaal, South Africa', *S.A.A.B.*, 37: 16–33.

Eyo, E. 1974, 'Odo Ogbe Street and Lafogido: contrasting archaeological sites at Ile Ife, Western Nigeria', *W.A.J.A.*, 4: 99–109.

Eyo, E. and Willett, F. 1980, *Treasures of Ancient Nigeria*, New York.

Fagan, B. M. 1964, 'The Greefswald sequence: Mapungubwe and Bambandyanalo', *J.A.H.*, 5: 337–61.

    1967, *Iron Age Cultures in Zambia – I*, London.

Fagan, B. M. and van Noten, F. 1971, *The Hunter-Gatherers of Gwisho*, Tervuren.

Fagan, B. M. and Yellen, J. 1968, 'Ivuna: ancient salt-working in southern Tanzania', *Azania*, 3: 1–43.

Fagan, B. M. *et al.*, 1969, *Iron Age Cultures in Zambia – II*, London.

Fage, J. D. (ed.), 1978, *Cambridge History of Africa – II*, Cambridge.

Fagg, A. 1972, 'A preliminary report on an occupation site in the Nok Valley, Nigeria', *W.A.J.A.*, 2: 75–9.

Fagg, B. 1979, *Nok Terracottas*, London.

Fagg, B. *et al.*, 1972, Four papers on the Rop rockshelter, *W.A.J.A.*, 2: 1–38.

Flight, C. 1976, 'The Kintampo culture and its place in the economic prehistory of West Africa', in Harlan *et al.*, 1976: 211–22.

Fosbrooke, H. A. *et al.*, 1950, 'Tanganyika rock paintings', *Tanganyika Notes and Records*, 29: 1–61.

Gallay, A. 1966, 'Quelques gisements néolithiques du Sahara malien', *J. Soc. Africanistes*, 36: 167–208.

Garlake, P. S. 1973a, *Great Zimbabwe*, London.

    1973b, 'Excavations at the Nhunguza and Ruanga Ruins in northern Mashonaland', *S.A.A.B.*, 27: 107–43.

    1974, 'Excavations at Obalara's Land, Ife: an interim report', *W.A.J.A.*, 4: 111–48.

    1976, 'An investigation of Manekweni, Moçambique', *Azania*, 11: 25–47.

    1977, 'Excavations on the Woye Asiri family land in Ife, western Nigeria', *W.A.J.A.*, 7: 57–96.

    1978a, *The Kingdoms of Africa*, London.

    1978b, 'Pastoralism and Zimbabwe', *J.A.H.*, 19: 479–93.

    1982, 'Prehistory and ideology in Zimbabwe', *Africa*, 52(3): 1–19.

Gau, F. C. 1822, *Antiquités de la Nubie, ou Monuments Inédits des Bords du Nil*, Stuttgart.

Gerster, G. 1970, *Churches in Rock*, London.

Gibbs, J. L. (ed), 1965, *Peoples in Africa*, New York.

Gowlett, J. A. J. *et al.*, 1981, 'Early archaeological sites, hominid remains and traces of fire from Chesowanja, Kenya', *Nature*, 294: 125–9.

Gramly, R. M. 1976, 'Upper Pleistocene archaeological occurrences at site GvJm/22, Lukenya Hill, Kenya', *Man (N.S.)*, 11: 319–44.

Gramly, R. M. and Rightmire, G. P. 1973, 'A fragmentary cranium and dated later Stone Age assemblage from Lukenya Hill, Kenya', *Man (N.S.)*, 8: 571–9.

Greenberg, J. H. 1963, *The Languages of Africa*, The Hague.

Hall, M. and Vogel, J. C. 1980, 'Some recent radiocarbon dates from southern Africa'. *J.A.H.*, 21: 431–56.

Hansen, C. L. and Keller, C. M. 1971, 'Environment and activity patterning at Isimila *karongo*, Tanzania', *Am. Anthrop.*, 73: 1201–11.

Harlan, J. R. 1969, 'Ethiopia: a centre of diversity', *Econ. Bot.*, 23: 309–14.

  1971, 'Agricultural origins: centers and non-centers', *Science*, 174: 468–74.

Harlan, J. *et al.*, (eds.), 1976, *Origins of African Plant Domestication*, The Hague.

Harris, J. R. (ed.), 1971, *The Legacy of Egypt*, Oxford.

Harris, J. W. K. and Isaac, G. L. 1976, 'The Karari industry', *Nature*, 262: 102–7.

Harvey, P. and Grove, A. T. 1982, 'A prehistoric source of the Nile', *Geog. J.*, 148: 327–36.

Hassan, F. A. 1980, 'Prehistoric settlements along the main Nile', in Williams and Faure, 1980: 421–50.

Hay, R. L. 1976, *The Geology of Olduvai Gorge*, Berkeley.

Heine, B. 1978, 'The Sam languages', *Afro-Asiatic Linguistics*, 6.

Heine, B. *et al.*, 1977, 'Neuere Ergebnisse zur Territorialgeschichte der Bantu', in Möhlig *et al.*, 1977: 57–72.

de Heinzelin, J. 1957, *Les Fouilles d'Ishango*, Brussels.

Helgren, D. M. 1980, 'The Vaal river chronology: an up-to-date summary', in R. E. Leakey and Ogot, 1980: 222–4.

Henige, D. P. 1974, *The Chronology of Oral Tradition*, Oxford.

d'Hertefelt, M. 1965, 'The Rwanda of Rwanda', in Gibbs, 1965: 405–40.

Hiernaux, J. 1968, *La Diversité Humaine en Afrique sub-Saharienne*, Brussels.

  1974, *The People of Africa*, London.

Hiernaux, J. and Maquet, E. 1968, *L'Age du Fer à Kibiro, Uganda*, Tervuren.

Hiernaux, J. *et al.*, 1972, 'Le cimetière protohistorique de Katoto, Vallée du Lualaba, Congo-Kinshasa', in Hugot, 1972: 148–58.

Hoffman, M. A. 1980, *Egypt before the Pharaohs*, London.

Hours, F. 1973, 'Le Middle Stone Age de Melka-Kunturé: résultats acquis en 1971', *Documents pour Servir à l'Histoire des Civilisations Ethiopiennes*, 4: 19–29.

Howell, F. C. 1976, 'An overview of the Pliocene and earlier Pleistocene of the lower Omo basin, southern Ethiopia', in Isaac and McCown, 1976: 227–68.

  1982, 'Origins and evolution of African Hominidae', in J. D. Clark, 1982b: 70–156.

Howell, F. C. and Coppens, Y. 1976, 'An overview of Hominidae from the Omo succession, Ethiopia', in Coppens *et al.*, 1976: 522–32.

Howell, F. C. *et al.*, 1962, 'Isimila: an Acheulian occupation site in the Iringa highlands', in Mortelmans, 1962b: 43–80.

Howells, W. W. 1966, '*Homo erectus*', *Scientific American*, 215: 46–53.

Huffman, T. N. 1974, *The Leopard's Kopje Tradition*, Salisbury.

  1978, 'The origins of Leopard's Kopje: an 11th-century *Difaqane*', *Arnoldia*, 8: no. 23.

  1982, 'Archaeology and ethnohistory of the African Iron Age', *Ann. Rev. Anthrop.*, 11: 133–50.

Hughes, A. R. and Tobias, P. V. 1977, 'A fossil skull probably of the genus *Homo* from Sterkfontein, Transvaal', *Nature*, 265: 310–2.

Hugot, H. (ed.), 1972, *Actes du 6e Congrès Panafricain de Préhistoire*, Chambéry.

Humphreys, A. J. B. 1970, 'The role of raw material and the concept of the Fauresmith', *S.A.A.B.*, 35: 139–44.

Huntingford, G. W. B. 1980, *The Periplus of the Erythraean Sea*, London.

Inskeep, R. R. 1962, 'The age of the Kondoa rock paintings in the light of recent excavations at Kisese II rock shelter', in Mortelmans, 1962b: 249–56.

　1978, *The Peopling of Southern Africa*, Cape Town.

Inskeep, R. R. and Maggs, T. 1975, 'Unique art objects in the Iron Age of the Transvaal, South Africa', *S.A.A.B.*, 30: 114–38.

Isaac, G. L. 1967, 'The stratigraphy of the Peninj Group', in Bishop and Clark, 1967: 229–57.

　1972, 'Chronology and the tempo of cultural change during the Pleistocene', in Bishop and Miller, 1972: 381–430.

　1976, 'The activities of early African hominids', in Isaac and McCown, 1976: 483–509.

　1977, *Olorgesailie*, Chicago.

　1978, 'The food-sharing behaviour of protohuman hominids', *Scientific American*, 238, 4: 90–9.

　1982, 'The earliest archaeological traces', in J. D. Clark, 1982b: 157–247.

Isaac, G. L. and Curtis, G. H. 1974, 'The age of early Acheulian industries from the Peninj group, Tanzania', *Nature*, 249: 624–7.

Isaac, G. L. and Harris, J. W. K. 1978, 'Archaeology', in M. G. Leakey and R. E. Leakey, 1978: 64–85.

Isaac, G. L. and McCown E. (eds.), 1976, *Human Origins: Louis Leakey and the East African evidence*, Menlo Park.

Isaac, G. L. *et al.*, 1972, 'Stratigraphic and archaeological studies in the Lake Nakuru basin, Kenya', *Palaeoecology of Africa*, 6: 225–32.

　1976, 'Archaeological evidence from the Koobi Fora formation', in Coppens *et al.*, 1976: 533–51.

Jaeger, J. J. 1973, 'Un pithécanthrope évolué', *Recherche*, 39: 1006–7.

James, T. G. H. (ed.), 1979, *An Introduction to Ancient Egypt*, London.

Jodin, A. 1959, 'Les grottes d'El Khril à Achakar, Province de Tanger', *Bull d'Arch. Maroc.*, 3: 249–313.

Johanson, D. C. and Edey, M. A. 1981, *Lucy – the Beginnings of Humankind*, London.

Johanson, D. C. and White, T. 1979, 'A systematic assessment of early African hominids', *Science*, 203: 321–30.

Johanson, D. C. *et al.*, 1978, 'Geological framework of the Pliocene Hadar Formation (Afar, Ethiopia) with notes on palaeontology including hominids', in Bishop, 1978: 549–64.

Jolly, C. (ed.), 1978, *Early Hominids of Africa*, London.

Kalb, J. E. *et al.*, 1982, 'Fossil mammals and artefacts from the Middle Awash Valley, Ethiopia', *Nature*, 298: 25–9.

Keeley, L. H. 1980, *Experimental Determination of Stone Tool Uses*, Chicago.

Keller, C. M. 1969, 'Mossel Bay: a re-description', *S.A.A.B.*, 23: 131–40.

　1973, *Montagu Cave in Prehistory*, Berkeley.

Kendall, R. L. and Livingstone, D. A. 1972, 'Palaeoecological studies on the East African plateau', in Hugot, 1972: 386–8.

Kirwan, L. P. 1960, 'The decline and fall of Meroe', *Kush*, 8: 163–5.

　1974, 'Nuba and Nubian origins', *Geog. J.*, 140: 43–51.

Klapwijk, M. 1974, 'A preliminary report on pottery from the north-eastern Transvaal', *S.A.A.B.*, 29: 19–23.

Klein, R. G. 1973, 'Geological antiquity of Rhodesian man', *Nature*, 244: 311–2.

1974, 'Environment and subsistence of prehistoric man in the southern Cape Province, South Africa', *World Archaeology*, 5: 249–84.

1978, 'Stone Age predation on large African bovids', *J. Arch. Sci.*, 5: 195–217.

von Koenigswald, G. H. R. (ed.), 1958, *Hundert Jahre Neanderthaler*, Utrecht.

Krzyzaniak, L. 1978, 'New light on early food-production in the central Sudan', *J.A.H.*, 19: 159–72.

(ed.), in press. *Origin and Early Development of Food-Producing Cultures in North-Eastern Africa*, Poznan.

Lancaster, J. B. 1975, *Primate Behaviour and the Emergence of Human Culture*, New York.

Law, R. C. C. 1978a, 'North Africa in the age of Phoenician and Greek colonisation', in Fage, 1978: 87–147.

1978b, 'North Africa in the Hellenistic and Roman periods', in Fage, 1978: 148–209.

Leakey, L. S. B. 1931, *The Stone Age Cultures of Kenya Colony*, Cambridge.

1943, 'Industries of the Gorgora rock shelter, Lake Tana', *J. E. Afr. and Uganda Nat. Hist. Soc.*, 17: 199–203.

1965, *Olduvai Gorge – I*, Cambridge.

Leakey, L. S. B. *et al.*, 1964, 'A new species of the genus *Homo* from Olduvai Gorge', *Nature*, 202: 7–9.

Leakey, M. *et al.*, 1969, 'An Acheulian industry with prepared core technique and the discovery of a contemporary hominid mandible at Lake Baringo, Kenya', *P.P.S.*, 35: 48–76.

Leakey, M. D. 1945, 'Report on the excavations at Hyrax Hill, Nakuru, Kenya Colony', *Trans. Roy. Soc. S. Afr.*, 30: 271–409.

1970, 'Stone artefacts from Swartkrans', *Nature*, 225: 1222–5.

1971, *Olduvai Gorge – III*, Cambridge.

1975, 'Cultural patterns in the Olduvai sequence', in Butzer and Isaac, 1975: 477–94.

1976, 'A summary and discussion of the archaeological evidence from Bed I and Bed II, Olduvai Gorge, Tanzania', in Isaac and McCown, 1976: 431–59.

1978, 'Olduvai fossil hominids: their stratigraphic position and associations', in Jolly, 1978: 3–16.

Leakey, M. D. and Hay, R. L. 1979, 'Pliocene footprints in the Laetolil Beds at Laetoli, northern Tanzania', *Nature*, 278: 317–23.

Leakey, M. D. and L. S. B. 1950, *Excavations at Njoro River Cave*, Oxford.

Leakey, M. D. *et al.*, 1948, *Dimple-based Pottery from Central Kavirondo, Kenya Colony*, Nairobi.

1972, 'Stratigraphy, archaeology and age of the Ndutu and Naisiusiu Beds, Olduvai Gorge, Tanzania', *World Archaeology*, 3: 328–41.

1976, 'Fossil hominids from the Laetolil Beds', *Nature*, 262: 464–6.

Leakey, M. G. and R. E. (eds.), 1978, *Koobi Fora Research Project – I*, Oxford.

Leakey, R. E. and Ogot, B. A. (eds.), 1980, *Proceedings 8th Panafrican Congress of Prehistory*, Nairobi.

Leakey, R. E. and Walker, A. C. 1976, '*Australopithecus*, *Homo erectus* and the single species hypothesis', *Nature*, 261: 572–4.

Lebeuf, J. P. 1962, *Archéologie Tchadienne*, Paris.

Lee, C. *et al.*, 1976, 'Amino-acid in modern and fossil woods', *Nature*, 259: 183–6.

Lee, D. N. and Woodhouse, H. C. 1970, *Art on the Rocks of Southern Africa*, Cape Town.

Lee, R. B. 1963, 'The population ecology of man in the early Upper Pleistocene of southern Africa', *P.P.S.*, 29: 235–57.

1968, 'What hunters do for a living', in R. B. Lee and DeVore, 1968: 30–48.

Lee, R. B. and DeVore, I. (eds.), 1968, *Man the Hunter*, Chicago.

Levtzion, N. 1973, *Ancient Ghana and Mali*, London.

1977, 'The western Maghrib and Sudan', in Oliver, 1977a: 331–462.

1978, 'The Sahara and the Sudan from the Arab conquest of the Maghrib to the rise of the Almoravids', in Fage, 1978: 637–84.

Lewis, H. S. 1966, 'The origins of the Galla and Somali', *J.A.H.*, 7: 27–46.

Lewis-Williams, J. D. 1981, *Believing and Seeing*, London.

Linares de Sapir, O. 1971, 'Shell middens of Lower Casamance and problems of Diola protohistory', *W.A.J.A.*, 1: 23–54.

Littmann, E. 1913, *Deutsche Aksum Expedition*, Berlin.

Lubell, D. 1974, *The Fakhurian: a late palaeolithic industry from Upper Egypt*, Cairo.

McBurney, C. B. M. 1960, *The Stone Age of Northern Africa*, Harmondsworth.

1967, *The Haua Fteah (Cyrenaica)*, Cambridge.

1975, 'The archaeological context of the Hamitic languages in northern Africa', in J. and T. Bynon, 1975: 495–515.

MacCalman, H. R. 1963, 'The Neuhoff–Kowas Middle Stone Age, Windhoek district', *Cimbebasia*, 7.

MacCalman, H. R. and Viereck, H. 1967, 'Peperkorrel, a factory site of Lupemban affinities from central South West Africa', *S.A.A.B.*, 22: 41–50.

McIntosh, R. J. and S. K. 1981, 'The inland Niger delta before the empire of Mali: evidence from Jenne-Jeno', *J.A.H.*, 22: 1–22.

McIntosh, S. K. and R. J. 1980, *Prehistoric Investigations in the Region of Jenne, Mali*, Oxford.

Maggs, T. M. O'C. 1971, 'Pastoral settlements on the Riet River', *S.A.A.B.*, 26: 37–63.

1976, *Iron Age Communities of the Southern Highveld*, Pietermaritzburg.

1980, 'The Iron Age sequence south of the Vaal and Pongola Rivers', *J.A.H.*, 21: 1–15.

de Maret, P. 1977, 'Sanga: new excavations, more data and some related problems', *J.A.H.*, 18: 321–37.

1981, 'L'évolution monétaire du Shaba central entre le 7e et le 18e siècle', *African Economic History*, 10.

1982, 'New survey of archaeological research and dates for West-Central and North-Central Africa', *J.A.H.*, 23: 1–15.

de Maret, P. *et al.*, 1977, 'Radiocarbon dates from West Central Africa: a synthesis', *J.A.H.*, 18: 481–506.

Marks, A. E. 1968, 'The Khormusan' and 'The Halfan', in Wendorf, 1968: 315–460.

Masao, F. T. 1979, *The Later Stone Age and the Rock Paintings of Central Tanzania*, Wiesbaden.

Mason, R. J. 1962, *The Prehistory of the Transvaal*, Johannesburg.

1974, 'Background to the Transvaal Iron Age: discoveries at Olifantspoort and Broederstroom', *J. S. Afr. Inst. Mining and Metallurgy*, 74: 211–6.

1976, 'The earliest artefact assemblages of South Africa', *U.I.S.P.P.*, Nice.

1981, 'Early Iron Age settlement at Broederstroom 24/73, Transvaal, South Africa', *S.A.J.S.*, 77: 401–16.

Mauny, R. 1973, 'Datation au carbone 14 d'amas de coquillages des lagunes de Basse Côte d'Ivoire', *W.A.J.A.*, 3: 207–14.

1978, 'Trans-Saharan contacts and the Iron Age in West Africa', in Fage, 1978: 272–341.

Megaw, J. V. S. (ed.), 1977, *Hunters, Gatherers and First Farmers beyond Europe*, Leicester.

Mehlman, M. J. 1977, 'Excavations at Nasera Rock, Tanzania', *Azania*, 12: 111–8.

Merrick, H. V. and J. P. S. 1976, 'Archaeological occurrences of earlier Pleistocene age from the Shungura formation', in Coppens *et al.*, 1976: 574–84.

van der Merwe, N. J. 1980, 'The advent of iron in Africa', in Wertime and Muhly, 1980: 463–506.

van der Merwe, N. J. and Scully, R. T. K. 1971, 'The Phalaborwa story: archaeological and ethnographic investigation of a South African Iron Age group', *World Archaeology*, 3: 178–96.

Michalowski, K. 1964, 'Polish excavations at Faras, 1962–63'. *Kush*, 12: 195–207.

Miller, J. C. 1972, 'The Imbangala and the chronology of early Central African history', *J.A.H.*, 13: 549–74.

1976, *Kings and Kinsmen*, Oxford.

Miller, S. F. 1972, 'The archaeological sequence of the Zambian later Stone Age', in Hugot, 1972: 565–72.

Möhlig, W. J. G. *et al.* (eds.), 1977, *Zur Sprachgeschichte und Ethnohistorie in Afrika*, Berlin.

Mokhtar, G. (ed.), 1981, *UNESCO General History of Africa – II*, London.

van Moorsel, H. 1968, *Atlas de Préhistoire de la Plaine de Kinshasa*, Kinshasa.

Mori, F. 1965, *Tadrart Acacus: arte rupestre e culture del Sahara preistorico*, Turin.

1978, 'Zur Chronologie der Sahara-Felsbilder', in Stehli, 1978: 253–61.

Mortelmans, G. 1962a, 'Vue d'ensemble sur la préhistoire du Congo occidental', in Mortelmans, 1962b: 129–64.

1962b, *Actes du 4e Congrès Panafricain de Préhistoire*, Tervuren.

Mturi, A. 1976, 'New hominid from Lake Ndutu, Tanzania', *Nature*, 262: 484–5.

Munson, P. J. 1976, 'Archaeological data on the origins of cultivation in the southwestern Sahara and their implications for West Africa', in Harlan *et al.*, 1976, 187–210.

Naville, E. 1898, *The Temple of Deir el Bahari*, London.

Nelson, C. M. and Posnansky, M. 1970, 'The stone tools from the re-excavation of Nsongezi rock shelter', *Azania*, 5: 119–72.

Nenquin, J. 1963, *Excavations at Sanga, 1957*, Tervuren.

1967, *Contributions to the Study of the Prehistoric Cultures of Rwanda and Burundi*, Tervuren.

Nordström, H. A. 1972, *Neolithic and A-Group Sites* (Scandinavian Joint Expedition to Sudanese Nubia, III, 2), Stockholm.

van Noten, F. 1971, 'Excavations at Munyama Cave', *Antiquity*, 45: 56–8.

1977, 'Excavations at Matupi Cave', *Antiquity*, 51: 35–40.

1978, *Rock Art of the Jebel Uweinat (Libyan Sahara)*, Graz.

1979, 'The Early Iron Age in the Interlacustrine Region: the diffusion of iron technology', *Azania*, 14: 61–80.

1982, *Prehistory of Central Africa*, Graz.

O'Brien, T. P. 1939, *The Prehistory of the Uganda Protectorate*, Cambridge.

Odner, K. 1971, 'Usangi Hospital and other archaeological sites in the North Pare mountains, north-eastern Tanzania', *Azania*, 6: 89–130.

Oliver, R. (ed.), 1977a, *Cambridge History of Africa – III*, Cambridge.

1977b, 'The East African interior', in Oliver, 1977a: 621–69.

1982, 'The Nilotic contribution to Bantu Africa', *J.A.H.*, 23: 433–42.

Owen, R. B. *et al.*, 1982, 'Palaeolimnology and archaeology of Holocene deposits north-east of Lake Turkana, Kenya', *Nature*, 298: 523–9.

Parkington, J. E. 1972, 'Seasonal mobility in the Later Stone Age', *African Studies*, 31: 223–43.

Partridge, T. C. and Brink, A. B. A. 1967, 'Gravels and terraces of the lower Vaal basin', *S. Afr. Geog. J.*, 49: 21–38.

Peabody, F. E. 1954, 'Travertines and cave deposits of the Kaap escarpment of South Africa and the type locality of *Australopithecus africanus*', *Bull. Geol. Soc. America*, 65: 671–705.

Phillipson, D. W. 1968a, 'The Early Iron Age in Zambia: regional variants and some tentative conclusions', *J.A.H.*, 9: 191–211.

1968b, 'Cewa, Leya and Lala iron-smelting furnaces', *S.A.A.B.*, 23: 102–13.

1970, 'Excavations at Twickenham Road, Lusaka', *Azania*, 5: 77–118.

1972, 'Zambian rock paintings', *World Archaeology*, 3: 313–27.

1974, 'Iron Age history and archaeology in Zambia', *J.A.H.*, 15: 1–25.

1975, 'The chronology of the Iron Age in Bantu Africa', *J.A.H.*, 16: 321–42.

1976, *The Prehistory of Eastern Zambia*, Nairobi.

1977a, *The Later Prehistory of Eastern and Southern Africa*, London.

1977b, 'The excavation of Gobedra rockshelter, Axum: an early occurrence of cultivated finger millet in northern Ethiopia', *Azania*, 12: 53–82.

1977c, 'Lowasera', *Azania*, 12: 1–32.

in press, 'Aspects of early food production in northern Kenya', in Krzyzaniak, in press.

Phillipson, D. W. and Fagan, B. M. 1969, 'The date of the Ingombe Ilede burials', *J.A.H.*, 10: 199–204.

Phillipson, L. 1978, *The Stone Age Archaeology of the Upper Zambezi Valley*, Nairobi.

Posnansky, M. 1968, 'The excavation of an Ankole capital site at Bweyorere', *Uganda J.*, 32: 165–82.

1969, 'Bigo bya Mugenyi', *Uganda J.*, 33: 125–50.

1973, 'Aspects of early West African trade', *World Archaeology*, 5: 149–62.

1976, 'Archaeology and the origins of the Akan society in Ghana', in Sieveking *et al.*, 1976: 49–59.

Posnansky, M. and McIntosh, R. 1976, 'New radiocarbon dates for northern and western Africa', *J.A.H.*, 17: 161–95.

Ralph, E. K. *et al.*, 1973, 'Radiocarbon dates and reality', *MASCA Newsletter*, 9, no. 1.

Ravise, A. 1970, 'Industrie néolithique en os de la région de S. Louis, Sénégal', *Notes Afr.*, 128: 97–102.

Reisner, G. A. 1923, 'Excavations at Kerma', *Harvard African Studies*, 5–6.

van Riet Lowe, C. 1952, 'The Vaal River chronology', *S.A.A.B.*, 7: 135–49.

Rightmire, G. P. 1970, 'Iron Age skulls from southern Africa re-assessed by multiple discriminant analysis', *Am. J. Phys. Anthrop.*, 77: 28–52.

1975, 'New studies of post-Pleistocene human skeletal remains from the Rift Valley, Kenya', *Am. J. Phys. Anthrop.*, 42: 351–70.

1978, 'Human skeletal remains from the southern Cape Province and their bearing on the Stone Age prehistory of South Africa', *Quat. Res.*, 9: 219–30.

1979, 'Implications of Border Cave skeletal remains for later Pleistocene human evolution', *Curr. Anthrop.*, 20: 23–35.

Robbins, L. H. 1974, *The Lothagam Site*, East Lansing.

Robbins, L. H. *et al.*, 1980, *Lopoy and Lothagam*, East Lansing.

Robert, D. 1970, 'Les fouilles de Tegdaoust', *J.A.H.*, 11: 471–93.

Robertshaw, P. and Collett, D. 1983, 'A new framework for the study of early pastoral communities in East Africa', *J.A.H.*, 24: 289–301.

Robinson, J. T. 1967, 'Variation and the taxonomy of early hominids', *Evolutionary Biology*, 1: 69–100.

Robinson, J. T. and Mason, R. J. 1962, 'Australopithecines and artefacts at Sterkfontein', *S.A.A.B.*, 17: 87–126.

Robinson, K. R. 1959, *Khami Ruins*, Cambridge.

1966, 'The Leopard's Kopje culture: its position in the Iron Age in Southern Rhodesia', *S.A.A.B.*, 21: 5–51.

1973, *The Iron Age of the Upper and Lower Shire, Malawi*, Zomba.

Robinson, K. R. and Sandelowsky, B. 1968, 'The Iron Age in northern Malawi: recent work', *Azania*, 3: 107–46.

Roche, H. and Tiercelin, J. J. 1980, 'Industries lithiques de la formation plio-pleistocène d'Hadar, Ethiopie', in R. E. Leakey and Ogot, 1980: 194–9.

Roche, J. 1971, 'La grotte de Taforalt', *Bull. Soc. Histor. Maroc*, 3: 7–14.

Roubet, C. 1979, *Economie Pastorale Préagricole en Algérie Orientale: le néolithique de tradition capsienne*, Paris.

Roubet, C. *et al.* (eds.), 1981, *Préhistoire Africaine*, Paris.

Rudner, J. 1968, 'Strandloper pottery from South and South West Africa', *Annals South African Museum*, 49: 441–663.

    1971, 'Painted burial stones from the Cape', *S.A.J.S.*, *Special issue* 2: 54–61.

Saban, R. 1977, 'The place of Rabat man (Kebibat, Morocco) in human evolution', *Curr. Anthrop.*, 18: 518–24.

Sampson, C. G. 1968, *The Middle Stone Age Industries of the Orange River Scheme Area*, Bloemfontein.

    1974, *The Stone Age Archaeology of Southern Africa*, New York.

Sandelowsky, B. *et al.*, 1979, 'Early evidence for herders in the Namib', *S.A.A.B.*, 34: 50–1.

Sandford, K. 1934, *Palaeolithic Man and the Nile Valley in Upper and Middle Egypt*, Chicago.

Sandford, K. and Arkell, A. J. 1933, *Palaeolithic Man and the Nile Valley in Nubia and Upper Egypt*, Chicago.

Sausse, F. 1975, 'La mandibule atlanthropienne de la carrière Thomas I (Casablanca)', *L'Anthropologie*, 79: 81–112.

Saxon, E. *et al.*, 1974, 'Results of recent investigations at Tamar Hat', *Libyca*, 22: 49–91.

Schild, R. and Wendorf, F. 1975, 'New explorations in the Egyptian Sahara', in Wendorf and Marks, 1975: 65–112.

    1977, *The Prehistory of Dakhla Oasis and the Adjacent Desert*, Warsaw.

Schmidt, P. 1978, *Historical Archaeology*, Westport.

Schweitzer, F. R. 1974, 'Archaeological evidence for sheep at the Cape', *S.A.A.B.*, 29: 75–82.

Sergew, H. S. 1972, *Ancient and Medieval Ethiopian History*, Addis Ababa.

Shaw, T. 1944, 'Report on excavations carried out in the cave known as Bosumpra at Abetifi, Kwahu, Gold Coast Colony', *P.P.S.*, 10: 1–67.

    1969, 'The Late Stone Age in the Nigerian Forest', *Actes 1e Colloque International d'Archéologie Africaine*, Fort Lamy: 364–73.

    1970, *Igbo Ukwu*, London.

    1971, 'Africa in prehistory: leader or laggard?', *J.A.H.*, 12: 143–53.

    1977, 'Hunters, gatherers and first farmers in West Africa', in Megaw, 1977: 69–126.

    1978, *Nigeria*, London.

    1981a, 'The Late Stone Age in West Africa and the beginnings of African food production', in Roubet *et al.*, 1981: 213–35.

    1981b, 'The Nok sculptures of Nigeria', *Scientific American*, 244: 154–66.

Shinnie, P. L. 1967, *Meroe*, London.

    1978, 'The Nilotic Sudan and Ethiopia', in Fage, 1978: 210–71.

Shinnie, P. L. and Bradley, R. 1980, *The Capital of Kush – I*, Berlin.

Shinnie, P. L. and Shinnie, M. 1978, *Debeira West*, Warminster.

Sieveking, G. de G. *et al.*, (eds.), 1976, *Problems in Economic and Social Archaeology*, London.

Silberbauer, G. B. 1965, *Bushman Survey Report*, Gaborone.

Simons, E. L. 1972, *Primate Evolution*, New York.

    1977, 'Ramapithecus', *Scientific American*, 236: 28–35.

Simoons, F. J. 1965, 'Some questions on the economic prehistory of Ethiopia', *J.A.H.*, 6: 1–13.

Sinclair, P. 1982, 'Chibuene – an early trading site in southern Mozambique', *Paideuma*, 28.

Singer, R. J. 1958, 'The Rhodesian, Florisbad and Saldanha skulls', in von Koenigswald, 1958: 52–62.

Singer, R. J. and Wymer, J. 1968, 'Archaeological investigations at the Saldanha skull site in South Africa', *S.A.A.B.*, 23: 63–74.

1969, 'Radiocarbon date for two painted stones from a coastal cave in South Africa', *Nature*, 224: 508–10.

1982, *The Middle Stone Age at Klasies River Mouth in South Africa*, Chicago.

Smith, A. B. 1974, 'Preliminary report of excavations at Karkarichinkat, Mali', *W.A.J.A.*, 4: 33–55.

1975, 'Radiocarbon dates from Bosumpra Cave, Abetifi, Ghana', *P.P.S.*, 41: 179–82.

1980, 'The neolithic tradition in the Sahara', in Williams and Faure, 1980: 451–65.

Smith, H. F. C. 1971, 'The early states of the central Sudan', in Ajayi and Crowder, 1971: 158–201.

Smith, P. E. L. 1967, 'New investigations in the late Pleistocene archaeology of the Kom Ombo Plain, Upper Egypt', *Quaternaria*, 9: 141–52.

1982, 'The late palaeolithic and epipalaeolithic of northern Africa', in J. D. Clark, 1982b: 342–409.

Smolla, G. 1956, 'Prähistorische Keramik aus Ostafrika', *Tribus*, 6: 35–64.

Soper, R. C. 1965, 'The Stone Age in Northern Nigeria', *J. Hist. Soc. Nigeria*, 3: 175–94.

1967a, 'Kwale: an Early Iron Age site in south-eastern Kenya', *Azania*, 2: 1–17.

1967b, 'Iron Age sites in north-eastern Tanzania', *Azania*, 2: 19–36.

1971, 'A general review of the Early Iron Age in the southern half of Africa', *Azania*, 6: 5–37.

1976, 'Archaeological sites in the Chyulu Hills, Kenya', *Azania*, 11: 83–116.

1979, 'Iron Age archaeology and traditional history in Embu, Mbeere and Chuka areas of central Kenya', *Azania*, 14: 31–59.

Soper, R. C. and Golden, B. 1969, 'An archaeological survey of Mwanza region, Tanzania', *Azania*, 4: 15–79.

Spaulding, A. C. 1960, 'The dimensions of archaeology', in Dole and Carnero, 1960: 437–56.

Speth, J. D. and Davis, D. D. 1976, 'Seasonal variability in early hominid predation', *Science*, 192: 441–5.

Stehli, P. (ed.), 1978, *Sahara*, Cologne.

Street, F. A. and Grove, A. T. 1976, 'Environmental and climatic implications of late Quaternary lake level fluctuations in Africa', *Nature*, 261: 385–90.

Summers, R. (ed.), 1959, *Prehistoric Rock Art of the Federation of Rhodesia and Nyasaland*, London.

1969, *Ancient Mining in Rhodesia*, Salisbury.

Sutton, J. E. G. 1968, 'Archaeological sites in Usandawe', *Azania*, 3: 167–74.

1973, *The Archaeology of the Western Highlands of Kenya*, Nairobi.

1974, 'The aquatic civilization of middle Africa', *J.A.H.*, 15: 527–46.

1978, 'Engaruka and its waters', *Azania*, 13: 37–70.

Sutton, J. E. G. and Roberts, A. D. 1968, 'Uvinza and its salt industry', *Azania*, 3: 45–86.

Suzman, I. M. 1980, 'A new estimate of body weight in South African australopithecines', in R. E. Leakey and Ogot, 1980: 175–9.

Szalay, F. and Delson, E. 1978, *Evolutionary History of the Primates*, New York.

Szumowski, G. 1956, 'Fouilles de l'abri sous roche de Kourounkorokale, Soudan français', *Bull. I.F.A.N.*, 18: 462–508.

Taieb, M. *et al.*, 1974, 'Découverte d'hominides dans les séries Plio-Pleistocene d'Hadar', *C.R. Acad. Sci. Paris*, 279: 735–8.

Thilmans, G. *et al.*, 1980, *Protohistoire du Sénégal: I – Les sites megalithes*, Dakar.

Thomassey, P. and Mauny, R. 1951, 'Campagne de fouilles à Koumbi Saleh', *Bull. I.F.A.N.*, 13: 438–62.

1956, 'Campagne de fouilles à Koumbi Saleh' *Bull. I.F.A.N.*, 18: 117–40.

Tobias, P. V. 1949, 'The excavation of Mwulu's Cave, Potgietersrust district', *S.A.A.B.*, 4: 2–13.

1967, *Olduvai Gorge – II*, Cambridge.

1976, 'African hominids: dating and phylogeny', in Isaac and McCown, 1976: 377–422.

1978a, 'The place of *Australopithecus africanus* in hominid evolution', in Chivers and Joysey, 1978: 373–94.

1978b, 'The South African australopithecines in time and hominid phylogeny with special reference to the dating and affinities of the Taung skull', in Jolly, 1978: 45–84.

1978c, *The Bushmen*, Cape Town.

1980, '*Australopithecus* and early *Homo*', in R. E. Leakey and Ogot, 1980: 161–5.

Trigger, B. 1976, *Nubia under the Pharaohs*, London.

Turnbull, C. M. 1961, *The Forest People*, New York.

1965, *Wayward Servants*, London.

Turton, E. R. 1975, 'Bantu, Galla and Somali migrations in the Horn of Africa', *J.A.H.*, 16: 519–37.

Tylecote, R. F. 1975, 'The origin of iron smelting in Africa', *W.A.J.A.*, 5: 1–9.

1982, 'Early copper slags and copper-base metal from the Agadez region of Niger', *J. Hist. Metal. Soc.*, 16: 58–64.

Ucko, P. J. and Dimbleby, G. W. 1969, *The Domestication and Exploitation of Plants and Animals*, London.

Vansina, J. 1965, *Oral Tradition*, London.

1966, *Kingdoms of the Savanna*, Madison.

Vinnicombe, P. 1976, *People of the Eland*, Pietermaritzburg.

Voigt, E. A. (ed.), 1981, *Guide to Archaeological Sites in the Northern and Eastern Transvaal*, Pretoria.

Wai-Ogusu, B. 1973, 'Was there a Sangoan industry in West Africa?', *W.A.J.A.*, 3: 191–6.

Walker, A. and Leakey, R. E. 1978, 'The hominids of East Turkana', *Scientific American*, 239: 54–66.

Walter, R. C. and Aronson, J. L. 1982, 'Revisions of K/Ar ages for the Hadar hominid site, Ethiopia', *Nature*, 296: 122–7.

Wandibba, S. 1980, 'The application of attribute analysis to the study of Later Stone Age/Neolithic pottery ceramics in Kenya', in R. E. Leakey and Ogot, 1980: 283–5.

Wendorf, F. (ed.), 1968, *The Prehistory of Nubia*, Dallas.

Wendorf, F. and Hassan, F. A. 1980, 'Holocene ecology and prehistory in the Egyptian Sahara', in Williams and Faure 1980: 407–19.

Wendorf, F. and Marks, A. E. (eds.), 1975, *Problems in Prehistory – North Africa and the Levant*, Dallas.

Wendorf, F. And Schild, R. 1974, *A Middle Stone Age Sequence from the Central Rift Valley, Ethiopia*, Warsaw.

1976, *Prehistory of the Nile Valley*, New York.

Wendorf, F. *et al.*, 1980, *Loaves and Fishes: The prehistory of Wadi Kubbaniya*, Dallas.

Wendt, W. E. 1966, 'Two prehistoric archaeological sites in Egyptian Nubia', *Postilla*, 102: 1–46.

1972, 'Preliminary report on an archaeological research programme in South West Africa', *Cimbebasia*, B2: 1–61.

1976, '*Art mobilier* from the Apollo 11 Cave, South West Africa: Africa's oldest dated works of art', *S.A.A.B.*, 31: 5–11.

Wertime, T. A. 1980, 'The pyrotechnologic background', in Wertime and Muhly, 1980: 1–24.

Wertime, T. A. and Muhly, J. D. (eds.), 1980, *The Coming of the Age of Iron*, New Haven.

White, T. D. 1980, 'Evolutionary implications of Pliocene hominid footprints', *Science*, 208: 175–6.

Willcox, A. R. 1963, *The Rock Art of South Africa*, Johannesburg.

Willett, F. 1962, 'The microlithic industry from Old Oyo, Western Nigeria', in Mortelmans, 1962b: 261–71.

1967, *Ife in the History of West African Sculpture*, London.

Williams, M. A. J. and Faure, H. (eds.), 1980, *The Sahara and the Nile*, Rotterdam.

Wilson, M. 1969, 'The hunters and herders', in Wilson and Thompson, 1969: 40–74.

Wilson, M. and Thompson, L. (eds.), 1969, *The Oxford History of South Africa – I*, Oxford.

Witthof, J. 1967, 'Glazed polish on flint tools', *American Antiquity*, 32: 383–8.

Wood, B. A. 1978, 'Classification and phylogeny of East African hominids', in Chivers and Joysey, 1978: 351–72.

Zohary, D. 1969, 'The progenitors of wheat and barley in relation to domestication and agricultural dispersal in the Old World', in Ucko and Dimbleby, 1969: 47–66.

ADDENDA

Clark, J. D. and Brandt, S. A. (eds.), 1984, *From Hunters to Farmers: the causes and consequences of food production in Africa*, Berkeley.

Crader, D. C. 1984, *Hunters in Iron Age Malawi*, Lilongwe.

Denbow, J. R. 1984, 'Cows and kings: a spatial and economic analysis of a hierarchical Early Iron Age settlement system in eastern Botswana', in Hall *et al.*, 1984: 24–39.

Denbow, J. R. 1986, 'A new look at the later prehistory of the Kalahari', *J.A.H.*, 27: 3–28.

Eggert, M. K. H. 1984, 'Imbonga und Linganda: zur früheston Besiedlung des zentralafrikanischen Regenwaldes', *Beiträge zur Allgemeinen und Vergleichenden Archäologie*, 6: 247–88.

Ehret, C. 1982, 'The first spread of food production to southern Africa', in Ehret and Posnansky, 1982: 158–81.

Ehret, C. and Posnansky, M. (eds.), 1982, *The Archaeological and Linguistic Reconstruction of African History*, Berkeley.

Hall, M. *et al.*, (eds.) 1984, *Frontiers: southern African archaeology today*, Oxford.

Klein, R. G. (ed.), 1984, *Southern African Prehistory and Palaeoenvironments*, Rotterdam.

Lewis-Williams, J. D. 1983, *The Rock Art of Southern Africa*, Cambridge.

Maggs, T. M. O'C. 1984, 'The Iron Age south of the Zambezi', in Klein, 1984: 329–60.

de Maret, P. 1985, 'Recent archaeological research and dates from central Africa', *J.A.H.*, 26: 129–48.

de Maret, P. 1986, 'The Ngovo Group: an industry with polished stone tools and pottery in Lower Zaire', *African Archaeological Review*, 4: 103–33.

Morais, J. 1984, 'Mozambican archaeology: past and present', *African Archaeological Review*, 2: 113–28.

Muzzolini, A. 1986, *L'Art Rupestre Préhistorique des Massifs Centraux Sahariens*, Oxford.

Peyrot, B. and Oslisly, R. 1986, 'Recherches récentes sur le paléoenvironnement et l'archéologie au Gabon', *L'Anthropologie*, 90: 201–16.

Smith, P. E. L. 1968, 'Problems and possibilities of the prehistoric rock art of northern Africa', *African Historical Studies*, 1: 1–39.

Walker, N. J. 1983, 'The significance of an early date for pottery and sheep in Zimbabwe', *S.A.A.B.*, 38: 88–92.

Wendorf, F. 1984, 'Addendum' (to paper by F. Wendorf and R. Schild), in J. D. Clark and Brandt, 1984: 101.

Willcox, A. R. 1984, *The Rock Art of Africa*, London.

Wilson, A. C. *et al.*, 1985, 'Mitochondrial DNA and two perspectives on evolutionary genetics', *Biological Journal of the Linnaean Society*, 26: 375–400.

INDEX

References in parentheses are to maps

Abkan 119
absolute chronology 5, 8
Abu Simbel, Egypt (118), 122
Acacus, Libya (100), 107
acephalous societies 188
Acheulian 32–57, 60, 86, 97
Adamawa-Eastern
 languages 6, 7
Adrar Bous, Niger (76), 88–
 90, 94, (100), 106, (118), 133
Adulis, Ethiopia (159), 160
Adwuku, Ghana (76), 87
Aegyptopithecus 11–12
aerial photography 208–9
aesthetics, Acheulian 56
Afalou bou Rhummel,
 Algeria (76), 92
Afar 19
Afikpo, Nigeria (118), 136
Afroasiatic languages 5–6, 41
Afro-Mediterranean *see*
 Mediterranean
Afyeh, Egypt (118), 119
Agadez, Niger 163, (169)
Agau 194
Agordat, Ethiopia (118), 140
A-group 119–20
Ain Hanech, Algeria (43),
 52–4
Akan 166, 191
Akhenaten, Pharaoh of
 Egypt 129
Akira, Kenya (118), 144
Akjoujt, Mauritania 163, (169)
Akyekyema Buor, Ghana 166
al-Bakri 188–9
Albany industry 64, 70
Alexander the Great, King of
 Macedon 154
Alexandria, Egypt 154, (159),
 161
Ali, sultan of Songhai 190
al-Masudi 198
Almoravids 189
Amanzi, South Africa (43), 49
Amekni, Algeria (100), 107
Amhara 196
Amharic language 5
amino-acid recemisation 45,
 47, 61
Amratian *see* Nakada

ancestral African physical
 type 110, 112
Ankole 199
Anthropoidea 11–12
Aphilas, King of Axum 161
'Apollo 11 Cave',
 Namibia 68, 73, (77)
Arabic language 5, 194;
 writings 188, 191, 198
Arabs 154–5
archaeology, evaluation of
 3–5, 8–10, 188
Arkin, Sudan (76), 94
Arlit, Niger (118), 133
Armah, King of Axum 161
Asante 191
Asselar, Mali (118), 134
Assyrians 154, 156
Atbara river 156
Aterian 88–90, 92, 94, 96
Atwetwebooso, Ghana 166,
 (169)
Australopithecus 11, 13, 15,
 18–19, 28, 30
Australopithecus afarensis 14,
 16, 19
Australopithecus africanus
 14–17, 23, 28–30
Australopithecus boisei 14–17,
 23, 40–1
Australopithecus robustus 14–
 16, 28
Awdaghast, Mali 169, (169),
 (190)
Axum, Ethiopia 10, 157, (159)
 160–2, 194
Axumite architectural
 style 196

baboon 42
Bachwezi 199–200
backed-blade industries 9
Badari, Egypt (118), 124
Badarian 123–4
Bambandyanalo, South
 Africa (195), 200
Bambata, Zimbabwe 67–8,
 (77)
Bambata industry 61, 65, 68,
 80–1

Bambuk, Guinea 169, (169),
 189–90, (190)
bananas 114, 198
Bantu languages 6–7, 136,
 146, 170–1, 179–81, 194,
 197, 199, 210
Barbary sheep 92, 114, 130
barley 99, 101, 113, 119, 124,
 131, 139–40
beads 116, 198, *see also* glass
 beads
beans 178
Begho, Ghana 166, (190), 191
Beli, Nigera (43), 50
bellows 165, 170, 202
Bemba 201
Benadir coast 198
Benin, Nigeria 136, 169,
 (190), 193–4
Berber language 5–6
Berbers 130, 150–3, 155, 189
bifaces 32ff
Bigo, Uganda (195), 200
Bioko Island, Equatorial
 Guinea (118), 136
Bir el Ater, Algeria (76), 88–9
Bir Sahara, Egypt (76), 90
Bir Terfawi, Egypt (76), 88
Blackburn, South
 Africa (195), 209
blood groups 109
Boomplaas Cave, South
 Africa 63–4, 69, (77), (184)
Border Cave, South
 Africa/Swaziland 61–2,
 64–5, 75, (77)
Borkou 133
Bornu 138, 190, (190)
Bosumpra Cave,
 Ghana (118), 135
brass 193
brine 208
Broederstroom, South
 Africa (174–5), 177
Broken Hill mine,
 Zambia (43), 47–9, 56, 65,
 67, (77), 81
Brong 191
bronze 127, 150, 168, 192–3
buffalo 63, 75
Buganda 199

Buhaya 172
Buhen, Sudan (118), 121
bulrush millet 114, 134–5
Bunyoro 199
Bushmen see San
Bushman Rock, South
    Africa 69, (77)
Buvuma Island, Uganda (77),
    82
Bwana Mkubwa mine,
    Zambia (195), 201
Bweyorere, Uganda (195),
    200
Byneskranskop, South
    Africa (184)
Byzantines 154

calibration of radiocarbon
    dates 5
camel 140, 143, 150, 155–6
Cape coastal pottery 185–6
Cape Hangklip, South
    Africa (43), 49
Capeletti Cave, Algeria (118),
    130
Cape Three Points,
    Ghana (118), 136
Capsian 93, 110; Kenya
    Capsian see Eburran;
    Typical Capsian 92–3;
    Upper Capsian 93–4, 106
Cap Vert, Senegal (76), 85
cardium shell 130
Carthage, Tunisia (151),
    151–3
Casablanca sequence 51–6
Casamance estuary,
    Senegal (118), 136
cassava 114
casting 149, 168, see also lost
    wax
Catarrhini 12
Catfish Cave, Egypt (100),
    101
cattle 90, 94, 99, 117, 119–20,
    124, 130–1, 134, 137,
    139–41, 146, 156, 163, 166,
    178, 181, 184–5, 194, 198–
    200, 203–5, 208–10
caucasoids 110, 146
cavalry 190
Cave of Hearths, South
    Africa (43), 49, 56, 60–1,
    64–5, (77)
cemeteries 92, 99, 110, 119,
    175, 202
cereals 96, 106, 113, 115, 136,
    139–41, 143, 151, 182, see
    also under names of species
C-group 119–20, 122, 140
Chabbe, Ethiopia (118), 140
Chadic languages 6

Chalbi Lake 143
Charaman 47, 67
Chari tuff 22, 37
Chebka phase 134
Chemeron formation 19
Chewa 201
chickens 208
chickpeas 140
Chifumbaze,
    Mozambique 171, (174–5)
Chifumbaze complex 171–83,
    186, 199–204, 207–10
China 198
Chondwe group (174)
Christianity 154, 157–8,
    160–1, 194, 196
Chyulu Hills, Kenya (195),
    200
circumnavigation of
    Africa 151
cleavers 33ff
client relations 180
cloth 198, see also cotton,
    linen
coins 160–1, 198, 205
Coldstream Cave, South
    Africa 73, (77)
Columnata, Algeria 58, (76),
    92–3
Columnatan 92–3
Congo-Kordofanian
    languages 6–7
Congo basin 34, 78, 97, 194
Congo river 147
copper 119, 124, 127, 148,
    150, 158, 163, 170, 178, 201,
    203–8
cotton 203–4
cowpeas 137, 178, 203
crocodile 24
currency 178, 201, see also
    coins
Cushitic languages 5–6, 141,
    146, 158, 163, 194
Cyrene, Libya (151), 152

Dabba, Libya (78), 90
Dabban 90–1, 95
Daima, Nigeria 108, (118),
    138–9, 166, (169), 170
Dambwa group (174)
Dar es Soltan, Morocco (76),
    90
Darfur 156
date palm 131
Debeira West, Sudan 157,
    (159)
Deir el Bahari, Egypt 140, 142
desertification 3
Developed Oldowan 38, 40,
    48, 53–5

Dhar Tichitt,
    Mauritania (118), 134
Die Kelders, South
    Africa (184)
Diepkloof, South Africa (184)
Dikbosch, South Africa (184)
dog 124
Doian 84
dom palm 131
donkey 124
Doornkloof, South Africa 74,
    (77)
Dryopithecus 11–13
Dundo, Angola (77), 80

Early Iron Age 171, see
    Chifumbaze complex
Early Khartoum,
    Sudan (100), 101–3, 106,
    110, 116, 131
east coast of Africa 10, 187,
    197
Eastern Cushitic
    languages 196
Eastern Highland group of
    Bantu languages 179–80
Eastern Oranian 91
Eburran 82–3
Edfuan 96
edge wear 34, 99, 136
Egypt 3, 10; pre-
    dynastic 116, 119, 123–5;
    dynastic 1, 59, 121–2,
    125–9, 148, 154; Ptolemaic
    and later 154–6
Egyptian language 156
einkorn 113
eland 63, 75
Eland's Bay, South
    Africa (184)
Ele Bor, Kenya (110), 108,
    (118), 143
elephant 25, 78–9
El Guettar, Tunisia (76), 89
El Khril, Morocco (118), 130
Elmenteitan 144
Elmolo 104
emmer 124
Engaruka, Tanzania (195),
    197
engravings 72–4, 140
ensete 114, 139–40
Epi-Pietersburg 64
Erg Tihodaine, Algeria (43),
    51
Erythraic languages see
    Afroasiatic
Esh Shaheinab, Sudan
    116–17, (118), 119, 134
Esna, Egypt 99, (100)
Ethiopic script 161

exchange systems 187, *see also* trade
Ezana, King of Axum 157, 160
Eze Nri 168

Fakhurian 96
Faras, Sudan 157–8, (159)
Fauresmith, South Africa (77)
Fauresmith industry 49
Fayum, Egypt 12, (100), 101–2, (118), 122–4, 131
finger millet 114, 119, 139–40, 203
finger prints 109
fire, Acheulian 45, 56
fishing 63, 84, 94–6, 99, 101–4, 106, 108, 113, 116, 119, 124, 133–4, 139, 141, 163, 178–9, 185, 210
flax 113, 119, 124
Florisbad, South Africa (43), 56, 65, (77)
fonio 114, 135
food-production 113ff
forest kingdoms, West African 191–4
forging iron 149
Fort Ternan, Kenya 13
furnaces, copper 170
furnaces, iron, natural draft 202
furnaces, iron *see* smelting
FxJj 50, Kenya 37

Gadamotta, Ethiopia (76), 81
Gadeb Plain, Ethiopia 42, (43)
Galla 197
Gambia river 85
Gamble's Cave, Kenya (77), 82–3
Gao, Mali 190, (190)
gazelle 24–5, 90, 127–8, 131
Gedi, Kenya (195), 198
Ge'ez language 160
Genda Biftu, Ethiopia 141
Gerzean *see* Nakada
Ghana, Kingdom of 169, (169), 188–9
Gikuyu 200
giraffe 127, 131–2
glass 151, 162, 197–8, 205; glass beads 168, 178, 193, 200, 203–5, 210
glottochronology 8
goat 114, 117, 119, 124, 134, 137, 139, 163, 178, 208
Gobedra rock-shelter, Ethiopia 76, 82–4, (118), 139–40, 143
Gogo Falls, Kenya (118), 146
Gokomere/Ziwa group (174)
gold 127, 148, 169, 178, 188, 191, 198–9, 203–6, 208

Gombe Point, Zaire (77), 80, (118), 136
gongs, iron 202
Gorgora rock-shelter, Ethiopia (76), 84
gorilla 14–15
gourd 144
grain impressions 134
graves 60, 71–2, 92, 99, 110, 119, 121, 123–4, 126–7, 129, 175, 188, 202–4
Great Zimbabwe, Zimbabwe (195), 204–7
Greek language 160–1
Greeks 151–2, 154
groundbeans 203
groundnuts 114
Gumanye phase 205–6
Gumban A *see* Nderit ware
gums 162
Guomde formation 22
Gure Makeke, Somalia (76), 84
Gure Warbei, Somalia (76), 84
Guruhuswa, Kingdom of 207
Gwisho hotsprings, Zambia 70–2, (77), 112

Hadar, Ethiopia (18), 19, 21, 30
Hadrumetum, Tunisia (151)
Hadza language 6
hafting of stone tools 58–9
Hafun, Somalia (159), 162
Hagfet et Tera, Libya (76), 91
Halfan 95–6
Hamamiya, Egypt 124
hand-axes 32ff
Hargeisa, Somalia (76), 83
Hargeisan 82–4
Harmony, South Africa (195), 208
Ha Soloja, Lesotho 66, (77)
Hatshepsut, Queen of Egypt 142
Haua Fteah, Libya (76), 90–1, 94, (118), 130
Hausa 190
Hawston, South Africa (184)
Hebrew language 5
Helwan, Egypt (118), 124
Herodotus 127, 150–1, 154
Hierakonpolis, Egypt (118), 124
hieroglyphic script 125–6, 156
Himyaritic script 159–60
Hippo, Tunisia (151)
hippopotamus 24–5, 134
hoes 86–7, 135, 140
Holocene 10
hominids 12–13
hominoids 12

Homo 12–13, 15, 23, 29–30, 49
Homo erectus 15–16, 22–3, 40–2, 47, 49, 54–6
Homo habilis 15–18, 22–3, 30, 40–1
Homo sapiens 12, 16, 47, 49, 56, 60
Homo sapiens neanderthalensis 47, 60, 90
Homo sapiens rhodesiensis 47–9, 56, 60, 81
Homo sapiens sapiens 9, 47, 60, 64–5, 92, 97
Hopefield, South Africa (43), 49, 56
horn 197
horses 150, 156, *see also* cavalry
Hottentots *see* Khoi
houses 103, 119, 123, 166, 175, 192, 197, 200, 203, 205, 208–9
Howieson's Poort, South Africa 68, (77)
Howieson's Poort industry 61–5, 75, 84, 97
hunting strategy 49, 56, 75, 78, 92
Hwang Ho valley 10
Hyksos, rulers of Egypt 129
Hyrax Hill, Kenya (118), 145

Iberomaurusian 91–3, 98, 110
ibn Battuta 199
Ife, Nigeria 169, (169), (190), 192–4
Igbo 168
Igbo Ukwu, Nigeria 166–7, (169)
Ileret, Kenya (118), 141, 143
India 198–9
Indian Ocean trade 161, 178, 197, 206
Indus Valley 10
Ingombe Ilede, Zambia (195), 206–7
ingots 201–2, 207
interlacustrine kingdoms 199–200
iron 127, 134, 143, 148ff, *see also* forging, smelting
Iron Age 5
Ishango, Zaire (100), 104–5, 110
Isimila, Tanzania 45
Islam 154–5, 188–90, 194, 196, 198
ivory 119, 151, 160, 162, 167, 170, 197–8, 204
Ivuna, Tanzania (195), 200
Iwo Eleru, Nigeria (76), 86–7, 110–11, (118), 136

Jebel et Tomat, Sudan 156, (159), 162–3
Jebel Ighoud, Morocco (76), 90
Jebel Moya, Sudan 156, (159)
Jebel Sahaba, Egypt 99, (100), 110
Jebel Uweinat, Libya (118), 131–2
Jenne, Mali (190), 191
Jenne-Jeno, Mali (118), 139, 164, (169)
Jos Plateau, Nigeria (43), 50, (76), 86

Kabambian 202
Kabwe see Broken Hill mine
Kadero, Sudan 117, (118), 119, 134
Kagera Valley, Uganda/Tanzania (77), 81
Kainji Dam 166
Kairouan, Tunisia 154–5
Kalabsha, Egypt 128
Kalahari Desert 70
Kalambo Falls, Zambia/Tanzania (43), 45–7, 67, 70, (77), 78, 81
Kalambo group (174)
Kalemba rock-shelter, Zambia 68–9, 71, (77)
Kalenjin 197
Kalundu, Zambia (174–5), 178
Kalundu group (174)
Kamabai, Sierra Leone (118), 136
Kamba 200
Kanapoi, Kenya (18)
Kanem, Kingdom of 169, 188, 190, (190)
Kansanshi mine, Zambia (195), 201
Kansyore Island, Uganda (118)
Kansyore ware 145–6, 173
Kaposwa industry 70
Kapthurin, Kenya (43), 56
Kapwirimbwe group (174)
Karari industry 22, 37–8, 54–5
Karkarichinkat, Mali (118), 134
Katoto, Zaire (174–5), 175
Katuruka, Tanzania 172, (174–5)
KBS industry 22, 27, 37, 56
KBS site, Kenya 22–3, 25–6, 30
KBS tuff 22–3
Kebibat, Morocco (43), 55
Kenya Capsian see Eburran

Kerma, Sudan (118), 121–2, 129
Khami, Zimbabwe (195), 206
Kharga Oasis, Egypt (100), 106, (118), 131
Khoi 7, 184
Khoisan languages 6–7, 84, 147, 184
Khoisan physical type 109–12
Khor Musa, Sudan (76), 94
Khormusan 95–6
Khufu, Pharaoh of Egypt 127
Kibiro, Uganda (195), 200
Kilwa, Tanzania (195), 197–9, 205
Kinangop plateau, Kenya (77), 81
Kinshasa plain, Zaire 78–9
Kintampo industry 137–8
Kintampo rock-shelter, Ghana (118)
Kipushi, Zaire (195), 201
Kisalian 202
Kisese rock-shelter, Tanzania (77), 82, 84
Klasies River Mouth, South Africa 61–5, 73, 75, (77)
Kliplaatdrif (43), 49
Kom Ombo, Egypt 99, (100)
Kondoa, Tanzania (77), 84
Koobi Fora, Kenya 16–17, (18), 22–7, 37–8, 41, (43)
Koobi Fora formation 22–3
Kordofanian languages 7
Koro Toro, Chad 166, (169)
Kourounkorokale, Mali (76), 86, (100), 107
Kromdraai, South Africa (18), 28–30
Kubi Algi formation 22
Kumbi Saleh, Mauritania 169, (169), 188–9, (190)
Kunkur Oasis, Egypt (100), 106
Kush 121–2, 130, 154, 156
Kwa languages 6
Kwale, Kenya (174–5)
Kwale group (174), 175, 200
Kwale ware 173

lacustrine sediment cores 173
Laetoli, Tanzania (18), 19, 21
Laga Oda, Ethiopia 72, (76), 84
Lake Baringo 19
Lake Besaka, Ethiopia (118), 140
Lake Chad 49, 106
Lake Edward 104–5
Lake Eyasi, Tanzania (77), 81
Lake Kisale 202

Lake Nakuru, Kenya (100), 104
Lake Ndutu, Tanzania 56
Lake Turkana (18), 19–20, 22, 103, 141, 144, 146
Lake Victoria 145, 173
Lalibela, Ethiopia (195), 196
Lalibela Cave, Ethiopia (118), 140
Lamu archipelago 197
language 1, see also linguistics
language, Acheulian 56
Lasta 194, (195)
Late Stone Age 5, 58
Lelesu, Tanzania (174–5), 175
Lelesu group (174)
leopard 28, 128
Leopard's Kopje industry 203
Lepcis, Libya (151)
Levalloiso-Mousterian 86, 88, 90–1, 94
Levallois technique 35–6, 51, 54, 56, 58, 96, 97
Libyan pre-Aurignacian 90–1
Libyco-Capsian 94, 130
linen 124
linguistics 2–3, 5–8, 146, 173, 177, 181, 187
Linnaean terminology 15
Lixus, Morocco (151)
loanwords 7
long-horned cattle 203
Lopoy, Kenya (100), 104
last wax casting 168, 193
Lothagam, Kenya (18), 19, 110
Lowasera, Kenya (100), 103–5
Luangwa tradition 200–1, 203
Luangwa Valley, Zambia (77), 79
Luba 203
'Lucy' 19
Lukenya Hill, Kenya (77), 81–2, 84
Lungwebungu tradition 201
Luo 197
Lupemban 68, 78–9, 81, 85–6, 94, 97
Lydenburg, South Africa (174–5), 177

Maasai 197
Macedon 154
maize 114
Makapansgat, South Africa (18), 28–9
Makgwareng, South Africa 195
Makwe, Zambia (174–5), 180
Makwe, Zimbabwe 73, (77)
Malebo Pool, Zaire (77), 78
Mali, Empire of 189–90, (190)

Malindi, Kenya (195), 198
Manda, Kenya (195), 197–8
Mande 189–90
Mande language 6
Manekweni,
　Mozambique 205
manioc *see* cassava
Mapungubwe, South
　Africa 204
marine sediment cores 61
Maringishu, Kenya (118), 144
Massinissa, King 153
Matara, Ethiopia (159), 161
material culture groupings 4
Matola, Mozambique
　(174–5), 175
Matupi Cave, Zaire (76), 80,
　82
Mbire 206
Mecca 190
Mechta-Afalou type 90, 92,
　94, 110
Mechta el Arbi, Algeria (76),93
Mediterranean type 109–10,
　130
megaliths 166–7, 196
Mejiro, Nigeria (76), 87
Melka Kunture, Ethiopia 42,
　(43), (76), 80–1
Merimde, Egypt (118), 123–4
Meroe, Sudan 10, 156–7,
　(159), 160–1, 163
Meroitic language 156
Mesopotamia 10
Messina, South Africa (195),
　208
metals 203, *see also* bronze,
　copper, gold, iron, tin
Mexico 10
microlithic industries 9, 58ff
Middle Stone Age 58
milking 146
millet 156, 198, *see also*
　bulrush millet, finger millet
mines 178, 198, 201, 203, 206,
　208
Miocene 11–13, 18–19
Mirabib, Namibia (184)
Mogadishu, Somalia 198
Mogador, Morocco 151, (151)
monkeys 128
Montagu Cave, South Africa
　33, (43), 49, 60, 63, (77)
Moshebi's rock-shelter,
　Lesotho 65, (77)
mosques 155, 188
Mossel Bay, South Africa 64,
　(77)
Mossi 191
Mousterian 88, 94
Mpongweni, South
　Africa 211

Mufo, Angola (77), 78
mules 150
Mumbwa Cave, Zambia 68,
　(77)
Musa, ruler of Mali 190
Musolexi, Angola (77), 79
Mwabulambo group (174)
Mwanganda, Malawi (77), 78
Mwari 205
Mwulu's Cave, South
　Africa 65, (77)

Nabta Playa, Egypt (100),
　106, (118), 131
Nachikufan I 69–70, 98
Nachikufan industries 70
Nachikufu, Zambia (77)
Naghez phase 134
Nakada, Egypt (118), 124
Nakada industry 123–4
Nakapapula, Zambia (174–5),
　180
Naletale, Zimbabwe (195),
　206–7
Nana-Mode, Central African
　Republic (169), 170
Napata, Sudan 156, (159)
Naqa, Sudan 157
Narosura, Kenya (118), 144
Nasera Rock, Tanzania (77),
　81, 84
Natal group (174)
Naukratis, Egypt (151), 154
Nderit, Kenya (118), 144
Nderit Drift, Kenya (77), 82
Nderit ware 141, 145
neanderthaloids 81, 97, see
　also *Homo sapiens
　neanderthalensis*
negroids 82, 86, 109–12, 146,
　204
Nelson Bay Cave, South
　Africa 64–5, 69–70, (77),
　(184)
Neolithic 5
Neolithic of Capsian
　tradition 130
Nhunguza, Zimbabwe (195),
　205–6
Niger-Congo languages 7
Niger delta, inland 90, 139
Nile gravels 37
Nilo-Saharan languages 5–6
Nilotic languages 5, 146, 163,
　194, 197, 199
Nilotic negroids 110
Njoro River Cave, Kenya 144
Nkope, Malawi (174–5)
Nkope group (174)
Nok, Nigeria 164–6, (169),
　192
noog 114, 139

North Horr, Kenya (118),
　143, (159), 163
Nsenga 201
Ntereso, Ghana (118), 138
Nthabazingwe,
　Zimbabwe (195), 203
Ntusi, Uganda (195), 200
Nubians 154, 157
Nyang'oma, Tanzania (118),
　145

Oba of Benin 194
oil palm 137
Okote tuff 37
Oldowan 26–7, 34, 38, 40,
　50–1, 56–7, *see also*
　Developed Oldowan
Olduvai Gorge,
　Tanzania (18), 40, (43), 56,
　(77); Bed I 17, 22–8, 30, 38,
　40; Bed II 37–9, 40–1, 48;
　Beds III and IV 40; Ndutu
　Bed 81; Naisiusiu Bed 82
Olifantspoort, South
　Africa (195), 208
Oligocene 11–12
Oligopithecus 11
Olorgesailie, Kenya 42, (43),
　44–5, 56
Oman 198
Omo valley, Ethiopia (18),
　20–1, 30, (100), 103
oral tradition 1–3, 8, 10, 180,
　187–9, 191, 194, 197, 199,
　202–3, 205–7, 209
Orangia, South Africa 65–6,
　(77)
Orangian industry 65
Oranian *see* Iberomaurusian
oryx 127
Osiris 126
ostrich 128, 131
Oued Guettara,
　Algeria (118), 130
Oueyanko Valley, Mali (118),
　136
Ounanian point 101, 106
Outeidat, Mali (100), 107

paintings 60, 72–3, 84, 133,
　140–1, 150, 181–3, 210–11
panicum 119
Pastoral Neolithic 143–4
Peninj, Tanzania 41, (43)
*Periplus of the Erythraean
　Sea* 161, 197–8
Phalaborwa, South
　Africa (195), 208
pharaohs 125–9, 154
Phoenicians 149–52, 170
Pietersburg, South Africa (77)

Pietersburg industry 62, 64–5, 67–8, 75
pig 24, 124
pilgrimage 190
Pleistocene 9, 11
Pliocene 11, 13, 19
plough 141
pollen analysis 46–7, 99, 115, 173
Pomongwan 70
Pomongwe, Zimbabwe 61, 67–8, (77)
Porc Epic, Ethiopia (76), 81
porcupine 24
Portuguese 194, 199, 203, 206–7
potassium/argon dating 17, 29, 41, 44, 48, 81
pottery, Chinese 205; Persian 205; imported 151, 197–8; for locally produced pottery see under names of individual sites
pre-Axumite 158–60
primates 11–12
Ptolemais, Libya (151)
Ptolemy I, ruler of Egypt 154
pumpkin 165
Punt, Land of 129, 140, 142
pygmies 181
pyramids 126–8

Qadan 99, 110
Qarunian 102

Ra 126
Rabat 54
radiocarbon dating 4–5, 45, 67ff
Ramapithecus 11, 13, 18
Ramesses II, Pharaoh of Egypt 122
raw material, effect on stone-tool typology 49, 65, 84
Redcliff, Zimbabwe 68, (77)
relic house 168
Relilai, Algeria/Tunisia (76), 92–3
Rendille 197
Rhapta 162
rhinoceros 134, 162
rice 114, 135, 139
Rift Valley 12, 16, (18), 19
Rim, Upper Volta (76), 87, 164, (169)
Robberg industry 64, 69–70
rock art 131, 210, see also engravings, paintings
Romans 152–4, 157, 160
Rooidam, South Africa (43), 48, 75

Rop, Nigeria (76), 86–7
roulette 170, 194, 199–200
Ruanga, Zimbabwe (195), 205

Sabi river 206
sagittal crest 15
Saharan languages 6
Saint Louis, Senegal (118), 136
Sakwe, Zambia (174–5), 183
Salé, Morocco (43), 55
salt 151, 188, 200, 203
Samun Dukiya, Nigera 165, (169)
San 7, 75, 184
Sandawe language 6
Sanga, Zaire (174–5), 175, (195), 202–3
Sango Bay, Uganda 67
Sangoan 67, 78–9, 81, 85, 97
Sanhaja 189
Sao 166
savanna kingdoms, southern 202–3
Scott's Cave, South Africa (184)
sea levels 51–4, 62, 70, 92
seasonality 4, 71, 119, 185, 210
Sebilian 99
Sehonghong, Lesotho 65, (77)
Semitic languages 5–6, 141, 158, 196
Semna, Sudan (118), 121
sense of identity 5
Septimius Severus, Emperor of Rome 153
Seti I, Pharaoh of Egypt 127
Shaba 201
Shamarkian 101, 103, 106
sheep 114, 117, 119, 124, 163, 178, 181, 184–5, 210
sheep/goat 115, 121, 124, 130–1, 133, 140–1, 143, 200, 203
shell mounds 92, 136, 166
shelters 45–6, 65–6, see also houses
ships 127, 151, 197, 210
Shirazi dynasty 198
Shoa 194, (195), 196
Shona 205–7
shorthorn cattle 133, 156
Shum Laka, Cameroon (118), 136
Sidi Abderrahman quarry, Morocco (43), 63–4
Sidi Okba mosque, Kairouan 155
Sidi Zin, Tunisia (43), 52
Siga, Algeria (151)

Silozwane, Zimbabwe (174–5), 181–2
Sine Saloum, Senegal 167
Singida, Tanzania (77), 84
Siraf 197
Sirte, Gulf 152
skins 119, 151, 160, 197
slaves 151, 170, 197
smelting iron 148–9, 152, 165, 173, 178, 202
Sofala, Mozambique (195), 198–9
Somali 197
Somali language 5, 146
Songhai 190
Songhai kingdom 190, (190)
Songhai language 5–6
sorghum 114, 119, 131, 134–5, 156, 163, 166, 178, 200, 203, 209
Sotho 208–9
South African Khoisan languages 6
South Arabia 161
South Arabians 158
Southern Cushitic languages 146
spices 162
squash 178
state formation 169, 171, 187–8, 200–1
steenbok 63
stelae 161–2
Sterkfontein, South Africa 17, (18), 28–9, (43), 48
stone bowls 140–1, 143–5
strandlopers 210
sudanic kingdoms 168–71, 187, 190
Sudanic languages 5–6, 181, 194
Suregei tuff 22
Swahili 197
Swartkrans, South Africa (18), 28–30, (43), 48
Sweitzer Reneke, South Africa 74, (77)
symbolism 4

Taba Zikamambo, Zimbabwe (195), 203
Tachengit, Algeria (43), 51
Tada, Nigeria (190), 193
Taforalt, Morocco (76), 92–3
Tagra, Sudan (100), 103
Tamar Hat, Algeria (76), 92
Tamaya Mellet, Niger (100), 107
Taruga, Nigeria 165–6, (169)
Taung, South Africa (18), 28–30

teff 114, 139
Ténéré Desert 106
Ténéréan 133
Ternifine, Algeria (43), 54–5
Thandwe, Zambia (174–5), 180
This, Egypt (118), 124–5
Thomas quarry, Morocco 54, 56
thorium/uranium dating 48
Three Rivers, South Africa (43), 49
Tibesti 117
Tiemassas, Senegal (76), 86–7
Tigre 158, (195), 196
Tilemsi valley, Mali 134, 138
Timbuktu, Mali 189
Timgad, Algeria 152
tin 208
trade 116–17, 119, 126, 128, 151, 169, 171, 187–91, 200–1, 203, 205–6
Transvaal groups (174)
tribalism 3
Tripolitania 152
tsetse fly 139
Tshangula, Zimbabwe (77)
Tshangula industry 61, 68–9, 80
Tshitolian 80, 97, 111
Tuareg 189
tubers 87, *see also* yams
Tunis 155, 169
Tutankhamun, Pharaoh of Egypt 129
Tuthmosis III, Pharaoh of Egypt 129

Twickenham Road, Zambia (195), 200
Tzaneen, South Africa (174–5), 175

Uan Muhuggiag, Libya (118), 133
Ubangian languages 7, 170, 181, 194
Upper Lualaba group (174)
Urewe, Kenya (174–5)
Urewe group 171–4, (174)
Utica, Tunisia (151)
Uvinza, Tanzania (195), 200

Vaal gravels 37
Vandals 153–4
vegeculture 87, *see also* tubers, yams
Venda 209
Victoria Falls, Zambia/Zimbabwe 36, (43), (77)
Volta gravels 50, 85
Voltaic languages 6

Wadi Halfa, Sudan 54, (76), 120–1
Wadi Kubbaniya, Egypt (76), 96, 99
Waqwaq 198
warthog 134
waterbuck 24
West Atlantic languages 6
Western Highland group of Bantu languages 179–80
wheat 113, 119, 139, *see also* einkorn, emmer

wheeled vehicles 150
Wilton, South Africa 70, (77)
Wilton industry 70, 98
Winam Gulf 172–3
windbreak 25–6
Wonderboompoort, South Africa (43), 49
written records, availability of 1
Wun Rok, Sudan (159), 163, 194, (195)

X-group 157
Xhosa 209

Yagala, Sierra Leone (118), 136
Yala Alego, Kenya (77), 82
yams 114–15, 135, 137, 139
Yayo, Chad (43), 49
Yeha, Ethiopia (159), 160
Yelwa, Nigeria 166–7, (169)
Yemen 161
Yengema, Sierra Leone (76), 87
Yoruba 192–3

Zaghawa 169
Zagwe 194, 196
Zambezi gravels 37
Zambezi valley 70, 200, 206
Zande 194
zebra 90
Zeila, Somalia (195), 196
Zenebi Falls, Nigeria (76), 86
Zenj 198
Zombepata, Zimbabwe (77)